ABBEYLARA:

e Tragic Shooting of John Carthy

REGINA HENNELLY covered the Barr Tribunal as a freelance reporter for the *Irish Examiner*, the *Irish Independent*, RTÉ, the 'Tonight with Vincent Browne' show on RTÉ Radio 1, Shannonside Radio and the *Longford Leader*. She also featured on a 'Prime Time' special on the Abbeylara incident and is acknowledged as one of the leading commentators on the shooting of John Carthy. Originally from Castlebar in County Mayo, she now lives in Dublin where she is studying for a Masters Degree in Political Theory at UCD.

ABBEYLARA

THE TRAGIC SHOOTING OF JOHN CARTHY

REGINA HENNELLY

THE O'BRIEN PRESS
DUBLIN

First published 2007 by The O'Brien Press Ltd,
12 Terenure Road East, Rathgar, Dublin 6, Ireland.
Tel: +353 1 4923333; Fax: +353 1 4922777
E-mail: books@obrien.ie
Website: www.obrien.ie

ISBN: 978-1-84717-017-0

British Library Cataloguing-in-Publication Data
Hennelly, Regina
Abbeylara : the tragic shooting of John Carthy
1. Carthy, John - Death and burial 2. Carthy, John
3. Police shootings - Ireland 4. Depressed persons - Ireland - Biography
I. Title
363.2'32

1 2 3 4 5 6 7
07 08 09 10 11

Typesetting, editing, layout and design: The O'Brien Press Ltd
Printing: Creative Print and Design, Wales

Picture Credits
Front cover © Photocall Ireland. Back cover © Barr Tribunal Report. Picture
section, p1: (top & bottom) family pictures courtesy of Keith Heneghan; pp2-5 ©
Barr Tribunal Report; p6 (top) © Keith Heneghan, (bottom) © Photocall Ireland;
p7 (top & bottom) & p8 © Photocall Ireland.

For my father, PJ, with love and happy memories.

ACKNOWLEDGEMENTS

This book has been over two years in coming to fruition, and I owe much thanks to those who have continued to encourage me and to stand by me.

Firstly, my thanks to the management and editors at The O'Brien Press, who provided much guidance in making this book the best that it could be.

The Barr Tribunal was a huge turning point in my journalistic career, and I wish to thank all those broadcasters and newspapers who gave me the opportunity to cover the inquiry for them: Caroline O'Doherty of the *Irish Examiner*, Dave Halloran of the *Irish Independent*, Joe Finnegan of Shannonside Radio and Eugene McGee of the *Longford Leader*.

I must especially thank Vincent Browne, for whom I reported for the 'Tonight with Vincent Browne' show on RTÉ Radio, who was the first to suggest I write this book, and who kindly agreed to pen the foreword.

Marie Carthy has always been most helpful to me, and was gracious enough to grant me a lengthy interview at her family home in Abbeylara. I thank her for giving me an insight into her feelings on what happened and I again extend my condolences to Marie, her mother Rose and to their extended family on their tragic loss.

Olivia Kelly of *The Irish Times* became a great friend to me in the long weeks and months at the Barr Tribunal, and I am pleased to say that that friendship continues.

My most heartfelt thanks in all of this however must go to those who know me best and longest, particularly Julie and Colleen – and on the other side of the world, Aisling – who kept me sane and listened to my concerns and my troubles from the outset of this project. Thanks also to my brother John and sister-in-law Triona for providing relief from the task of book writing on my frequent trips home.

I can safely say that had it not been for the invaluable and unconditional support and love of my boyfriend, Mick, this book would never have made it to the bookshelf. He has been my proof-reader, my sounding board and my strength.

Finally, my sincerest gratitude to my mother, Peig, whose positive attitude to life has contributed much to my ability to start out on a project like this and to see it to fruition. She has been my rock, my greatest fan and my best friend. Thanks, Mam.

Foreword

The killing of John Carthy was not just a tragedy. It represented significant failures on the part of An Garda Síochána, the media and the mental health services. It also illustrated the depth of ignorance and insensitivity there is on mental illness, notably on the part of the gardaí and the media.

The Abbeylara 'siege' involved a mentally distressed young man – who had been drinking heavily over the previous few days, who had become distraught at the prospect of leaving his old, dilapidated family home, with which he so associated his late father – blockading himself into the house and firing a few shots in the air occasionally.

He was no threat to anybody but himself. Even if he was considered to be a threat to the nearby house and its occupants – the house where his mother, Rose, went on being asked to leave the home by John Carthy – that threat could have been dealt with by positioning one or two gardaí between John Carthy's home and that other house.

John Carthy was known to have had problems with the gardaí, so the intrusion of gardaí on the scene at all was going to be a problem. It was known he was distressed and yet no attempt was made until close to the end to get his psychiatrist on the scene. He was known to be very close to his sister – he had telephoned her dozens of times over the previous few days – and yet when she eventually got to the site she was not allowed approach her brother.

Instead the emergency response unit of An Garda Síochána – the unit trained to repel major security threats to the State – was called in. They were accompanied by a recently trained negotiator. These heavily armed gardaí were positioned around the home in a way that almost required John Carthy to be shot dead were he to emerge from the house while still armed.

Inexplicably, the chairman of the Tribunal that was established to examine the events leading to John Carthy's death, the former High Court judge, Robert Barr, found nothing inappropriate about the call-up of the emergency response unit. But he was very critical of how the gardaí positioned themselves around the house and about the naiveté of the negotiation.

The lack of criticism of the Garda handling of the media in relation to the tragedy was a curious oversight of Robert Barr. For instance, why did the gardaí not ask the media to avoid reporting on the incident at all until John Carthy was in safe medical care? Why, instead of doing that, was every facilitation given to the media in its coverage of the event, given that the distress of John Carthy was likely to be heightened by such tension? Why, particularly, were the media facilitated to the extent of being brought on a tour of the 'siege' area by the gardaí? Was there nobody in senior positions in the force who would have thought this was a grossly insensitive intrusion on John Carthy's distress and privacy and that it was likely to cause further upset and danger?

Then there is the media itself. How could it be that the major item on the news from around 9.00pm on the evening of 20 April 2000 for twenty-one hours afterwards was the not unusual actions of a mentally disturbed man, dealing with his demons? While it is true that John Carthy did not have access to a television after the first night of the incident, he did have access to radio throughout it all, and the presentation of his predicament as the major news item of that day must have been horrific for him.

Why did it make the news at all? That question is particularly pertinent to the public service broadcaster, RTÉ. There was no need to broadcast or publish anything at all about the Abbeylara incident while it was continuing. The only reason for the publicity was the titillation of public prurience in the furtherance of profit and market share.

Finally, on the mental health services. Conditions in parts of St Loman's Hospital in Mullingar in 1996 were deplorable, a situation referred to repeatedly in the reports of the Inspector of Mental Hospitals but consistently ignored by the health boards and the Department of Health. John Carthy was almost hysterical at the prospect of being lodged there again.

This book by Regina Hennelly tells the sad story of John Carthy vividly and compassionately. It highlights the sheer rank incompetence of the gardaí in handling the crisis and the killing of a kind, gentle, troubled man who could be alive today, giving joy and comfort to his loving mother, sister and friends, were it not for the combination of ineptitude, crassness and indifference of so many.

Vincent Browne
January 2007

Prologue

When I bought my first car in May 2005, the first trip I took was to Abbeylara. Everything about my recent life to that point had been consumed by this place, the people in it and one young man in particular, John Carthy. For over two years, my time had been spent hearing of, reporting on and writing about a troubled life that ended suddenly and tragically. Now, it was time to put flesh on the bones of a story that existed to now as shorthand notes and one picture of a pale, drawn young man.

I parked the car in the large yard in front of St Bernard's Church in the heart of the village. Everything was quiet. The wind fluttered through the yellow and white bunting hanging across the yard and on my radio Neil Young found some words to fit,

See the lonely boy,
out on the weekend
Trying to make it pay.
Can't relate to joy,
he tries to speak and
Can't begin to say.

A laneway along the side of the church led to a small grave-yard perched on a little hill. On this summer's day it looks like a peaceful resting place, full of birdsong and shaded by great trees. At the end of the graveyard, I find what I'm looking for. The large, black headstone stands boldly out from the rest. The grave is lined by tattered wreaths and some fresh flowers. John Carthy has been dead for more than five years now, but people haven't forgotten him.

A month later, I return to meet John's sister, Marie. I have been invited to the new bungalow in Toneymore, Abbeylara, where her mother lives, where Marie was spending most of her weekends and where John would have resided had he still been with them. Even after years of staring at maps of the area, finding the house is difficult. The only indication of the house's significance is a neat plaque on the front wall of the Carthy property, which reads:

'In loving memory of John Carthy whose life was taken tragically on April 20th, 2000 aged 27 years
Do not stand by my grave and weep
I am not there, I do not sleep
I am a thousand winds that blow
I am the diamond glint upon the snow
I am the sunlight on ripened grain
I am the gentle autumn rain
I am the soft star that shines so bright
In Abbeylara late at night'

The plaque is black, and alongside the words, there is a picture of John.

It is situated close to the spot where he fell on the road when the final bullet hit him.

At the front door, Rose welcomes me and invites me in, but then she goes out to the kitchen, leaving Marie to show me in to the front room. Photographs are dotted along the cabinets and the mantelpiece. Normal family pictures track the lives of two children from infancy onwards. Marie points at a picture sitting on a sideboard in the corner of the room.

'That one was when John won a local handball competition. He loved handball, and football and hurling.'

She moves to the mantelpiece.

'There's the two of us when we were young.'

'You look really alike.'

'Yeah, a lot of people say that. I suppose we did. But then, there was only a year and two months between us in age. We were very close.'

Settling down on the sofa in the comfortable living room, Marie is willing to bring me through her memories of John and her memories of the day he died, but she asks that I don't make her cry. For support, her partner sits in on the interview. But where do we start? The beginning of this story came at the end. John Carthy's life was only remarkable because of the way in which it ended.

A very ordinary young man, for twenty-seven years John Carthy was known only to those who were part of his small circle of family and friends. His life revolved around his mother and sister. His world was set on a parochial compass, keeping him close to home at all times. His hobbies were few, his working life was sporadic and consisted of short-term labouring jobs here and there. It was only on Holy Thursday 2000 that the name John Carthy reached a wider audience, through a tragic event that became known as 'The Abbeylara Siege'.

On that day – 20 April 2000 – John Carthy was shot four times by members of An Garda Síochána after he emerged from his home following a twenty-five-hour stand-off, during which he fired thirty shots. The shooting provoked anger and raised awkward questions for the police force. Persistent calls for an independent investigation into the incident were made and eventually heeded, and over the course of a lengthy Tribunal of Inquiry, the short life of John Carthy was deconstructed and revealed for the whole country to see.

What emerged was a sad account of a young man who suffered from bipolar affective disorder, or manic depression. But that was just one dimension of his story. Other aspects of his character were also revealed, finally doing justice to his memory. For so long, John Carthy had existed in the public consciousness only in the context of his final hours, his name was synonymous with a tragedy, a shooting, a scandal. The in-depth examination of his life introduced the real John Carthy to those who wished to know him as more than the man at the centre of the incident at Abbeylara. It unveiled his caring nature, his intelligence, his ability to express himself and his determination to cope with his manic depression.

Sitting in the family living room, Marie asks that we don't dwell on the more upsetting elements of that day when John died. Years after that horrible day, it still makes her cry. The ordeal of the past few years has taken its toll on her. Now each Easter season, on Holy Thursday, Marie marks the deaths of her grandfather, her father and her brother. Three generations of Carthy men all dead on the same day, two of them through simple coincidence and the third through a tragedy that has changed their lives in so many ways.

The life Marie has led since John died has been a strange one. She has been grieving in the public eye. People on the street recognise her from her appearances in the media. Some feel the need to speak to her, to express their sympathy and to tell her about someone they know who suffers from a mental illness. Both she and Rose have received hundreds of letters of sympathy, and that support has meant a lot.

Marie travels home as frequently as possible to visit her mother, but for the most part Rose passes the days and nights in the new house on her own. It is lonely for her. This was the house that she and John had planned together, and now it is empty without him. The void in her life is immense.

When mother and daughter are together however, they talk about John. Not about the way he was taken from them, but about the way he was. Marie remembers his sense of humour, his intelligence and his easy-going manner. In spite of the reams of newsprint and legal transcripts that have analysed his life in recent years, she remembers him as being just like any other young man.

She insists there was never a time in his battle with manic depression that he was suicidal, and feels that the emphasis on his mental illness has wrongly implied to people that he was always either elated or depressed. Some of the evidence she heard during the tribunal didn't tally with the brother she loved. To hear his personality distorted into an angry, unsettled young man hurt.

'They have tried to blacken his name by saying his only outlet was drinking and smoking,' she said. 'His memory has been tarnished.'

In her mind and in her memory, he was just a big brother, and while he may have battled with highs and lows, for long periods he was just himself.

She misses John greatly. They were so close in age. They started school on the same day in St Bernard's National School in Abbeylara. They sat beside each other in the classroom. They walked home together. They played together. It was a childhood bond that grew stronger as they got older and as they went their separate ways in adulthood, they were still tightly bound together.

Marie still has many questions about what happened to her brother; the only time there is any indication of bitterness in the things she says is when she is pressed for her opinion on the gardaí who responded to what happened here in Abbeylara in 2000.

The only garda who was present at the siege with whom they ever have any contact is Sergeant Mary Mangan. She was one of the officers who sat with Rose for many hours from the time the gardaí were called to the moment when news came that John was dead. After the incident was over, after John had been laid to rest, after Rose had moved into the new house and after Marie had reluctantly gone back to resume her working life, Sergeant Mangan continued to call in from time to time to see how Rose was doing. At least, Marie thinks, that was something.

Marie's ill-feeling towards the force was aggravated greatly by the press coverage that was given to the allegation that she was drunk on the night of the siege.

'[Drinking] was the last thing you'd be doing. I was never drunk in my life. And all that stuff was printed in the papers. People that wouldn't know me, they would probably believe it and I couldn't blame them if they did.'

From the conversation, it becomes clear quite quickly that Marie is critical of everything the gardaí did throughout the course of the incident. She still doesn't understand why there was a need for such a large garda presence at the scene and she is adamant that if they had been subtler in their approach, the end result would have been very different. John would have simmered down, she would have talked to him and the episode would have passed.

'If they had just kept away and left him alone, he would have been fine,' she insists.

If Marie had had her way there would have been no garda presence at all at her old home that evening. She remains certain that if she had been at home when John fired the first shots that evening, she would never have called the guards.

Having had years to dwell on the issue, Marie has her own thoughts on why John emerged when he did and why the gardaí reacted as they did. Marie was sitting in a car with Dr Shanley up the road from the cottage when John came out and she believes there are two possible reasons why John chose to suddenly come out after being holed up in the house for twenty-five hours. In her view, he was either leaving to buy cigarettes or else he was making his way up the road to talk to her.

'Why he didn't get the cigarettes? He could have been coming out for cigarettes – he was a chain smoker. Plus, they told him I was up the road with Dr Shanley, so he could have been coming up to talk to me,' she says.

I urge her on. What else does she remember of those moments. All she recalls, or perhaps all she wants to recall is the sight of guards running up the road. She feels there was 'definitely panic there', but that's as much as she wants to say about it.

'You're going to make me cry now.'

Driving back through Abbeylara after my visit to Marie and Rose Carthy, I see again all the familiar sights and landmarks that have now been immortalised in the column inches that were devoted to the death of John Carthy. Progress over the coming years will add and subtract elements from the place it was when it first became famous. New developments will spring up, and perhaps most relevant to what John Carthy's life might have been, a new handball alley was built a few years after his death. He would have been there, working on the new alley, if he had survived, but to honour him an annual competition is now held there where players compete for the John Carthy Memorial Cup. A fitting tribute in itself.

Like Abbeylara, Marie Carthy has moved on. She is currently in the second year of a four-year counselling degree at NUI Maynooth. She has come full circle, from dealing with a major tragedy herself, through the grieving process, and back to the point where she wants a career where she can help others to cope with their own traumas. In particular, she is hoping to specialise in counselling those who suffer from depression.

♎ ♎ ♎

Much of the content in this account of the life and death of John Carthy is based on detailed notes taken throughout the proceedings of the Barr Tribunal of Inquiry set up to investigate the shooting at Abbeylara, and also the comments, criticisms and praise contained in the official Report on the incident compiled by the Honourable Mr Justice Robert Barr.

The Tribunal of Inquiry examined the garda operation that was put in place by the officers tasked with responding to the incident. It was quickly noted and accepted that what unfolded at Abbeylara was unique in the history of policing in this country, and the garda response had to be appreciated in such a context. Due recognition was paid to the undoubted pressure that was placed on those officers who were instructed to man the front line of an incident involving an armed and volatile man, and in particular, the tough decisions that faced the Emergency Response Unit officers who were on duty that day.

In his Report, Justice Barr refers repeatedly to the incident as 'the disaster at Abbeylara', and while he pays tribute to certain gardaí and certain garda actions, his seven hundred and forty-four page analysis reaches one overall conclusion – the death of John Carthy should never have happened.

1.

Rose Carthy closed the door behind her when she left. John had asked her to leave him alone in the cottage the two of them shared, not in an aggressive tone, but in a voice that was sad and serious. She always did as he asked, unable to break the hold that an only son has over his mother, but she hated leaving him that evening. There was an air about him that was dark, and the scene she left behind in the kitchen would remain with her forever. Her son, sitting silently, focused only on the shotgun in his hand.

Rose hurried down the driveway, heading for the home of her sister, Nancy Walsh. It was a short walk up the Abbeylara road, and for once the slight incline in the road didn't trouble her. Her mind was preoccupied with worry as she re-ran the events of the day to try to find something, anything, that would explain the state John was in and why her twenty-seven-year-old son wanted to be alone with his gun.

She knew he had been in bad form for a long time and that the first months of the new millennium had dealt him some rough blows. The only real relationship he ever had had delighted and destroyed him in the space of a few weeks, he had found it difficult to find and hold on to labouring jobs and he had been openly down on himself. Rose could see it in him, and it tortured her.

When he joined her in the kitchen for some breakfast that morning, he ate his food and didn't say much, but young men can be like that and Rose didn't push him to make small talk.

As usual, it was just mother and son in the house all day. John's sister and only sibling, Marie, had been living and working in Galway for some time. She would visit home at weekends, but for the most part Rose and John had settled into a routine where it was just the two of them.

John had spent that afternoon watching television, while Rose pottered around, doing her chores out of habit rather than necessity. She knew it was a pointless exercise for her now. In a few weeks' time, she and John were due to leave the old house that had reared generations of Carthys and the run-down cottage would be torn to the ground. The council had finally agreed to build them a new home, which was almost ready.

The move was long overdue. The cottage had not been fit to live in for years now. It had reached a stage of severe dilapidation, and no amount of housekeeping could disguise the damp patches and the worn-away flooring. Nothing could brighten up the gloom that was ever present in the small hallway and the three cramped bedrooms. There was no living room, just a small kitchen, and that was where they cooked, ate and watched television.

The new house was progressing at pace, and when Rose looked out the hall window of the cottage she could see it coming along nicely. It was being built just a few yards away on the same site as the old cottage, a modest but modern bungalow.

They were all looking forward to the move. John had been planning for it for months, trying to organise furniture, and telling friends and relatives that he was happy that his mother especially would finally have some comfort. He wanted the place to be perfect, and the new house was all he and Rose had talked about in the winter evenings just past. They went through every detail time and again, and by all accounts the move just couldn't come soon enough.

But on that particular day, second thoughts seemed to be forming in John's mind. When Rose made mention of the new house, as she did on a daily basis, she could see he wasn't pleased. Her excitement seemed to annoy him, and she heard him mutter something about wanting to remain in the old dwelling. It was a complete turn-around, but he was adamant. He told her no one was going to put him out of his home.

She left it at that, but continued to wonder about his sudden negativity on the move. She could only conclude that it was down to the week and the day that was in it, Wednesday, 19 April 2000. It was Easter Week, and Holy Thursday marked the anniversaries of the deaths of both John's father and his grandfather.

The following day, the Carthys would commemorate the death of John senior for the tenth time. He had passed away in 1990, and despite the fact that he was seventy-two, his passing was unexpected, and the sudden trauma was more than John junior could deal with. He was seventeen at the time, and in the months that followed the bereavement those around him noticed that his grieving process was not progressing as it should and he was not coping at all with the loss of his father. The upset had exposed a weakness in him, and it sparked a re-curring battle with depression. The various doctors who would come into contact with him in the following years would all eventually conclude that his father's death had been the 'life trigger' that set off his mental illness.

Down through the years since, John always faltered when it came to Holy Week, and that was the time when Rose would pray for him most. She knew he was burdened by grief and that he was sensitive to the most minor reminders of his father's death. In the early years of his depression, he had experienced frequent auditory hallucinations, many of which left him convinced that he could hear his father calling him to get up for school. But those days had passed, and Rose knew he was much better now. Doctors had treated him and he was conscientious about taking his medication.

The anniversaries were the only explanation Rose could find to explain John's Holy Week anger at the pending move, and she could understand how he would become nostalgic for the ancestral home on the eve of such a sad day. The cottage had been built in 1906 and had been home to three generations of her husband's family. John was fond of the old house; it held memories of the earlier Carthy men. When the council had agreed to their request for the construction of a new home in 1998, John had attempted to convince council officials to leave the old place standing as well. He wrote a letter, which Rose signed, asking the council not to demolish the cottage, but his request was denied.

Rose could understand John's attachment to the cottage, and knew they would all shed a tear when the old place was knocked down, but practicality had to overrule their sentiments. She could have said all this to John, but on this day she knew it would make little difference. Today, he was adamant he was going nowhere and she would leave him be. Now he told her again, nobody was going to put him out.

With those words said, and meant, he went to get his shotgun from its cabinet in the hall. That was not unusual – he had been an avid shooter for years, ever since he went to purchase his first gun at the age of twenty. Rose watched and winced as he went to the door of the house and fired a few shots at nothing in particular. John had never done this before. His mood was increasingly worrying her. He was angry and agitated, and she didn't know what she could do to help.

It was at that point that he asked her to leave the house and pay a visit to the Walsh household up the road. Rose says she did as he asked, not because she was frightened of him, but out of a feeling that it was best to leave him be. As she walked out the door, she heard him say 'good luck'.

There was much to concern Rose on the short walk to the Walsh house. In the last few weeks John had been drinking too much; he had even slept rough one or two nights after having too much beer, and everyone who came into contact with him had commented on his bad form. Neighbours and friends who met with him had been struck at how down he was, and more than one had felt a fleeting concern for the way he was and the things he said.

Abbeylara shares the same gossiping characteristics as any rural village. Its houses and inhabitants live in arcs around a crossroads that is the heart of the town. On a sunny day, it's a pretty place, bedded with flowers and shaded by evergreens. The houses that line its modest main street are quaint and well kept, and shadowed graciously by the soaring stature of St Bernard's Church. The only other imposing building in the village is the handball alley, a place where John Carthy and every youth in Abbeylara spent many lazy hours in the summer holidays. The alley stands just above the crossroads, almost equidistant from the two pubs in the village, Crawford's and McCormack's.

It's the kind of place where familiarity is inbuilt and everyone has a vast knowledge of everyone else. The Carthy cottage stood a few hundred yards on the Cavan side of the church, in a townland called Toneymore, just fifteen miles short of the border with Ulster. There is a dab of Cavan in the accents that air there; words are rolled out with a hint of a lilt and with an emphasis on the broad vowel.

John Carthy was well known in Abbeylara, a familiar figure at the handball alley, in the pubs and out on the Granard road, thumbing a lift. Most knew he suffered from a form of depression. Some who knew the full story of his illness looked out for him and gave him advice; the more narrow-minded exploited his problems and made fun of him.

During that Holy Week and on the weekend preceding it, John had been making remarks that were causing concern to those who heard them. All his thoughts seemed concentrated on those who had wronged him in the past, and particularly on certain people in the village who he believed were constantly mocking him. He was bitter and easily aggravated, and was clearly struggling to control his illness.

♎ ♎ ♎

Saturday, 15 April 2000

John Carthy rose very early. He wasn't sleeping well, a symptom of something stirring in his mind. By a quarter past eight that morning, he was walking around Abbeylara village, waiting for the shops to open so that he could buy a packet of cigarettes. He had been barred from Crawford's pub a few years previously, and that was the only place open at such an early hour. Hanging around, he bumped into a local man by the name of Larry Boland, and he told him he would shoot the publican Willie Crawford were it not for the fact that his mother had to live in the area.

John spent much of that Saturday helping Brendan and Pat McLoughlin to lay some foundations for a new house. He talked while he worked, and the McLoughlin brothers didn't know if they should take what he was saying seriously. He was in bad form, and was 'giving out hell' about the fact that they had to wait for the delivery of some materials. He told Brendan McLoughlin that a man should be in the pub at three o'clock on a Saturday, rather than spreading concrete. He complained to them about a number of locals, saying there were a lot of people in Abbeylara that he did not like. He told Pat McLoughlin that they were a 'shower of cunts' and he would like to 'shoot a heap of them'.

That evening, he walked down to the village to have a drink in McCormack's pub. Sitting at the bar, he tuned in to the banter going on around him and became paranoid that a group of youngsters were making comments about him. He confronted the group, an altercation ensued, and John stormed out of the pub. He decided to continue his evening out in Longford town, and he phoned his friend Bernard Reilly for a lift.

Over the course of that Saturday, John phoned his sister Marie a total of nineteen times between half past eight in the morning and five o'clock in the evening. Phone records show that only two of the calls were of any significant duration.

Sunday, 16 April

After a late night out in Longford, John stayed home all the next day, watching television. As evening approached, he decided to go out drinking again, but didn't feel he could go back to McCormack's after the row on the previous night. Again he called on Bernard Reilly and asked him for a lift to the Town & Country pub in Castlepollard.

While there, he met another acquaintance of his, Sean Farrell, and the two of them chatted for a while. Farrell thought John Carthy looked very down in himself, and he recalled him saying that his mother had been giving out to him about his drinking. Mr Farrell, who was something of a father figure to Carthy, advised his young friend to go home early that night, just to keep his mother happy.

In spite of this advice, and despite the fact that he was supposed to be working at a site in Longford the next morning, John decided to go on to another pub, and he hailed a taxi to bring him to Oldcastle. He entered the Mountain Dew pub, where he sat alone and drank four pints of Guinness while reading a newspaper. When closing time came, he asked bar staff if there was any accommodation in the town. He staggered away into the dark, but never made it to any of the B&Bs or hotels in the area. Instead, it is suspected that he slept rough in some quiet corner of the town.

He phoned Marie on two separate occasions that evening. According to his sister, there was nothing to cause her concern from any of these conversations, and all that was discussed were plans for the forthcoming Easter weekend, when Marie was returning home for a visit.

Monday, 17 April

Although John was up and about early the next morning, he was far from where he was supposed to be. Gerard Delaney, his boss at the site in Longford, waited for him to clock in, but there was no sign of him and no phone call of explanation. John was in no rush to get back to Abbeylara, and spent half the day in the hostelries around Oldcastle.

At eight o'clock, he ate breakfast at the Finn Court, and washed his food down with four bottles of Budweiser. According to staff, John was in chatty form. He tried to engage them in conversation, and also asked them to turn on the jukebox. Mid-morning he moved on to the Napper Arms and drank some more. The owner of the Arms, Adelle Leary, kept an eye on him, concerned by his demeanour. She recalled that he had his feet up on chairs, and that he was 'rough and untidy, he had big boots on him and he looked like he could be after sleeping out.' He snoozed on a chair in the bar for a few hours.

In the afternoon, John took a taxi back to Abbeylara and called again on the McLoughlin brothers, who were still working on their foundation. When John arrived, the McLoughlins were trying to convert metric measurements, and he told them they should just go and buy a 'fucking conversion ruler' and make the task simpler for themselves. Pat McLoughlin thought he looked very pale. He had known John Carthy for years, and liked him. He was aware of John's depression and knew he wasn't supposed to mix alcohol with his daily course of medication. Expressing concern, he advised John to cut down on his drinking. John didn't appreciate the interference and he became very agitated. In an angry outburst, he asked Pat McLoughlin if he was 'fucking insinuating that I cannot drink?' Pat McLoughlin told him to cool down and go for a walk, and with that John moved on.

After his sudden departure, the McLoughlin brothers discussed John Carthy and both expressed the view that he had changed a lot in that past year. They were concerned about him, and Pat told his brother Brendan that he should 'ring the gardaí and get him lifted'. That call was never made.

John made numerous phone calls again that day, two of

which were to the office of his solicitor, Mark Connellan. When the secretary in the Connellan office answered his first call, John was told that his lawyer was away on holidays, and would not be back until 2 May. He hung up, waited a minute, and phoned the office again just to be sure. Speculating on this call to his solicitor, Rose Carthy would later explain that her son was probably ringing Mr Connellan to arrange some help with a loan they were seeking to buy furniture for the new house.

'John and myself were worrying about getting money to furnish the new house. I went to the Bank of Ireland in Granard for a loan and they wouldn't give it to me. John then got on to Mark Connellan's solicitor's office and made an appointment for 2.5.00 and he was away on holidays. He was John's solicitor, and he thought he might help him with a loan to furnish the house,' she said.

That Monday, John also phoned Marie's mobile twenty-two times. Marie had always talked to her brother every day on the phone since she had left home, but she has been unable to account for the dozens of calls made to her that week. From the phone records, it would appear that John actually dialled her voicemail on numerous occasions, but he never left her a message.

John also phoned a friend of his by the name of Kevin Ireland on two occasions that day. Despite the fact that he was at home in Abbeylara, he told Ireland that he was in Dublin for the day. According to Kevin Ireland, John would frequently call him to say he was in the capital city.

Tuesday, 18 April
That morning, John Carthy thumbed a lift to work and was picked up by a local electrician, John Scally. Mr Scally was

employed at the Enplast factory in Granard, and John made several references to one of the headmen at the plant and another local businessman. His mood was still angry, and he told Scally that 'both of them should be shot'. Scally dropped his passenger off and thought no more about it.

John worked away for the morning, but at lunchtime he drank two pints of Guinness with his food. He returned to work briefly after his break, but left the site again at three o'clock and didn't reappear for two hours. During this time, he went to the shopping centre in the town and at some point he went to a pharmacy to purchase his anti-depressant and mood stabilising medications for the month. When he returned to the site at five o'clock to collect his stuff, he was met by his boss, Gerard Delaney, and was quizzed as to why he hadn't been at work all afternoon. John told him he had been having a few drinks down town, to which Delaney responded that he had better go home. According to a workmate, Kieran Lennon, John seemed to think he had been dismissed from the job for good, but he didn't appear too bothered by it. He told Kieran Lennon he 'might as well go to the bookies' while he waited for the six o' clock bus home.

That day, John made another phone call to the office of Mark Connellan, and was told for the third time that his solicitor was away. Ann Doyle, the secretary at the office, recalled that John was very anxious on the phone, and she asked if he would like to speak to any of the other lawyers at the firm. He refused the offer and would not give her any idea of what was bothering him.

The Carthys had a visitor later that evening. A neighbour, Alice Farrell, called to see Rose, but it was John who met her at the door. Ms Farrell attempted to make conversation, saying she knew John must have been home because she had heard music coming from the kitchen.

'I says, "I was thinking you were here John when I heard the rock music" – you know, joking like. He says "Alice", he says, "the party is over, no more laughing and the guards won't be here anymore". I took it up. I says, "John, I never sent the gardaí to you or what are you worrying about?" He says, "the guards won't be here anymore".'

Ms Farrell was baffled by the replies she received from her young neighbour. But she left it at that. She knew just by looking at John that he wasn't well, that he was perhaps a bit high and felt it was best to leave him be.

That night, John entered McCormack's pub again, hoping to be served. However, he was refused alcohol on the basis of the altercation he had had there the previous weekend. Accepting the punishment, he drank two cans of 7Up and went home.

When he awoke on the Wednesday morning, he was teetering even closer to the edge of despair. The hours dragged by, the world seemed no brighter a place, and he finally reached the point where he took out his gun and asked his mother to go.

Nancy Walsh, her daughter Ann, and their neighbour, Alice Farrell, were all in the Walsh house when Rose arrived to the door in what they later described as a hysterical state. She was crying and they strained to decipher what she was trying to say. Ann Walsh asked her aunt 'Is it John?' and believed Rose replied to the effect that she was afraid 'John would shoot himself'.

The recollections of those frantic minutes in the Walsh house have intermingled to form different accounts of the exact fears Rose Carthy expressed to her relations that evening. Nancy

Walsh formed the view that her nephew John had 'told Rose to go up to me for a couple of hours and the first garda to come was going to get it'. Rose denies ever saying this, and is certain that her son made no mention of the gardaí before she left the house.

Whatever was or was not said, the picture that emerged to the women in the Walsh house was that John Carthy was in the house with the gun and something in what he had said or done had sent his mother into this panic. They had always known Rose to be reserved and sedate, and seeing her in such a state of fear was enough to infuse them all with a similar sense of alarm. Within minutes, the women had worked themselves up into a type of terror, and they decided the only thing they could do was to phone the gardaí.

2.

When the phone rang in Granard garda station that evening, it interrupted what was otherwise a quiet day. There were three gardaí sitting in the main office when the call came through. Garda Maeve Gorman had been there all day, on duty as the station orderly. It was now 5.25 pm, and she had been joined in the main office by Garda John Gibbons and Garda Colin White, two patrol members who had dropped by the station for a break. Gorman went to answer the call, and was immediately snapped out of the Holy Week monotony. The woman on the other end of the line was frantic, to the point that Garda Gorman had difficulty understanding what Rose Carthy was saying. She was crying, and making little sense.

After a few seconds, Rose was unable to speak anymore and she handed the phone over to Ann Walsh, who quickly gave Garda Gorman the basic details of what was unfolding. Scribbling down notes, Garda Gorman assured Ms Walsh that a unit was on the way, and hanging up, she made the first entry in relation to the Abbeylara siege into the station's occurrence book, writing 'the caller reported that her son had locked himself into the house, that he had a loaded shotgun and had fired a few shots.'

Hearing part of the conversation, White and Gibbons knew something was stirring, and they awaited instructions from Gorman. She told them all she had heard from the frantic caller, and she asked them to leave straight away to travel to the home of John Carthy. The officers responded, and went to gather what they would need for such a call-out. Gibbons, who was now in his twenty-seventh year at the station, quickly changed out of his uniform and back into plain clothes. As the senior member, he armed himself with a Smith & Wesson revolver and put on a flak jacket underneath his civilian garments. His colleague, Garda White, was unarmed and was in uniform. This was only his second year as a garda.

White was doing the driving, and he turned the patrol car in the direction of Abbeylara to respond to what was his first ever firearms incident. He had no knowledge of John Carthy, and on the way to Toneymore, Gibbons filled him in on what he knew of the young man from Abbeylara. As one of the senior members at Granard station, Gibbons had acquired a good store of information on the people of the region and particularly of those who had any dealings with the gardaí. He knew that John Carthy had suffered bouts of depression in the past, and also that there had been some difficulties over his shotgun licence one or two years previously. He had met Carthy a few times socially, and wondered what it was that had sent him into this spin.

It took the two gardaí ten minutes to reach Abbeylara, and the women in the Walsh household were finding it difficult to stay calm. They were straining to hear any noise coming from down the road, and were starting to imagine the different scenarios that could unfold if John had reached a new low in his depression. As the minutes ticked by, Ann Walsh phoned Garda Gorman on a number of occasions, dialling the garda station out of desperation, asking why it was taking the gardaí so long to respond. Garda Gorman felt that Ms Walsh was sounding increasingly petrified on the phone. She claims Ms

Walsh told her there was only a field between the Carthy cottage and their own home, and she was afraid that Carthy might come over the field to them.

By this time, John's cousin, Rosaleen Mahon, had also called down to the Walsh house and she brought a sense of practicality to the situation. She had a really soft spot for Carthy, and had always had a good relationship with him. Contrary to what some in the village would say about him, she always found him to be a sweet young man, and that was one of the reasons he was often called upon by relatives to babysit their children. Young children adored his easy manner and the way he never tired of their games, and he relaxed with the kids because they took him for what he was. She had half a mind to go down to the Carthy cottage herself to try and calm John down, but the other women persuaded her that it was too dangerous. She tried to calm the fears of the other women, and decided to make a phone call herself to someone who could shed a better light on why her cousin was acting in such an aggressive manner.

♎   ♎   ♎

Dr Patrick Cullen was just finishing up at his surgery in Coole, County Westmeath when he got the urgent call. He was surprised to hear it was a cousin of one of his patients, John Carthy, and he barely had time to take in what was being said before the line went dead again. He was told that Carthy was 'high', and that he was firing his shotgun. Rosaleen Mahon asked him to come as quickly as he could to Abbeylara.

Dr Cullen was well aware of John's problems. He was in fact the one who had first diagnosed Carthy with depression back in 1992. John was only nineteen then, and Dr Cullen had hoped that he was just another troubled teen who would overcome his problems after a short course of pills. That wasn't to be the case.

Dr Cullen had been John's GP since the eighties, and had seen the change in him after his father died. He had become withdrawn and sensitive and had started drinking too much. The most minor life stresses caused him undue amounts of anguish and he worried about everything. Watching this hyper-sensitivity progress and worsen, Dr Cullen was not surprised when he heard in the spring of 1992 that John had dropped out of his first year at Warrenstown Agricultural College. John had an appointment with Dr Cullen shortly after he left the course, and he admitted he had yearned for the familiarity of home, and also that he had been thinking a lot about suicide. He told his GP that he had been 'down' since the Christmas of his first year at college, that he thought a lot about his father's death and was worried about how his sister, Marie, would get on with her Leaving Certificate exams. Dr Cullen advised the young man to voluntarily admit himself to St Loman's psychiatric hospital in Mullingar to get some help with the constant low he was experiencing.

John was first admitted to St Loman's on 25 March 1992 and he remained in the care of the hospital for almost two weeks. Records of that admission by consultant psychiatrist Dr John McGeown stated that John Carthy had been having suicidal ideas for two months, mostly centring on thoughts of drowning himself. The psychiatrist recorded that John 'at times has a death wish. He had suicidal ideas for two months ... had thought of going to the nearby lake and jumping in.' The psychiatrist concluded that he had unresolved morbid grief in relation to the death of his father, and in the discharge summary, the following was written:

'He has become preoccupied with memories of his father's death and has had pseudo-hallucinations of his father, vivid visual and auditory imagery in which he sees him and hears his voice.'

Carthy was prescribed a combination of anti-depressant and tranquilliser medications to deal with his moods, but just four months later, he was back in St Loman's again for his second voluntary admission. Altogether, he was admitted to hospital on five different occasions in the course of the nineties, and his condition fluctuated until a suitable combination of drugs was found for him.

His doctors began to see patterns in his behaviour and his moods as the years passed by, and those trends led them to diagnose John with bipolar affective disorder, or manic depression, when he was just twenty years old. He displayed symptoms of the highs and lows of the illness, forever contradicting himself, one minute telling doctors he felt his left side was paralysed, the next saying he felt he could run a marathon.

Bipolar affective disorder affects about one per cent of the Irish population, and is equally diagnosed in both men and women, regardless of their backgrounds. The illness is characterised by episodes of both depression and elation, hence the use of the term bipolar. Most who suffer from the illness will experience their first episode of either a high or a low before the age of thirty.

The condition manifests itself in various ways, but for John Carthy, one sure sign of his mental unrest was a physical complaint, and his psychological problems would often lead him to grumble over pain from non-existent physical injuries. He became obsessed by his health, and in times of elation or depression he would often feel pain for no reason. In April 1993, he suffered a knee injury while working at the Pat the Baker factory in Granard – the accident occurred on a Holy Thursday, suggesting again that that particular day and its significance as the anniversary of his father's death triggered a surge in his mental unrest. He complained of pain in his knee and back for months after the incident. Doctors at first prescribed something for the physical discomfort, and even put him on a course of physiotherapy. After the accident, he remained off work on sick leave related to his injuries for six months. When his complaints continued however, doctors concluded that his symptoms were 'inconsistent' with the minor accident he had had, and concluded that the problem was almost entirely psychological.

John demonstrated extremes of both mania and depression. He would swing between feelings of being 'high' for sustained periods to being depressed, but there were also times when he was perfectly normal. In the first years of his illness doctors found him very sensitive and extremely vulnerable. He was tearful at times. On his third voluntary admission to St Loman's, he was again treated by Dr John McGeown, who recorded that six months after the accident at the Pat the Baker factory, John was still obsessed by what had happened. By this time, Dr McGeown had formed the view that John was a very insecure young man, who was easily upset by any kind of physical or emotional trauma. The psychiatrist reiterated his view that it was the death of his father that was the dominant issue preying on his young patient's mind. He wrote at that time that John 'had not entirely gotten over his father's death.'.

John would also regularly display signs of extreme paranoia. On his fourth voluntary admission to St Loman's in 1994, he confessed he was worried about catching disease from rats in the cottage, and said he felt his relatives were plotting to get rid of him. He told doctors that he had been afraid he would catch an infection in his own house and that he had spent the previous night at his aunt's house. He could not sleep there either however. He said, 'the doors were rattling ... I thought they wanted to get rid of me so that they could get the land'. This was something that preoccupied him from time to time over the years, a suspicion that his family wanted him out of the picture so that they could have 'the land'. John in fact did not own any land, but was due to inherit about fifteen acres from his mother in the future.

As the years passed, a suitable course of drugs was found and they stabilised his highs and lows. A combination of the mood stabiliser, lithium, and the major tranquilliser, Stelazine, worked best for him and brought him back to some degree of normality. Added to the right combination of drugs, John helped himself by gaining a great insight into his illness. He understood what was wrong with him, and tried to deal with it. He became interested in the work of AWARE, and attended some lectures by the psychiatrist who had founded the organisation. He took his medications as prescribed, never failing to pick up prescriptions from Dr Cullen and always buying his tablets on the first day of every month. He wanted to overcome his illness, if only to guarantee that he would never have to set foot inside St Loman's Hospital again. He had developed a serious dislike of the hospital in the time he had spent there over the years, and the hope that he would never be a patient there again was incentive enough for him to take his medication and to keep himself well.

The only major setback he had came in 1997, when he was involved in a car accident. He received some minor physical injuries in the crash, but the trauma of the accident stayed with him and rattled his already weakened state of mind. His doctors came to regard it as another significant event in his life that triggered further psychological symptoms in him. He showed signs of post-traumatic stress, nightmares disturbed his sleep and he found it difficult and frightening to travel in cars.

After the accident, John pursued a personal injury claim, a symptom of another of his personality traits. He was extremely litigious, forever feeling he was at the brunt of injustice and seeking legal advice on the most minor issues. He had far more dealings than most young men with his solicitor, Mark Connellan, and he seemed to be obsessed by the legal practice in general.

His personal injury claim was, however, successful and in July 1998, he received compensation in the region of twenty thousand pounds. He lodged the money in the Bank of Ireland in Longford on 11 September 1998. Ten months later, all of the money had been spent, mostly frittered away in petty gambling.

Ω   Ω   Ω

It was close to six o'clock when Gardaí Gibbons and White arrived at the row of bungalows that surrounded the Carthys'. Everything was quiet, and they kept their speed to a minimum as they approached the shabby cottage that Gibbons knew to be the old Carthy home. On the journey out from Granard, they had discussed what they should do and decided to call first on the Walsh house to get the full story and an idea of the type of man they were dealing with. On their way there, they met and spoke with Michael Burke, a next-door neighbour of the Carthys. He was keeping an eye on the cottage, and was concerned. He told the gardaí that Carthy had fired a number of shots out the back while Rose was still in the house. He said he had heard four or five shots up to that point.

White drove around the Walsh house and parked at the rear. After knocking on the back door, the officers were left on the doorstep for a minute while one of the women ventured forth to ask who was there and eventually unlocked the bolted door. Inside, Gibbons and White found the five women huddled together in the kitchen. Nancy Walsh, her daughters Ann Walsh and Rosaleen Mahon, and their neighbour Alice Farrell were all gathered around a very distressed woman whom the gardaí took to be Rose Carthy. According to Gibbons, there was a sense of 'total panic' about the women. They were openly upset, their nerves having been eroded to nothing in the minutes since the first shots had been fired down the road. The women were all talking at once – the accounts of what was said and what wasn't said again differ between all who were present in the Walsh kitchen. Ann Walsh, for instance, believed she heard Gibbons ask, 'What are we up against here … is it a shoot-out or what?' a claim that is refuted by the senior officer. Alice Farrell believed she gave the gardaí the name of John's psychiatrist and told them where he was based, but neither Gibbons nor White have any recollection of this.

The gardaí learned that John was on anti-depressants and that Dr Cullen was on his way. They also asked the women who would be the best person to talk to Carthy and calm him down, and were told that John's cousin, Tom Walsh, was the best candidate for that. He was working in Cork, and they had already tried to get in touch with him with no success, but they would keep trying. Garda Colin White had also managed to convince Rose to give them John's mobile number. He sensed that Rose was reluctant to do this, and recalled her saying 'he will know it was me who gave you this number.'

Emerging from the Walsh house, White and Gibbons were concerned at the possibility that John might have already taken his own life, and getting back into their patrol car, they decided it was their duty to make sure that he had not committed suicide. They hadn't heard any shots since they arrived in the area, and they didn't know if that was a good or bad sign. Maybe the deed was already done, or maybe he was having second thoughts. Both of the officers admit it did not occur to them to try phoning John on his mobile to check if he was okay, and both felt the right thing to do at that moment was to head straight for the Carthy cottage. White edged the marked patrol car the short distance from Walsh's to the Carthy gate, and drove straight up the driveway. Just as he was about to bring the car to a stop however, John discharged two shots from the house. The young officer fumbled to find reverse, and swung the car back out of the drive, as the realisation dawned on both officers that this might be something other than an attempt at suicide.

3.

As Dr Cullen made the journey to Abbeylara he thought of three people he had known who had killed themselves by putting a gun to their heads. Now he worried that John Carthy would be number four.

It was the time of year for it. Spring was always the worst time of year for suicides, the longer evenings serving only to further depress jaded minds. The doctor had never seen John in a seriously suicidal state, but some hid it better than others.

As Dr Cullen brought his car to a stop a little way up the road from the Carthy home, two shots exploded through the silence. A patrol car careered out of the Carthy driveway, aimlessly swerving backwards. Dr Cullen didn't know how to read the situation, unable to figure out if he had just heard John Carthy kill himself, or if he had just heard his patient attempt to put a bullet through a garda vehicle.

The patrol car emerged from the driveway and drove down the hill towards where Dr Cullen had parked, just outside Farrells' house on the Cavan side of the Carthy home. The doctor quickly jumped from his own car and ducked into the back seat of the patrol vehicle to introduce himself to the gardaí and tell them what he could. The conversation between the officers in the front and the doctor in the back took the form of questions and answers, the gardaí eager to get what information they could before the situation escalated any further. The answers came easily to Dr Cullen, and it calmed his nerves to revert back to making diagnoses and giving a patient history, rather than to think of what was going on inside the house.

Having known John Carthy since he was a teenager, there was a multitude of things the doctor could have divulged to the officers, but in the tense circumstances that prevailed that evening, he kept it simple. He told the gardaí he suspected that John had been drinking, because that often transformed his usually mild manner into something more aggressive. He told them that John was on medication and that he suffered from a severe form of depression. Garda White handed him John's mobile number and suggested the doctor try phoning his patient in the hope that this would calm him down. Dr Cullen obliged, but the phone rang out and John never answered.

Dr Cullen then gave Gardaí Gibbons and White a very important warning. He was keen to get it off his chest because it had been bothering him since Rosaleen Mahon had told him that the gardaí were on their way. The warning was crucial in the circumstances, and if he did nothing else to help, Dr Cullen wanted the officers to understand one thing. They were dealing with a young man who hated the gardaí.

John's difficult history with the local officers was well known amongst his family and acquaintances. It was the reason Rose had been reluctant to make that initial call to Granard station, and it was the reason she had worried about handing John's mobile number over to Garda White. She knew what had happened to turn John against the force, and so did Dr Cullen.

In September 1998, John was arrested and accused of an arson attack on a giant fibreglass goat in the town. The goat had been brought to Abbeylara to act as a mascot for the local gaelic football club in the county final, and over the weekend of the big match it was positioned on the village green for all to see. The night after the game, however, the goat was set alight and incinerated, and John was suggested as the guilty party. He was arrested and brought to Granard station, where he was questioned for a number of hours. He was eventually released without charge.

The arrest had been made largely on hearsay and no hard evidence existed that would place John Carthy in the frame. The publican Willie Crawford was the man who had arranged for the goat to be brought to the town, and anxious to find the guilty party, he made his own inquires into the malicious attack. Eventually two local youths came forward claiming that John Carthy was the man he wanted.

It wasn't long before the allegation started to spread throughout Abbeylara, and by lunchtime that day, John had heard the rumour himself. Vexed at the allegation, he presented himself at Granard Garda station to complain that Willie Crawford was wrongfully blaming him for the arson. Having lodged his complaint, he left the station, hoping that that would be the end of the matter.

Mr Crawford had also approached a member of the gardaí, however. He brought the allegation against John Carthy to Garda Dave Martin of Smear Garda Station. The information was passed down the line, and eventually landed on Garda Turlough Bruen's desk. There was nothing concrete to back up the allegation, but in spite of this, John became the number one suspect in the case of the burnt goat.

'It is evident that Garda Bruen accepted without question the information he had been given by Garda Martin and despite its paucity of detail and without any investigation by him, and that he firmly believed that Mr Carthy was responsible for the destruction of the goat mascot the previous night – a high profile crime which no doubt was of much interest to the people of Abbeylara. Garda Bruen did not regard it as necessary to interview any alleged eyewitnesses to the offence and appears to have decided that all required of him was to prevail on John Carthy to confess his guilt.' (Barr Tribunal Report)

Garda Bruen went to Toneymore to bring John to the station. John was not home, but he voluntarily presented himself at the station later that evening to try to clear his name. Garda Bruen informed him of the allegations that had been made against him, and accused him of being responsible for the burning of the goat. John protested his innocence and tried to leave the station, but was immediately arrested and brought into an interview room where he was questioned by Garda Bruen and Garda Frank McHugh. John was extremely annoyed, and in the course of the interview he expressed his dislike of various gardaí and people in the village who he felt had done him wrong.

When he calmed down, John was able to give the officers a record of his movements on the night of the arson, and he repeatedly and vehemently denied any involvement in the destruction of the mascot. After two hours of interrogation, a phone call was placed by Garda Dave Martin to one of the alleged witnesses, and it was discovered that he had not, in fact, ever seen John near the goat.

Gardaí released John, but the three hours he had spent in custody played greatly on his mind in the weeks and months that followed. He was embarrassed that he had been put through such an ordeal, and it added another dent to an already fractured sense of confidence.

When he was let go that night, John phoned his friend Bernard Reilly for a lift home. In the car, he explained what had happened, and told Reilly he had endured 'a rough time' in the station. He didn't go into detail, but the following day, he went to see Dr Cullen, alleging that he had been assaulted while in custody. He complained that his neck had been injured in the assault, and on examination, the doctor did find some tenderness but no evidence of bruising. Dr Cullen felt the type of tenderness he found on John's neck would be consistent with some trauma or the application of force to that area. John did not tell the doctor which of the gardaí had allegedly mistreated him.

The gardaí totally denied any wrongdoing, but their defence foundered on one crucial detail. Contrary to every regulation in the force, not one note was taken of what was said or what went on in the hours John Carthy spent in the interview room. (It was a serious oversight on the part of Gardaí Bruen and McHugh, and one that would cause them to come in for criticism from Justice Robert Barr when he came to examine the wrongful arrest of John Carthy.)

'Contrary to police practice and instruction, no notes were taken by either officer. Garda Bruen's explanation in evidence was that he intended to take notes but Mr Carthy was talking too quickly and he was anxious not to interrupt him as that might discourage him from giving his account. I do not accept that explanation'. (Barr Tribunal Report)

Justice Barr goes on to say it is his belief that John Carthy was assaulted in the hours he spent in garda custody, and this he states was a significant factor in fuelling Carthy's animosity towards the gardaí, which manifested itself again on the eve of Holy Thursday in the year 2000.

'…it appears that John Carthy was probably subjected to physical abuse while under interrogation … at Granard Station on the night of 23rd September, 1998 and falsely accused of burning the goat mascot … I do not accept the evidence of [the gardaí] that neither of them physically abused the subject while under interrogation after an unjustified arrest and charging with a substantial crime.'

Justice Barr contends that the issue of the wrongful arrest in 1998 was a serious hindrance in what unfolded at Abbeylara in Easter week 2000. He states in his Report that the embarrassment and distress it caused to Carthy meant that no garda would ever succeed in winning his trust and convincing him to leave his home quietly.

The issue of the arrest did indeed stay with John for a long time, and he frequently spoke about it in the same tone of annoyance and agitation. Those who enjoyed making fun of him often taunted him about the goat and the time he had spent in the station, and it bothered him greatly. Eventually, he paid a visit to his solicitor, Mark Connellan, and asked him to send a letter on his behalf to Willie Crawford. On the back of this, the solicitor sent the following letter to Mr Crawford:

'Our Client wants to make it absolutely clear that there is no basis whatsoever for such an allegation and our Client will simply not tolerate such an allegation being made about him. Our Client requires that you withdraw the allegation forthwith, and he wants to make it clear that if there is any repetition of the allegation by you, he will take steps as are necessary to protect his good name and reputation.'

In the days leading up to Easter week, the arrest and the embarrassment it had caused John was raised again, when he received a bill from Mark Connellan for £35 in respect of the above letter that was written to Willie Crawford. Both Rose and Marie knew the receipt of that bill brought it all back to John again, a fact verified from the conversation he had with Pat McLoughlin the weekend before he put his mother out of the house. As part of his outburst about the 'shower of cunts' that he felt occupied Abbeylara, John was giving out about one of the young men who blamed him for the arson and he also wasn't short of negative things to say about Garda Frank McHugh.

The arrest and its subsequent effect on John was a vital piece of information, and Dr Cullen was anxious to put it across to the first gardaí on the scene that evening; he told Gibbons and White that John had been greatly upset by the issue of the wrongful arrest, and he warned them that his patient 'might not be too happy' to see gardaí around his house.

The gardaí took the warning on board, but while they were listening to the doctor most of their attention was fixed on the road up ahead and on the entrance to the Carthy property. They were still shaken by the shots that were fired at them in the drive. That present danger had to be their first priority.

☊   ☊   ☊

While the doctor and the two gardaí were still sitting in the patrol car, back-up arrived in the form of Detective Garda Jim Campbell. He had been contacted by Garda Maeve Gorman and had decided to travel to Abbeylara himself. Gibbons got out of the car and consulted with his superior, telling him what had gone on, and what they knew of this twenty-seven-year-old man. Campbell swept an eye around the property, and suggested they attempt another approach to the house, only this time they would travel up the driveway in his unmarked car.

As the more senior officers, Gibbons and Campbell opted to make the journey on their own, leaving White to remain out on the road to keep an eye out for any traffic that might be passing. The officers were thankful for the fact that as part of the work on the new Carthy house, a strong concrete wall had been built to separate the Carthy property from the public highway. Mercifully, it was about five foot high, but the gardaí knew that if this situation was to continue in its present tense circumstance, all traffic on the road would have to be rerouted.

As Gibbons and Campbell prepared to make their approach, Dr Cullen remained in the back of the patrol car, unsure of what he should do. He had already attempted to phone John on his mobile phone, but got no answer. He would have been prepared to try talking to his patient, but while the shotgun was part of the equation, it wouldn't be safe for him to approach the cottage. All he could really offer was information, but the gardaí had now turned their attention to what action they could take to try and prevent the situation from worsening.

Garda White occasionally got back into the front seat of the car, but no real conversation passed between him and the doctor. The young officer was concentrating on watching his senior colleagues advance towards the Carthy driveway. He saw the unmarked car disappear through the gateway to the property, and was relieved when the silence around the cottage was not broken by another explosion from Carthy's shotgun.

♎ ♎ ♎

Gibbons and Campbell paused for a second when the car came to a stop, and absorbed the layout of the old house. It was positioned in an odd direction, the front door facing into the hedge at the opposite side of the garden from the driveway. The gable end of the house looked out on to the road, and at the back of the house – the side nearest the drive – there were one or two small sheds that seemed to be almost attached to the main building. The new house was under construction a few metres away.

With no idea of where John Carthy was in the house, the gardaí got out, drew their guns and crept quickly to the sheds. Nothing. The silence was welcome, if unnerving, and the gardaí took it as an invitation to edge further around the house. Moving with caution, they passed the windows in a crouched position and hovered at corners until they came to the front and only door at the side of the house. Pausing for a moment to again ensure all was quiet, Campbell decided to make the first move. Crouched at the side of the porch, he reached his hand around and knocked on the front door. He shouted in to John.

Nothing. The two gardaí waited, barely daring to breathe. Was he listening? Perhaps he was at the other side of the house and hadn't heard the question. Perhaps he was just inside the door, biding his time. Then, a noise. Glass breaking at some location that was uncomfortably close to where they were crouched. For one confused moment, the gardaí wondered why John Carthy was smashing out a window. Then they got their answer. To get a better aim.

A shot exploded through the silence, almost deafening the

two gardaí and confirming the dread they were feeling since they had left the safety of their unmarked car. Both Gibbons and Campbell were sure they were going to die, and they froze in their positions, pinned to the wall between the windows of the cottage. They were afraid to breathe or blink in case John would suddenly appear beside them, and that would be it. Any attempt at running back to the car would surely be lethal. They had no choice but to stay put and hope that John remained inside.

A few minutes passed. The house had gone quiet again; they decided they should move position to the back of the Carthy property. As they covered each other, and rushed to the rear of the house, another shot was fired from the front of the house. It seemed that Carthy was moving from room to room, breaking out panes of glass and firing shots into the distance. Campbell however, decided he had nothing to lose by making another attempt at talking to the young man and asking him to calm down.

He shouted in some assurances. He told John that they were members of the gardaí and they wanted him to throw out his shotgun. He assured him that no harm had been done and that nobody had been injured, so he should just throw out the gun and calm down. The response from the house was not encouraging.

'Fuck off', John Carthy shouted, 'Come in here, you fucker, I'm not coming out.'

Another approach was needed, and Campbell decided to offer John some help. He shouted in that Dr Cullen was there and would like to speak to him. Campbell told John that the doctor was 'outside in the car', but did not specify that he was actually in a patrol car that was further down the road. John immediately fired two shots from a window at the back of the house. The shots were aimed at the unmarked car in the driveway, and being a good marksman he managed to hit the front left wing of the vehicle. From that particular window, John would not have been able to see whether or not the car was occupied, which suggests he was shooting at the vehicle out of a belief that Dr Cullen was in it.

The situation was getting far beyond their control. Campbell and Gibbons sought the best protection they could find around the house, and Campbell phoned Garda Gorman on his mobile, requesting more back up. Truly fearing for their lives, there was nothing they could do but remain on bended knees away from the windows and the door.

Keeping their eyes peeled and their movements to a minimum, their minds were racked with worry. They were conscious that John Carthy could come out at any time. And worse still, they were conscious of the fact that their car was still in the driveway, and the keys were in the ignition in easy reach of John. The keys would remain there for a further ten hours, long after Campbell and Gibbons had been moved away to safety by their superiors. Had Carthy decided at any stage to leave the house, the unmarked garda car was there as an option.

Out on the roadway, Dr Cullen was growing increasingly anxious. He had heard the shots that were fired when his name was mentioned, and felt sure they were meant for him. Sitting in silence with Garda White one thing in particular was bothering him; he couldn't figure out how John had managed to get hold of the shotgun.

The last the doctor had heard, John Carthy's gun had been confiscated by the gardaí. That was back in 1998, after a number of people in the Abbeylara area had alleged that John was threatening to shoot locals. Dr Cullen couldn't understand what could have made the gardaí reconsider, and he wondered if John had got hold of another gun somewhere else.

4.

John Carthy's working life had been sporadic and variable. After he dropped out of agricultural college, he took up odd jobs in the area, labouring and helping out on local sites. He picked up some skills, but his career was a nomadic one that brought him all around Longford and also to Galway for a time. For one reason or another, he never stayed with any employer for too long. He would find fault with them, or they would tire of his mood swings. There were long periods of time when he was unemployed, and those were the worst days for Rose. She would have to watch him simmer, his boredom further frustrating him every day. It was a problem that was worsened by the fact that he had very few hobbies.

John's main interests were handball and shooting. He was known to have a talent for both, but while handball had occupied a lot of his time as a youngster, shooting became his passion once he reached his twenties. It was, and still is, a common pastime in the Abbeylara area. The village has its own active gun club, and a good percentage of young males get involved in the sport at one time or another. Carthy spent his teenage years watching men from the village setting out on shooting trips, and as soon as he was old enough, he purchased his own double-barrelled shotgun, a Baikal. The gun became his favourite possession, and he was fanatical about cleaning it and keeping it in perfect condition.

In his first years as a shooting enthusiast, he participated in the gun club activities, but he allowed his membership to lapse in the mid-nineties. He preferred to go shooting in his own time, and he continued to join relatives and friends on regular hunts. He loved the outings, and he was careful and competent with the weapon, always making sure it was safely broken open when it was not in use or when he was crossing a ditch or a gate. Those who accompanied him felt he had immense respect for the gun and its power, and he was admired as having a very good shot.

Difficulties arose, however, when Carthy allegedly began to use the gun as more than just an accessory for his hobby. Stories began to circulate around the village that he was threatening to shoot people. Word of these threats first surfaced in 1998 when Carthy was medically believed to be in a state of mania. The allegations reached the authorities, and they eventually led gardai to confiscate his gun.

In the August of that year, Carthy got into a row with some children at the handball alley. He was prone to being difficult if he wasn't winning or if he couldn't get a game, and on this particular summer day, he was alleged to have threatened those gathered in the alley, telling them he would go home and get his gun and shoot them.

'... the court [handball alley] was frequently occupied by children and John Carthy had difficulty in finding a convenient slot in which to play. This upset him and appears to have caused him significant annoyance. It was alleged that he threatened to shoot the children, but it was not suggested that he took any step to carry out that threat or to frighten the children with his gun.' (Justice Robert Barr)

Whether the threat was made or not, news of the allegation against Carthy was passed from one child to another and from one parent to another, eventually reaching the committee of the handball club and a meeting was convened to discuss what they should do about it.

The committee members took the rumours very seriously. All of them were troubled by what could happen and the guilt they would feel if John Carthy ever did decide to carry out his alleged threat. A motion was put forward and approved, the decision taken that they had to do something to reduce the apparent risk posed by Carthy. It was decided that a member of the committee should phone Granard garda station with their concerns and ask if there was any way that his gun could be taken away.

That kind of news made for good gossip in a village the size of Abbeylara, and it wasn't long before the alleged threat was blown out of all proportion. The rumour was passed along until it reached Evelyn McLoughlin, the wife of local builder Brendan McLoughlin. Brendan had employed John Carthy from time to time on various sites and found him to be a fairly good worker. But there were days when Carthy could be argumentative, and just a few weeks before the alleged incident at the handball alley, the two had got into a disagreement over something trivial, and Carthy was given his marching orders.

Shortly after that, the McLoughlins received a letter from Carthy, alleging that he had been unfairly dismissed. They had thought nothing of it at the time, but when Evelyn heard rumours of the alley threats, she began to worry that the former employee might try to inflict his own justice on her husband. She brought her fears to a local garda, and in an off-the-record chat, she inquired if there was any way that Carthy could be separated from his gun.

With this second complaint about Carthy and the potential

danger he posed, gardaí at Granard began to take the issue seriously. In a report to the sergeant in charge, dated 10 August 1998, Garda Oliver Cassidy stated that he was going to go to the Carthy home and seize the gun, writing, 'I feel he has become unfit to hold a firearm certificate.'

Taking the gun proved to be easy. Garda Cassidy drove out to the cottage in Toneymore. Carthy received him well and brought him inside. The officer had come up with a story to cover why he wanted the weapon, and after some idle chat, he broached the subject. He told John that all the guns in the county were being taken in for a routine check, and he asked him to comply with the request and hand over his own weapon. John bought the story, went to his gun cabinet and freely handed over his double-barrelled Baikal.

Carthy had an appointment with Dr Cullen later that same day. The doctor felt his patient's condition was starting to change for the worse. He appeared to be 'high' and he confessed to the doctor that he had been drinking a lot the previous weekend. Dr Cullen gave him the usual warnings about not drinking while on his medication, but he could see that his advice was barely registering. There appeared to be something playing on his patient's mind. He was unusually preoccupied, and seemed to be put out about something. Dr Cullen inquired as to what was bothering him.

It was the gun. As soon as Carthy had closed the door behind Garda Cassidy, he began to have doubts about why his gun had been taken away. He wasn't a stupid man, and thinking about it afterwards, he got the feeling that he had been singled out, that there was no routine county inspection, and that he wasn't going to get his gun back. He chided himself for not realising what was happening sooner, and determined that he would take whatever steps were necessary to convince the guards that they should return his weapon.

Sitting there with Dr Cullen, it occurred to Carthy that his GP might be able to help him and he interrupted the examination to tell the doctor the whole story of how his gun had been taken from him by the gardaí. The doctor was taken aback. In all his dealings with John Carthy over the years, he had never known that he owned a shotgun, and was surprised he had ever been deemed fit to possess such a deadly weapon. The memory of those others who had taken their own lives with a gun came to his mind. He felt there was probably a good reason why Carthy's weapon had been taken away, and, in fact, counted it as a blessing.

Carthy asked the doctor if he would write a letter to the gardaí, telling them it was his medical opinion that he was fit to have a shotgun. Dr Cullen felt there was no possible way that he could write such a letter, and he told his patient he was unwilling to help him. He could see that John was annoyed, but he continued to try and reason with him. He asked him what would happen if, after the firearm was restored to him, he became unwell again and the gardaí felt the need to confiscate it once more.

'The gardaí would have to take the gun off me,' the young man replied.

The doctor took this to mean that Carthy would not be so co-operative with the forces of law and order again. He had learned his lesson. Next time, he would put up a fight.

In the following days the gardaí at Granard station were looking for some concrete justification for keeping John Carthy from his gun. They knew he would come looking for it eventually, and Sergeant Desmond Nally ordered that further inquiries be made into Carthy's background and his medical history.

In his report, Garda Oliver Cassidy wrote:

'John Carthy has threatened a number of people in the Abbeylara area and said that he would use the gun. He spent some time in St Loman's Mental Hospital in Mullingar, and appears to be not well lately.'

Before the week was out, Carthy began his regular visits to the station. Every time he approached the front desk, his request was the same. He asked to have the gun back. When his request was refused, he asked to be given the reason why he had been singled out in such a manner. Each time, he was fobbed off and told to go home.

One month on, Carthy had yet to tire of his mission to retrieve his shotgun. He continued to drop by the station almost every day, asking to see the more superior officers, demanding an explanation for what he regarded as extremely unfair treatment. In reality, the gardaí had nothing other than hearsay to back up their case, and Sergeant Daniel Monaghan ordered that a file be prepared on the Carthy gun issue, with statements from those people who claimed to have been threatened by him. It was seen as a matter of urgency because Carthy's patience was running thin.

But none of those who had expressed their fears to gardaí in quiet moments and off-the-record chats would agree to sign any formal complaint in relation to John Carthy. When contacted by gardaí for a statement, their concerns suddenly decreased, they brushed off the fears they had had before, and stayed out of it.

Without statements, the police had no reason to keep the gun from Carthy any longer, but they stalled for a further few weeks. On 6 October Carthy brought his problem to the top, and went to see Superintendent Denis Cullinane. At the meeting, the superintendent informed him of the allegations of threatening behaviour that had been made against him. John denied it all.

He relayed his own version of events to the superintendent, telling him that while he had suffered from depression in the past, he was now fully recovered and his illness was regularly monitored by a psychiatrist in Dublin. With no statements on record, Superintendent Cullinane reached for the last resort. He told Carthy that he would need medical evidence to say he was fully fit to hold a lethal weapon.

Now Carthy had a means, and he intended to use it. All he needed was one doctor willing to certify him as being well, and he would have his firearm back. Dr Cullen was out of the question because he had already said no, but Carthy had a back-up, a man who was based in Dublin, who would not be aware of village rumours. That man was his psychiatrist, Dr David Shanley.

Ω   Ω   Ω

Carthy had always liked Dr Shanley. His obsession with his health was indulged from time to time by the added outlet in Dublin. He liked having a second opinion on his progress, and Dr Shanley took him seriously. He first began attending Dr Shanley in April 1995, after he himself had asked Dr Cullen to refer him to the specialist.

He opened up a little more to Dr Shanley. At their first appointment, he described an unhappy childhood and revealed some of his stranger hang-ups to the consultant. He told Shanley he felt he had developed breasts in puberty, and also said he sometimes felt there was a smell coming from him. He admitted that he sometimes drank heavily, and revealed the nature of the voices that came into his head whenever he had a hangover.

Dr Shanley listened, but felt that the symptoms being presented were not unusual, and he encouraged John to keep up treatment at his local psychiatric services in the Longford area. He did not feel it would be appropriate for the young man to continue commuting to the capital every few weeks to keep appointments with him. That would be time consuming and expensive. But a few days after that appointment, Dr Shanley received a call from a member of the Carthy family, and they begged him to continue seeing John. He agreed.

Over the following years, the regular visits continued. Carthy would attend at the psychiatrist's practice in Dublin every so often, and he would continue to see Dr Cullen from time to time, if only to pick up further prescriptions. As it would happen, Dr Shanley never saw Carthy in one of his severe bouts of elation or depression, and he never saw him in a hospital situation. To him, Carthy became one of those patients who was coping, who was taking his medication as prescribed, and who was dealing with the difficulties that manic depression could present.

With these positives forming the background to Dr Shanley's only dealings with John Carthy, the psychiatrist was sympathetic when he heard the tale of how the gun was taken away. He believed the story that the weapon was taken only as part of a routine check, and he did not question why, in these circumstances, John was having trouble in getting the gun back.

In his clinical notes from that appointment on 8 October 1998, the psychiatrist wrote:

'Superintendent indicates that he needs another letter to indicate that he is able to handle a firearm. No evidence of depression/elation … hopes to use gun to shoot pheasants and game pigeons. Has had gun for last seven years, but police took in guns from all over county for routine check.'

Before Carthy left the clinic that day, he had secured Dr Shanley's help, and had been assured that a letter would be written to the gardaí at Granard supporting his fitness to use a firearm. Dr Shanley did not phone the gardaí to check out Carthy's story.

His justifications for writing the letter were well meant. As a psychiatrist, he always encouraged patients to pursue hobbies and to develop interests that would keep them either physically or mentally active. In this vein, he felt that Carthy's interest in shooting was a positive, and he did not want to be the one who would deny him his favourite pastime. He himself would later account for his writing the letter by pointing out that he gave his support 'on the basis of knowing Carthy over a number of years; on the basis that he had been stable from a psychiatric point of view; on the basis that he was conscientious about coming to see me which involved long distance; on the basis that he took his serum of lithium regularly and that it was always within therapeutic range.'

A few days after Carthy's visit, Dr Shanley penned the following letter to the Superintendent in Granard:

October, 1998
Dear Superintendent,
Mr John Carthy has given me permission to write to you. He is a patient of mine for some years now and in my opinion is fit to use a firearm. When last seen on the 8th of October, 1998, he was very well. He has been treated for depression and elation

in the past, and should the situation change, his GP will be in touch with your office.

Yours, etc.

It is clear from the letter that there was meant to be an onus on Dr Cullen to be the key informant for the gardaí on John Carthy's condition. Unfortunately, the letter was never actually copied to Dr Cullen, so he was completely unaware of the responsibility. Not only that, he didn't even know that the gun had been returned to his patient until he was called out to the scene at Abbeylara. Subsequently Dr Shanley accepted that it was an omission on his part not to have copied the letter to Carthy's GP.

On receipt of the letter from Dr Shanley, the gardaí in Granard had no other option but to restore John Carthy's gun to him. As well as the medical reference, John had also presented them with a signed letter from his mother, supporting his case for return of the weapon. The guards did make an effort to consult Dr Cullen for a second opinion, but a phone call to his office at that time found that the doctor was away on holidays, and no further call was made to him in the following weeks. John Carthy's gun was finally restored to him in mid-November 1998.

Ω   Ω   Ω

Over the following months, John's condition began to deteriorate. As early as 30 November 1998, just weeks after he got his gun back, he was displaying symptoms of being unwell. He had an appointment with Dr Shanley on that day, and in his notes from that meeting, the psychiatrist noted that the young man was in a state of elation, that he had been drinking a lot, and that he was now entering a phase of depression. John told the doctor that he had been sleepless and full of energy, and estimated that he could well have spent a few thousand pounds on alcohol in the previous weeks.

Rose and John went to Marie's home in Galway for Christmas. It was meant to be a happy family time, but John wasn't well. Marie could see him flipping between highs and lows. On St Stephen's Day, she convinced him to go to the casualty department of the University College Hospital in Galway. On examination, he was thought to be hypomanic; his speech came in rapid bursts and the slightest movement or noise in the quiet casualty room distracted him. However, hospital records show that he denied he had any 'suicidal ideation, death wish or thoughts of self-harm'.

There was an obvious escalation in Carthy's condition, but because the letter Dr Shanley wrote had never been copied to Dr Cullen, there was nobody to inform the gardaí of this change in his illness, which might have caused them to reconsider his gun ownership.

In addressing the issue of the restoration of the gun, Justice Robert Barr adjudicated on whether or not the psychiatrist acted appropriately in penning his letter to the gardaí. Giving regard to the fact that Dr Shanley had never seen Carthy when he was seriously ill, Justice Barr contended that Dr Shanley acted reasonably through granting this support to his patient.

Justice Barr was far more critical of the fact that Carthy's gun was ever confiscated in the first place. In his report he states that the gardaí were 'premature' in their actions, and finds that there was 'no apparent justification' for them to separate Carthy from his gun.

' ... there was no apparent justification for obtaining possession of Mr Carthy's gun and for retaining it ... the local gardaí were premature in immediately securing possession of the subject's gun by subterfuge before investigating the matter.'

Justice Barr also contends that the matter of the gun confiscation, just like the issue of the wrongful arrest and assault while in custody, both only served to diminish any possible trust that may have helped solve the situation that arose at Abbeylara,

'An important consequence of the garda conduct is that the creation of one cause for Mr Carthy's distrust of and antagonism towards the gardaí (which loomed large at Abbeylara) would not have arisen.'

This is a statement that was supported by those who met with John Carthy in the weeks prior to the siege. Kieran Lennon, the young man who worked with Carthy in Longford town that April remembered that almost every day at lunchtime, he would turn the conversation around to the gardaí. He told Mr Lennon of the dealings he had had with them, and said he hadn't much time for them after he had been wrongfully arrested.

Dr Shanley saw John Carthy for the final time in June 1999. John was looking healthy, and he reported to the doctor that he was feeling well. When they parted company that day, Dr Shanley was happy with the progress the young man was making. He did not see Carthy at all in the following months and it was not until he was winding up his practice for the Easter break in 2000 that John Carthy's name cropped up again. That was when Dr Shanley received a phone call from a garda who was standing on a road in Abbeylara, asking him to confirm that he had a patient called John Carthy.

5.

Garda Maeve Gorman was busy dialling numbers. The call she had received from Detective Garda Jim Campbell as he crouched at the back of the Carthy house had been brief and barely audible, but from his tone alone it was clear that the situation was spiralling. He sounded terrified, and his request for back-up was desperate and urgent. She decided it was time for her to bring the situation to the notice of superior officers outside of her own station.

Her first call was to Superintendent Michael Byrne, the district officer for Granard. He answered the phone, heard the details of what was unfolding and knew he wasn't going to be of any immediate assistance. He was in Dublin for the day, and while he would be able to get to Abbeylara in a few hours' time, the initial response was going to have to be left to one of his colleagues. He told Garda Gorman to get in touch with Superintendent Joe Shelly at Athlone Garda Station.

Joe Shelly listened to the details of what was unfolding at Abbeylara. He knew this was serious. Firearms incidents always had that edge, and hearing that shots had already been fired at a patrol car, he resolved to throw every resource available into bringing the incident to an end. He informed his superior, Chief Superintendent Patrick Tansey, the divisional officer for the Longford/Westmeath region, of what was happening, and then set about organising his men. He formed the view that he would need in the region of ten armed officers, and, before leaving for Abbeylara, he sent out word to all the surrounding stations, requesting that whatever armed gardaí were available should be sent to Abbeylara as a matter of urgency.

The call was heeded in the Longford and Athlone stations, as well as in his own Mullingar division. The working armed gardaí were notified, and the understanding of them all was that they were to assist in a situation involving an armed man who had already discharged shots at a garda vehicle. Guns were loaded and checked, armoured jackets were collected and the first exodus to Abbeylara began.

♌   ♌   ♌

At the Carthy cottage, little had changed. Garda John Gibbons and Detective Garda Jim Campbell were still crouched behind the house, praying that backup would arrive soon. In the Walsh house, Ann Walsh had finally succeeded in contacting her brother, Tom, to tell him what was unfolding. The family regarded Tom as being John's best friend as well as his cousin, and were sure he would be able to persuade John to calm down. Tom Walsh said he would leave Cork straight away and would be home as soon as he could. Immediately after hearing the bad news from his sister, he placed a call through to Garda Dave Martin, whom he knew on a friendly basis. He enquired if there was any way Garda Martin could arrange to have his mother and other relations moved away to safety. Nancy Walsh had a heart condition, and Tom was worried that the upset and fear of the evening would be too much for her.

As it happened, plans were already being put in place to move the women from the Walsh house. After John Carthy had fired his last shots, and when his two senior colleagues hadn't returned from their approach to the cottage, Garda White decided that it was his duty to evacuate the neighbours in the houses around the Carthys'. He especially felt it necessary to move the women away from the immediacy of the scene. He made his way back to Walsh house and asked if there was anywhere they they could go. It was arranged that the women would be brought to the home of Mrs Patricia Mahon who lived on the Coole Road, about one mile from the Carthys'.

While all of this was going on, other local uniformed officers had started to arrive in the area. Dr Cullen had emerged from the patrol car again, and while the gardaí were busy with evacuations, he remained by the roadside, talking to some of the Carthy neighbours. Eventually, feeling as though he were starting to get in the way, he asked a passing garda if they thought it would be okay if he were to leave. Having been cleared to go, he got into his car and headed back to his clinic in Coole.

Ω   Ω   Ω

It was almost seven o'clock that evening when Superintendent Shelly arrived at Granard Garda Station. He was pleased to see that other senior officers were already there. He greeted Inspector Martin Maguire, Detective Garda Jack Kilroy and Detective Garda Gerard Barrins from Longford. Garda Maeve Gorman welcomed Superintendent Shelly, and told him what she knew: John Carthy was twenty-seven years old, he suffered from depression, he had put his mother out of the house, and had been firing shots.

Shelly was anxious to get to Toneymore to see the scene for

himself. He was fully aware that he would be the senior man at this incident – the scene commander – and it would be up to him to make the decisions. He had never been at a scene like this before and he had never been involved in an incident where mental illness was a factor, but as part of his training, he had attended an Operational Commander's Course in 1997 which laid out the basics of taking charge of a large scale operation such as this. The course even included a lecture entitled 'The Siege – Practical', which instructed commanders on how they should deal with the elements of a firearms incident such as the one at Abbeylara.

When he arrived at the scene, Shelly parked up the road from the Carthy property and saw that reinforcements were already arriving from all angles. He spoke first with Sergeants Tom Dooley and Mary Mangan, two local members who had arrived at the scene some minutes previously and were able to brief him on the location of Carthy inside the house, the number of shots fired so far, and the positioning of local gardaí at the scene. They also told him that the houses adjacent to the Carthy home had been evacuated, and that Rose Carthy and her relations had been relocated to the home of Patricia Mahon.

Hearing that Campbell and Gibbons were still behind the house, Shelly ordered that Gibbons be contacted on his mobile and told to forget about the garda car and to withdraw from their positions on foot. With that, Campbell and Gibbons hurried to the nearest hedge and edged away from the house with as much cover as they could afford themselves.

Once safely out on the road again, Gibbons informed Shelly of the conversation he had had with the women in the Walsh house when they first arrived at the scene, and of the fact that

Dr Cullen had been present for a time. Shelly had already heard from Garda Gorman that Carthy suffered from depression, and his queries on what was said by Dr Cullen were minimal. While Gibbons believed he remembered telling Shelly that Dr Cullen had indicated that Carthy might bear some animosity towards the gardaí, Shelly claimed it was not until much later that he heard anything of Carthy's issues with the force.

Feeling that he had an adequate amount of information, Shelly set about putting his plan in place. He assigned Sergeants Dooley and Mangan to be family liaison officers and to go and get as much information as possible from the women who were now gathered in the Mahon home. He appointed Inspector Martin Maguire to be his assistant in the on-scene command. Then he turned his attention to deploying the large gathering of armed officers he had assembled.

While John Carthy continued to pace back and forth through the rooms of the cottage, further up the Abbeylara road, Shelly gathered the group of armed officers and local men around him to inform them of what they needed to do. The policy he had in mind was one of isolation, containment and evacuation – John Carthy was to be isolated in the house, he was to be contained through the deployment of officers who would watch his every move, and all other areas around the scene would be evacuated for safety reasons.

'I told them that I wanted to put in place,' said Shelly, 'to achieve a cordon, an inner cordon of armed people, and I told them that my strategy was that I wanted to contain the situation, to contain John Carthy in the house. In so doing, I believed that while he was contained in the house the likelihood of danger or risk to anybody present was minimised.'

Shelly also told the officers that there were two scenarios to watch for – that of a controlled or an uncontrolled exit. The first of these described a situation where Carthy would come out without his weapon and in co-operation with the gardaí; the uncontrolled exit was one where Carthy would emerge with his shotgun, ignoring their pleas and leaving them guessing as to what he would do next.

Shelly then set about positioning the armed gardaí at points around the house that afforded some view of the property. Two were sent to the gable at the back of the house, another went to man a spot at the dividing hedge between Farrell's house and Carthys' garden, three more took up their posts at the side of the Burke house nearest to the Carthys'. Finally, a number of officers from the Athlone station were told to remain in and around an ESB pole that stood at the edge of the Carthy property on the Abbeylara side. All of these officers were in plain clothes, and they formed the inner cordon, the first ring of defence.

An outer cordon was also established, with the responsibility of manning checkpoints and generally ensuring that no unauthorised parties were given leave to approach the area around the Carthy home. Checkpoints were set up on both the Ballywillin and Abbeylara sides of the area, to turn away any approaching traffic. As well as this, a number of unarmed officers were sent to take up duty in the fields behind the Carthy house.

All of the gardaí were reliant on mobile phones for contact with each other. This was not the ideal situation. Mobiles can be temperamental, batteries can run low, and at that time in rural County Longford coverage was not at its peak. However, garda radios were never provided to the local officers at the scene.

It didn't take long for each of the officers to make their way to their assigned posts. Two hours after Rose Carthy made that first call to Granard, asking for an officer to come out to help her son, her home and the area around it had been transformed into a crime scene. Eleven gardaí surrounded her home, armed with Uzi sub-machine guns and Smith and Wesson revolvers. No traffic was allowed down her road, the place was a hive of activity, with uniformed men and garda cars going to and from the area.

The local men were only the first line of troops ordered to Abbeylara; the top men were still to come. While Shelly was busy organising his operation on the ground in Abbeylara, a decision had been taken further up the ranks in Dublin that the Emergency Response Unit should be deployed.

Ω   Ω   Ω

Chief Superintendent Patrick Tansey was keen to keep himself informed of everything that was going on at the scene. He maintained regular phone contact with Shelly in the first hour of what had now become a full-scale operation. It was difficult to get a real idea of what was going on, but it seemed that Carthy had now fired in the region of ten shots. Tansey decided to bring the situation to the attention of the most senior officer covering the region. He phoned the then Assistant Garda Commissioner, Tony Hickey, regional commander of the Garda Eastern Division.

Hickey was attending a family function that evening and wouldn't be able to make it to Abbeylara to make his own assessment of what was going on. His distance from the scene put him in an awkward position, requiring him to make a judgement on what needed to be done without actually seeing it with his own eyes. Widely respected, Hickey had the reputation of a sensible and measured officer, someone who would be unwilling ever to storm into any situation without first examining it from every aspect. But the word that was coming through from the officers at Abbeylara was worrying, and all the indications suggested an incident that could go on for some time. Not wishing to leave the local men without the appropriate help, he made the decision to call in the Emergency Response Unit.

The ERU was established as the Special Task Force in the 1970s to work specifically in the area of terrorism and the Troubles in Northern Ireland. Gradually, it evolved into a unit that provided specialist assistance in anything from firearms incidents to searches for missing people. The ERU is made up of four units comprising two sergeants and ten officers in each. Within An Garda Síochána, it is generally accepted that it is very difficult to meet the criteria for acceptance into the specialist branch. The selection of applicants to the unit is based on a two-week course at the specialist school at the Garda College. Successful candidates then undergo a six-week induction course, which focuses on firearms training, tactical training and driving skills.

While ERU officers still continue their regular duties as gardaí or detectives, they spend one week out of every month at intensive training with their ERU colleagues. Physical fitness is an essential part of their work. In addition to that, they are required to qualify three times a year in all firearms that are issued to them, and every member must attain proficiency in the use of five different firearms.

The work of the ERU rarely involves bullets whizzing overhead. Most of their time is spent protecting international VIPs who visit the country, or escorting dangerous prisoners to court. For all their firearms training they rarely have occasion to produce their weapons, and from one decade to another there are only a handful of incidents that really test their abilities.

Prior to Abbeylara, the only other similar incident the ERU had been involved in was a siege in Bawnboy, County Cavan in 1997. That case involved Jan Isenborger, a German man who became distressed and violent when he was visited by the County Registrar and a number of bailiffs who had come to serve an eviction notice on him.

Isenborger lived with his elderly mother who was suffering from chronic cancer, and he reacted very badly on hearing from the county officials that they were to be evicted. He chose a rifle from his arsenal of weapons and shot and injured three of the officials outside his home. He then locked himself and his dying mother into the house, and refused to come out and surrender.

The ERU were called in, and in some ways the events that followed were an example of how the perfect operation should be executed. The gardaí involved set up camp at a house next door; they made phone contact and gradually negotiated a peaceful conclusion to the siege. In the end, the man invited them into the house and gave a full statement. His mother had passed away during the incident.

Tony Hickey had seen the ERU in action at various incidents, and, weighing up the options, he judged that they would be helpful in the situation that was unfolding at Abbeylara. Thinking back to Bawnboy, he felt that negotiation would probably be necessary and he knew the ERU had negotiators at their disposal. Added to that, he felt the presence of the specialist unit would be a comfort to the local men, and would provide an extra safety net for whatever was going to happen at the scene. They were used to working as a team, and they also had more specialist equipment available to them.

The phone calls continued. Tansey got in touch with the powers at the Special Detective Unit, and authorisation was granted for two detective sergeants and four detective gardaí from the ERU to be sent to Longford. Most importantly, emphasis was placed on the need for the national negotiator, Detective Sergeant Michael Jackson, to travel immediately to the scene.

Ω   Ω   Ω

As well as contacting Hickey and others, Tansey also made it his business to ring the Garda Press Office. Almost as soon as he was notified of the incident by Shelly he had checked his watch, had seen that the top of the hour was approaching, and had informed the press officers on duty of the events down the country. So, by seven o'clock that evening, the Garda Press Office had been briefed on what was unfolding in Abbeylara.

Tansey said he made the call to the press office because he was aware that it was almost time for the hourly news, and he was afraid that the media might already have heard something and it might be broadcast before the press office had ever heard about it.

'There have been occasions where the press office wouldn't hear things until after the news and we have been called to task on that,' he said.

The practice in most newsrooms is for hourly calls to be made to the Garda Press Office for updates on the latest happenings. The press office is a major source of news, and the demand for information is such that there are currently six-teen gardaí employed there, and it operates seven days a week from 7.30am to 11pm.

The head of the press office at that time was Superintendent John Farrelly, a name that would have been familiar to every journalist. When word came through to Farrelly of what was developing at the Carthy house, he decided to leave Dublin immediately and travel to Abbeylara to assist with the media who would be making their way to the scene. This was seen as a priority. Journalists and cameramen can become loose can-nons in situations like this. They can cross lines and get in the way. It was seen as a necessity that Superintendent Farrelly would get there as soon as possible to keep control of the situation.

♎   ♎   ♎

At 7.12pm on that Wednesday evening, the new television sta-tion, TV3, broadcast as its breaking news item the story of the garda operation that was underway at Abbeylara. This was something that caused great concern to the relations of John Carthy.

When Sergeants Tom Dooley and Mary Mangan arrived at the Mahon household to check on Rose Carthy and the others, the women expressed concern about the media coverage. They felt that this would have been very upsetting for Rose, and they told the gardaí that it was going to be 'absolutely det-rimental' to John if he was 'hearing that on the news'. They were annoyed, and wanted to know who had informed the media of what was going on.

The two sergeants remained with the women for approxi-mately one hour, listening again to the only explanations the women could offer for what was unfolding back at the cottage. Rose was very upset and was unable to say why her son was acting in such an aggressive manner. The gardaí heard that Tom Walsh was on his way from Cork, and the conversation turned to the people John was closest to, bringing them around to his sister and only sibling, Marie.

It was now approaching eight o'clock and the family had not yet contacted Marie, who was in Galway at the time. Ann Walsh told Sergeant Mangan that they didn't want to upset Marie by telling her what was happening until they could provide transport for her to travel down to her home. Sergeant Mangan left to contact the gardaí in Galway so that they could arrange for a patrol car to bring Marie to the scene.

6.

Shelly was pleased when he was informed that the ERU were on their way; any reinforcements that were available would be welcomed into the operation. He too had worked with the ERU on previous occasions, and he knew them to be a capable and well-organised group of men. The problem was, however, that the assigned ERU officers were travelling down from Dublin. It would be at least two hours before they arrived in Abbeylara, and that was a long time for his men to be standing in a hedge waiting for more shots, and praying that Carthy wouldn't emerge. Five more shots had already been fired from the house since Shelly and the armed officers had arrived on the scene.

If only for the morale of the local men, Shelly needed to be proactive and try to make some headway towards a positive end to the incident. A megaphone had been brought to the scene, and Shelly decided he would make an attempt at initiating negotiations with Carthy. He had never received any formal training in negotiation, but something had to be done. He spoke on the phone to the ERU negotiator who was on his way to the scene, Detective Sergeant Michael Jackson, and received some advice on how best to handle his attempt at opening negotiations. There were other non-ERU negotiators in the Eastern region, in areas as nearby as Portlaoise, but Shelly decided against contacting one of them, and began communicating with Carthy himself.

Standing beside the ESB pole at the edge of the Carthy property, Shelly took up the megaphone and, as advised by Jackson, started with the basics. He told Carthy his name was Joe and he was with the gardaí. He shouted assurances that he was there to help, that he and his colleagues would assist Carthy in any way they could, and that there was nothing to be afraid of.

'I asked him to throw the gun out the window on a number of occasions,' said Shelly. 'I tried to explain to him that basically no matter what had happened, it wasn't the end of the world and we could sort something out. At all times, I conveyed to him that it was our wish to bring the matter to a peaceful resolution and I was hoping that that would be a quick resolution as well.'

The megaphone was perhaps not an ideal method of communication, and even the most sincere assurances from Shelly probably sounded threatening to Carthy when issued at such high decibels. Added to that, it was a one-way system of communication. The kitchen window was seventy feet from the ESB pole. Even if Carthy had wanted to reply, he had no loud-hailer to project his voice, and there was an April wind waiting to carry his words over the fields before they would ever make it to garda ears. That didn't mark out an equal playing field, and when Shelly continued to shout and holler, Carthy's only reply was to fire two shots.

♎︎   ♎︎   ♎︎

At her home in Galway, Marie answered the call that would change her life. It was her cousin Ann Walsh, and it was bad news. John had locked himself into the house. He was firing off rounds from his shotgun. The guards had had to be called.

Marie asked how her mother was and heard that she was fine. Shaken, but fine.

Shocked by what she was hearing, it was a relief to Marie to hear that everything had been arranged for her. A patrol car was on its way to pick her up at her house. They would bring her to Abbeylara. Was there anyone who would travel with her to keep her company? She would ask Martin Shelly, with whom both she and John were friendly.

Ω   Ω   Ω

With little success for Joe Shelly, there was a changing of the guard at the ESB pole, and Sergeant Tom Dooley stepped up to have a go. Like Shelly, Dooley had no negotiating experience, but he too had spoken with Detective Sergeant Michael Jackson and had some idea of what he needed to say to Carthy to calm him down.

Dooley introduced himself as Tom, and told Carthy there was nothing to worry about because nobody had been injured. Carthy immediately pulled his trigger and released another shotgun blast, firing at no particular target, but at what he perceived to be the general enemy that was lurking outside.

Shaken but determined, Dooley caught his breath and started again, almost afraid of what could come next. He took the congenial route once more, and in case Carthy missed it the first time, he repeated that his name was Tom, and that no harm had been done, that the gardaí were there to help, and that their concern was only for Carthy's own safety.

The lines were all the same, and no reply, or no audible reply, came from the house. The silence was nearly as frightening as the shotgun blasts, generating nothing but anxiety among the gardaí outside. Both Shelly and Dooley tried to break through the quiet, repeating their lines, but with each rendition of the worn-out script, they began to lose faith in their initial belief that Carthy couldn't hold out forever.

♎ ♎ ♎

At a few minutes past nine, the phone rang in the Carthy house. John picked it up, and heard a female voice. The voice on the line was familiar. It was Marie's friend, Patricia Leavy. She was caught by surprise when John actually answered the phone. She had heard about the incident and telephoned wishing to speak to Rose. She hadn't expected any reply, and she didn't really know what she should say to him. Trying to sound relaxed and normal, she asked him if he was all right and when he said nothing in reply, she kept chatting to herself about nothing in particular. Carthy lost interest, said nothing and hung up. Thinking she had made some kind of a break-through, Ms Leavy rang back again straight away. Again, Carthy picked up the phone, listened to the well-meant small talk, and hung up.

♎ ♎ ♎

It was around this time that the Garda Press Officer, Superintendent Farrelly arrived in Abbeylara. He stopped in the shop in the village to ask directions to the Carthy home and while there, he met Carthy's cousin, Ann Walsh. Having seen the media people already gathering at the outskirts of the scene, she told the press officer that something had to be done to curb the coverage of what was unfolding. Farrelly assured her that he would try his best 'to keep them at bay.'

Moving towards the scene, Farrelly found that the media

had chosen to gather in the small car park in front of St Bernard's Church. About five members of the media were present at that stage. By 10 pm, that number had swelled to between ten and twelve as the reporters continued to find their way to the scene. Farrelly spoke to the reporters as a group. Most of them had picked up the name of the man inside the house, but Farrelly asked them not to identify Carthy in any of their reports. To emphasise this point to them, he told the media gathered there was a chance that Carthy could be listening to the radio or watching television, and they should bear this in mind when they were airing their reports. He also told them Carthy suffered from depression.

Ω Ω Ω

Back at the ESB pole, time had brought Shelly a new possibility in the form of Tom Walsh, who had just arrived from Cork. This was the man the family believed would have the best chance of talking Carthy round, and no time was wasted in letting Carthy know that his cousin had arrived. This was a friend and a relative, and all thoughts were positive that Carthy would at least respond to him.

Mr Walsh spoke with the senior gardaí before he attempted to get through to his cousin. He told Shelly that Carthy suffered from manic depression, and it would aggravate him if he were to notice all the gardaí that were in the area. He also warned Shelly that his cousin had an exceptionally good shot, and there was a chance that if he caught sight of the gardaí who had been involved in his wrongful arrest at Granard station, he might shoot at them.

Anxious to move on with the negotiations, the gardaí escorted Mr Walsh to the ESB pole and tried to advise him on what he should say to Carthy. Garda John Gibbons told him to try and cheer Carthy up by speaking to him about positive things they had done together in the past. The most important thing, they said was to let Carthy know that no harm had been done and that the best thing would be for him to come out.

They handed Mr Walsh the megaphone, but he wasn't comfortable with the idea of shouting in at Johnny, as he called him. What he wanted was to speak privately with him on the phone. But calls to Carthy's mobile went unanswered, and eventually Walsh picked up the megaphone to tell his cousin that he was trying to phone him and that he should answer so that they could talk. No response. With concern growing that something may be seriously wrong, Walsh shouted in to the cottage, and asked Carthy to flick the light on and off, just to let him know he was okay. The request was ignored.

Desperate for a response of some kind, Walsh continued to repeatedly dial Carthy's number. Eventually, after countless attempts, the phone was answered, but the voice Walsh heard on the other end of the line was cold and bitter. The conversation that passed between the cousins was brief, but the implication from Carthy's side was that he no more wanted to speak to Tom Walsh than he did the gardaí.

Walsh: 'Johnny, it's me, are you alright?'

Carthy: 'What the fuck do you care?'

Walsh: 'Of course we care, we're all worried sick about you.'

Carthy: 'I was in Loman's several times, and I never seen you.'

Walsh: 'Of course you seen me there. I brought your mother up nearly every evening.'

Carthy: 'Don't disgust me Walsh.'

With the anger in his voice rising, Carthy hung up the phone leaving Walsh at a loss to explain what had been said or to identify anything familiar between the Johnny he knew and the detached man who had just abused him on the phone. He was upset by the exchange, and after a few more attempts at saying something comforting, he handed the loudhailer back to the gardaí, placing his cousin in their hands. He felt there was nothing else to do but to let Shelly and Dooley try their best. Seeing the response Walsh got, Shelly and Dooley felt there was nothing to do but to leave the negotiations to the arriving expert, Detective Sergeant Michael Jackson.

Ω   Ω   Ω

There were other things however that Shelly should have been doing at these initial stages of the incident. Best police practice instructs that in a situation where it is felt negotiations will be necessary, certain functional officers need to be appointed to run such a scene in an orderly manner. Organisation is paramount.

An intelligence officer is a necessity, a person whose sole purpose is to find out as much as possible about the subject of an incident, an officer who is tasked with compiling facts from every source, sharing the information and using it wisely. Shelly did not appoint an intelligence officer. He chose instead to take that role upon himself. He believed he was capable of carrying out this role as well as all his other functions as scene commander, because the incident involved just one man, who had no criminal record and whose family was readily available to provide any necessary information.

He thought that he had covered all the bases by sending Sergeants Dooley and Mangan to speak with the family and find out all they could, but there were many more sources of information that should have been contacted. In those first hours of the operation, an intelligence officer, in this case Shelly, should have been speaking to the family directly. In fact, Shelly never once spoke to the women gathered in the Mahon household at any stage over the course of the incident. Expert opinion later added that he should have gone to interview Dr Cullen himself, or had him interviewed by an experienced senior officer, so that he could find out everything in relation to Carthy's medical history. Again, Shelly never spoke to the doctor at any stage of the incident.

Shelly could also have appointed a log-keeper, an officer who would take note of everything that happened at the scene, of all the shots that were fired, but he didn't. Instead, Shelly chose to keep his own log, but this would later be judged by policing experts from around the world to be an inadequate record of events.

Because of his failures on the intelligence-gathering front, many of the key areas of Carthy's life went untapped until deep into the stand-off, or indeed until after the tragedy had come to an end.

Shelly's failure as an intelligence officer caused Justice Barr to suggest that the scene commander may have been concerned about the dignity of his own police force:

'The goat mascot episode was obviously embarrassing for the Garda Siochana,' wrote Justice Robert Barr. 'If he learned about it, which seems likely, Superintendent Shelly may have decided that, to avoid the risk of public disclosure at a later date, it was preferable not to go down that road and that the matter of Mr Carthy's distrust of and antagonism towards the police should not be pursued with Dr Cullen.

'Although Superintendent Shelly had the pivotal role of scene commander in a difficult situation of which he had no previous experience, he decided, contrary to his training, to take on personally the important function of intelligence co-ordinator rather than to appoint Inspector Maguire, or some other experienced senior officer such as Sergeant Monaghan, to perform the task. The unexplained and unnecessary decision to burden himself with a major additional chore which could have been performed by other competent officers, is credible if his motivation was to ensure as well as he could that embarrassing information was not obtained from Dr Cullen by another intelligent co-ordinator, if one had been appointed.'

Whether or not Shelly knew about John Carthy's history with the local police, he could tell the ERU little that they didn't already know. He couldn't tell them, for instance, of Carthy's recent problems, of his comments in the days before the incident to people in the village, of all the facets of Carthy's life that had led him to this juncture. All he had to tell them was that this was a manically depressed young man, and he had a gun. But that wasn't even half the story.

7.

The Emergency Response Unit officers were on the road to a place they had never heard of. There were six of them in all, and they travelled in three vehicles, separated by miles of road. Phone calls were exchanged between the cavalcades, and the chief officers discussed the scant amount of information they had. Their boss Superintendent Patrick Hogan only had time to tell them the basics before they left, but it was enough to inject urgency into their movements.

The last ERU vehicle held the national negotiator, Detective Sergeant Michael Jackson. He was running about twenty minutes behind his colleagues, and the miles were clocking reluctantly. He was happy to leave the driving to his assistant Detective Garda Michael Sullivan, freeing him up to think about the task ahead. He had a lot on his mind. He thought about the hours to come and rehearsed what he should say. A lot of responsibility would be placed upon him tonight, and he couldn't doubt himself even for a second. This was going to be a momentous task for him. The title of national negotiator had barely settled on his shoulders; he had not yet negotiated at an incident, having completed the National Hostage Negotiator Course with the London Metropolitan Police just a few short weeks ago.

Jackson knew he was capable of the job. He was a thinker and a man who was measured in every sense. He was admired by his colleagues, and there were many who would describe him as the most meticulous man you could ever hope to meet, textbook in his precision and his exactness. In appearance, in demeanour and even in his gait, he exuded that air of perfect confidence, never cocky but always definite. He was the perfect choice for the negotiating position, his calm nature and his intelligence marking him out for the job.

On the road that evening, Jackson wondered if he had brought everything he needed. Their departure from the HQ had been rushed and leaving for a scene where he was to be a negotiator was different. While he and Detective Garda Sullivan packed their ballistics equipment and radio sets into the back of their jeep, they also picked up some lighting material, flip charts, pens and a tape recorder from the HQ. Other equipment, such as field phones and CCTV technology, would also be available to the gardaí, but these were not brought to Abbeylara. As far as Jackson was concerned the most important tools he would need, at this his first scene as a negotiator, would be the right words and good timing.

He had been told that John Carthy suffered from a form of depression, and it was a factor he thought about a lot on the journey down the country. An avid reader, some of the greatest biographies he ever read had uncovered the lives of great men who had changed the world in spite of their own battles with mental illness. Winston Churchill was one of those, Abraham Lincoln was another, and Jackson was an admirer of both. He was well aware of the irrationalities that can accompany a mental illness, and as the garda vehicle navigated byroads and potholes towards Abbeylara, he resolved to keep sensitivity at the forefront of everything he would say and do in the coming hours.

On the journey to Longford, the phone calls continued. He

rang Shelly for an update on the situation and then his ERU colleague who was ahead on the road, Detective Sergeant Gerry Russell. Russell was to be in charge of tactical planning at the operation, and they exchanged views on the situation. That was all they could do at that stage: speculate and try to envisage the scene they were about to enter.

It had already been a long day for Jackson. On that morning of 19 April, when nothing was yet stirring in Abbeylara, he had started duty at 7am in Castlerea. It was a routine prison escort to the High Court, and when he was done with that he moved on to some diplomatic protective work. When he had set off from Roscommon early that morning, he was looking forward to getting home at a reasonable hour that evening. Thirty-four hours later, he would instead find himself on a by-road in Longford facing a life or death decision. To fire or not to fire.

Ω   Ω   Ω

Detective Sergeant Gerry Russell rolled his jeep into Abbeylara just before 10 pm. He had with him Detective Garda Oliver Flaherty, followed closely in another jeep by Detective Garda Ronan Carey and Detective Garda Tony Ryan. The ERU members attracted stares as they progressed through the village. Russell ignored the looks of the locals and of the first press people who were starting to gather at the edge of the scene. By that stage, another road cordon had had to be set up at the church about half a mile from the Carthy cottage to help contain the media.

It had been a long journey and Russell was anxious to get to the area around the Carthy cottage itself. The local gardaí waved his jeep through the cordons, relieved to see that the reserves had arrived. The tactical commander drove slowly and cautiously, eyes darting around the scene, taking it all in. The positions of the gardaí, the best positions of cover, the light in the kitchen where he presumed John Carthy was. It was much easier now to see what had to be done.

Bringing their jeeps to a halt, the ERU men jumped out of their vehicles, and began unloading their armoured jackets and weapons. Before leaving Dublin, each of them had gathered the equipment they deemed necessary. Carey had signed out two Uzi sub-machine guns, one Bennelli semi-automatic shotgun and one Heckler & Koch .33 rifle and the necessary ammunition. Flaherty had gathered first aid equipment, and some technical equipment that might come in useful, such as night vision equipment and pyrotechnic distraction devices. Ryan signed out the necessary equipment that would aid in any forced entry into the cottage.

Russell scanned the gardaí that were already in the area, and eventually found the familiar face of Joe Shelly. He had never worked with the superintendent before, but he knew him to see. The two men quickly greeted each other and then set about their plans. Russell listened to Shelly's description of the man inside the house. His name, his age, his depression – Russell stopped him there. This was the first he had heard about the presence of a mental illness, and it interested him greatly. Way back before he had signed up for the gardaí, Russell had trained as a psychiatric nurse, and for three years he had studied the mind in all its complexity. He had in fact worked for a time in St Loman's Hospital in his hometown of Mullingar, the same institution that John had come to despise. Russell had seen how depression could affect a person's behaviour and knowing that this man suffered from such a mental illness gave him a better understanding of the situation they were dealing with.

But he put the depression to the back of his mind, reminding himself that whatever about his experience of psychiatry, tactical planning was his job tonight. He paced around the area, taking in the scene. It was the little things that interested him. He eyed up every hedge and every possible route to and from the house. Darkness was fast falling on the midlands, and he needed to memorise a map of the area for what he feared might be a long night. A few things worried him. He looked at the sheds adjacent to the cottage and wondered if there might be a door or an entrance there that they couldn't see from the road. He wondered if Carthy might have access to the sheds from the house, and whether he could use them as an escape route once night fell.

He went back to his three officers, and gave them his instructions. He had a good relationship with all the men. They respected and liked him. His easy-going and friendly manner made him approachable and easy to work with. The plans he laid out for them were clear. Each of the officers would be placed where they could have a clear view of all the exits from the house, the windows and in particular the front door. He explained the possible scenarios to them. If Carthy should emerge they should try to disarm and arrest him, if that was a safe option for them at the time. He told them what he thought Carthy's possible exit routes might be, and the rest was left unsaid. He did not nominate one man to take on the task of arresting Carthy. Whichever officer was closest to him would be automatically selected for that. Similarly, he did not go beyond the basic instructions on how they should deal with him if a confrontation did arise. That would be up to each member, their levels of bravery and their breaking points. This was the kind of standard instruction that would normally be given at this stage in a siege situation.

The officers were told to be flexible, to bear in mind that they had a cordon around the house, that the neighbours had been evacuated and for a short distance at least, Carthy would not be an immediate danger to anyone. It was only if he did come to present a clear threat to life that any of the men would be justified in shooting at him. They knew this, it was in the garda code.

The instructions were given out quickly, priority being placed on getting the men in position and settling them down before night was upon them. The local armed men who had been manning the inner cordon points closest to the cottage were instructed to move back, allowing the ERU men to move into position. Detective Garda Ryan was sent to take up position at a mound of clay that was at the back of the house. It gave some cover, and would allow him to keep an eye on the front door. Flaherty was told to man a point at the corner of the new Carthy house so he could watch those sheds that Russell was worried about, while Garda Carey was positioned at the pillar between the Carthy garden and the Flaherty property next door. With darkness falling Russell had told them they had to tighten the cordon up, and all of the officers were as close to the house as safety would allow.

Russell discussed all his plans with Shelly. Regardless of the special skills of his unit, Russell still regarded Shelly as being the head man at the scene and everything had to be run by him, but that was where Russell's liaison with the local branch ended. He could see that a number of both armed and unarmed local members were still dotted around the immediate area of the scene. Some were standing at the ESB pole at the edge of the Carthy property, others were on the road, and two more were positioned at the Burke property next door. Russell did not have any direct conversation with these local officers, but he assumed that Shelly would inform them of what was going on. In theory at least, the local men were now assigned to a back-up role, a second line of defence in case Carthy came out and somehow got past the ERU men. That was the plan agreed between Russell and Shelly. Russell went to do his job and Shelly was responsible for informing the local personnel of what was going on.

He instructed the senior local officer, Detective Sergeant Aidan Foley to do the rounds and tell all the local men that the ERU were now in place and that their role now was as a back-up to the specialist force. But the lines of communication weren't ideal. Some of the local officers got the message, but others, like Detective Garda Jim Campbell who had remained in the area since he had been moved from the back of the house, stated that no one specifically instructed him 'one way or the other' as to what the new role of the local men was. There was no direct communication between the ERU and the local branch throughout the entire incident.

With his men safely in their positions, Russell set out along the wall in front of the gable end of the Carthy house. The light was still on in the kitchen, and taking occasional glances around pillars and bushes, Russell got his first look at the figure of Carthy. He could see him clearly through the window, a very slight young man, gun in hand. Russell felt better having seen him and having a better idea of what he was dealing with. Beyond the hype and the fear of what was happening, he could now bring this back down to practicalities and confirm

Left: John Carthy playing handball. He was a keen player and had helped in the rebuilding of the handball alley in Abbeylara.

Right: John Carthy receiving a sports trophy.

Aerial view towards Abbeylara showing a) the Farrells' house, b) the Carthys' old house; c) the Carthys' new house; d) the Burkes' house; e) the Walshs' house.

Above: The garda patrol car in the driveway of the Carthys' property. Note damage to left front wing where John Carthy fired at it.

Below: View of the boundary wall of the Carthys' old house. The central pillar served as the negotiation point. The loudhailers can be seen on the ground.

Members of the Emergency Response Unit in position outside the front wall of the Carthy house.

Above: The front gable window of the Carthy house, through which John Carthy fired shots.

Below: The disordered kitchen in the Carthy house after the siege had ended. The pillar that served as the negotiation point can be seen through the window.

Above: The scene of crime tent on the roadway outside the Carthy home.

Below: The Oireachtas sub-committee outside the front wall of the old Carthy house.

Above: Marie Carthy at a press conference to give the Carthy family's response to the findings of the Barr Tribunal.

Below: Rose Carthy outside her new cottage.

In Loving Memory Of
JOHN CARTHY *Toneymore Abbeylara*
Died 12th April 1990
His Son JOHN
Who Died Tragically 20th April 2000 Aged 27 Years

Also His Parents and Brother Terry
Rest In Peace

CARTHY

We Miss You
JOHN
Love Mammy & Marie

Though You Cannot S
Or Touch Me I Will
Always Be Near

In Loving Memory Of
A Dear
SON

John Carthy's grave in Abbeylara.

in his own mind that despite the dangers posed at this scene, they were dealing with a sick man who had reached a stage of unbearable insecurity.

♎ ♎ ♎

Jackson formed his own views when he arrived at the scene just after ten o'clock. He sized up the house and the area, his eyes delaying a few seconds on the light in the kitchen window. He listened carefully to Shelly. He heard again about the depression and about Carthy's behaviour so far and he felt sympathy for him. Shelly told him what he knew about Carthy's arrest for the goat-burning incident and that Carthy had issues with the gardaí on account of his wrongful arrest. There was no mention at this stage however of any allegations of physical abuse while Carthy had been in custody.

Other information was given to the negotiator at this point. He was informed that Marie Carthy was on her way to the scene from Galway and that John Carthy's doctor had been at the scene for a time, but had since left. He also learned that John had been having difficulty finding work and that he had broken up with his girlfriend. Detective Sergeant Jackson also believed he was told by Shelly that the family had been asked if Carthy had a treating specialist, but that they had said they weren't aware of any psychiatrist.

The two officers were standing at the ESB pole that stood at the edge of the Carthy property discussing the situation, and Shelly explained that he had chosen that spot for his own earlier attempts at negotiating. Now Jackson sized it up for himself. It was a reasonably good position, the kitchen window could be seen at an angle, it was close enough for communication to be possible and far enough away for comfort and safety. Studying the large area in front and around the Carthy cottage however, he estimated the pole to be about 70 feet to the left of the house and that distance bothered him. Negotiating at such a remove would be difficult. A lot of shouting would be required and there was a danger that if Carthy did respond, his replies would be lost in the no-man's land between them.

The position of the negotiating post was going to be crucial. Best police practice indicates that the safest position for such a post is in a remote cell away from the immediacy of the scene. Phone negotiations from a distance are the ideal method of communication, providing a secure set-up for the negotiator and also allowing the subject of the incident the space often required to return to logical thinking. The remote negotiating cell had been used to great effect at the siege in Bawnboy, the officers in that incident setting up base in the house next door and managing to negotiate a peaceful conclusion. But a remote cell was not a possibility unless Carthy became more agreeable to talking on the phone. He had a mobile, but when Dr Cullen had tried to phone it, he ignored the call and it also took several calls from Tom Walsh before Carthy eventually answered. There was a landline phone in the house, but it had been disconnected by Eircom some months previously. The family told them this, and the gardaí had arranged for it to be reconnected so that they could have it as a second option.

In his first half hour at the scene, Jackson tried ringing Carthy on a few occasions, but got no answer. Because of this, Jackson quickly dismissed the idea of moving the negotiation post to a remote location. He chose instead to take the same route followed by Shelly, to stand at the ESB pole and use the megaphone to try and get through to Carthy. Experts were later critical of Jackson for his impatience, and would also criticise the use of a loudhailer for communications.

Former FBI negotiator, Frederick J. Lanceley said that in the United States, negotiators would persist in trying to establish telephone contact with a subject, even if that took hours or days, because it was always the best method of communication. Highlighting the particularly personal problems Carthy had, Lanceley said the use of a loudhailer was not an appropriate means to discuss the turmoil in this young man's life.

'Shouting and using a loudhailer is not conducive to discussing and resolving such intimate and private issues as Mr Carthy's mental disorder, suicidal ideation, love life, job loss, loss of possible self-esteem and self-worth, anger, slagging he had been receiving, the feelings about the garda, guilt over self-inflicted blame for his father's death, the loss of the family home, etc.'

It was shortly after 10pm when Jackson spoke his first words to Carthy. Standing at the ESB pole, and making use of the garda loudhailer, he introduced himself to Carthy and repeated much the same words that had been iterated by both Shelly and Dooley earlier in the evening. The negotiator could see Russell crouched behind the wall in front of the house and he wondered if his colleague could see any reaction from the man inside. At 10.25 pm, he heard the reaction himself. Carthy fired a shot at the wall where Russell was hiding. As the cartridge disintegrated, the pellets hit off the concrete, and whizzed over Russell's head.

Russell was shaken, and as soon as he felt it was safe, he hurried away from the front wall and back to relative safety at the edges of the inner cordon. Coming around the property, he arrived at the pole to speak with Jackson and Shelly about how they were going to manage this. He had known Jackson for nearly twenty years before they were brought together to work at Abbeylara. The two officers had worked side by side at Kilmainham station in Dublin, and had also had many dealings with each other through their work with the ERU.

Russell had a great amount of respect for Jackson, but when he arrived at the ESB pole to speak with him that evening, he couldn't believe what he was hearing. Jackson wanted to move the negotiating post to the garden wall that stood right in front of the Carthy kitchen window, the same wall that had just felt the impact of the last shot Carthy had fired from his stronghold. The negotiator had only spent ten minutes at the ESB pole, but in that short time, he had come to the conclusion that he needed to get closer to the cottage.

Justifying his proposal to Russell, Jackson said he wanted to have a chance of making eye contact with Carthy and of hearing any response he might make to the attempts at dialogue. Russell wasn't convinced. While it was admirable for Jackson to want to get closer to Carthy, the definite risks of the move far outweighed the potential rewards that may have been gained by setting up camp right in front of the kitchen window.

But on that night, Russell was willing to at least consider Jackson's request. Looking at the front wall again, he estimated it to be about five foot high. It was a new wall, it was deep and sturdy, and he knew it would be of sufficient strength to withstand any future shots from Carthy. But it was very close to the cottage – only about thirty-eight feet of grass separated the gable window from the pillars. As tactical commander at the scene, Russell would never have suggested such a move himself, but accepting the wisdom that negotiation would be the key to a successful resolution, he eventually gave in to Jackson's request.

Within a few minutes, Jackson, his assistant Detective Garda Michael Sullivan and Russell had skirted their way along to the wall. Jackson was determined on this one, and confident that Carthy would eventually come round. His first aim was to set himself apart from the other gardaí that Carthy had encountered. He made a mental note that he would identify himself as being a garda from Dublin, disconnecting himself from the local members Carthy had dealt with before. To further mark himself out as a garda with a difference, he discarded his ballistics helmet, so that when he raised his head above the wall Carthy would see a friendly face rather than an armoured presence. Russell was particularly worried by that. He had caught a glimpse of Carthy's gun and he knew the lethal capabilities it held. One shot from its barrels could kill or injure many. That was the 'spray' effect that came from such a shotgun, a cartridge would explode and send bits of shrapnel shooting in several directions.

Ω   Ω   Ω

At the wall, Jackson chose a spot that was beside a pillar, directly opposite the kitchen window. The high pillar afforded enough cover and height to allow him to almost stand up straight behind the concrete barrier that would be his protection in the attacks that were to follow. For the most part however, he would remain crouched safely near to the ground. At times, he would use the loudhailer, sometimes he would just shout in, but all the time, the speech and the assurances were the same.

Settled at the wall, Jackson decided to start from the beginning again, and he re-introduced himself to Carthy, telling him again who he was.

'John, this is Mick, I'm here to help, I'm with the gardaí.'

Jackson stole a few quick glances over the wall. Carthy did not appear to have heard or heeded his introduction. He just paced the kitchen over and over again, oblivious. Jackson called out his mobile phone number, in case Carthy wanted to phone him at any stage, but the interest inside the house was in something other than the noise that was coming from outside. He seemed too preoccupied to respond. Jackson continued to introduce himself every few minutes, waiting for Carthy to respond.

Recognition finally came after twenty minutes. Carthy, seemingly suddenly aware of a new presence at his front wall, rushed to the window, and in almost excited tones, inquired as to who Jackson was.

Carthy: 'Who are you?'
Jackson: 'I'm Mick from the gardaí, I am here to help you.'
Carthy: 'Are you a guard?'
Jackson: 'Yes John, I am.'
Carthy: 'Go away and fuck off.'

Introductions over, Carthy moved away from the window again to resume pacing the circumference of the small family kitchen. Jackson, however, was encouraged to at least have had some form of dialogue with Carthy, even if it was in such negative tones. He wanted to keep Carthy talking, and he shouted in to him, asking if he would answer his telephone so that they could talk properly.

Carthy mumbled something unintelligible and turned up

the volume on the television to silence the speech that he had heard so many times at that stage. When Jackson didn't take the hint, Carthy walked to the window and levelled the gun at him through one of the panes that he had already smashed out. Seeing the double barrels of the shotgun for the first time, Jackson immediately ducked his head back down behind the wall. Carthy got the silence he wanted.

Preferring to keep the wall between them for a while, Jackson gave Carthy a few minutes, and then went back to ringing his mobile phone. He didn't expect an answer, but Carthy picked up almost straight away, and it seemed as though Jackson had interrupted a train of thought.

Carthy: 'Where is my solicitor? Get the fuck out of here.'

That was all he said before he hung up the phone again, but the snippet had given Jackson something very promising to work with, and it nourished his hopes of bringing the incident to a peaceful ending. It encouraged him to hear that Carthy was perhaps thinking beyond this bad day, planning how he would defend his actions and how he could minimise the penalty for what he had done. Using the loudhailer, he dwelt on the issue, promising he would get Carthy any solicitor he wanted. He asked for a name, but Carthy only ever replied in riddles.

'I want the best, the best, the best.'

The conversation went back and forth, Jackson promising Carthy any solicitor he wanted, whenever he wanted, Carthy seeming to muse on it for a time and then issuing grandiose demands. He told Jackson he wanted the solicitor to come and talk with him in the house, and he was firm about it. Banging the gun off the kitchen table to ensure his point was heard and heeded, he shouted out that he wanted the lawyer to come to him.

'I want him to come in here, in here.'

Allowing a civilian into the house was out of the question, but Jackson tried to come to a compromise. He offered to arrange for a solicitor to meet Carthy half way, in the garden. Jackson reasoned with him and pointed out that it would be impossible to allow a solicitor into the house while the gun was still in the equation. The negotiator put it in the simplest terms, walking Carthy through it. He told him to just leave the gun inside, to come out the door, and a lawyer would be waiting there for him.

Carthy, however, wasn't interested. Two parts of the plan bothered him, the part where he had to come out and the part where he had to leave the gun behind. The house was his last stronghold, and leaving it was not a possibility.

'I am not coming out, no way.'

Ω   Ω   Ω

Midnight approached, and Jackson decided to take a new route in his attempt at gaining the trust of John Carthy. He needed to reach him, to say something that touched him in some way, and launching into a prolonged monologue, he set out the few private details he knew of Carthy's life. He asked Carthy why he was doing this, and told him that his sister and mother and all his friends and neighbours just wanted him to leave the gun behind and to come out. The negotiator was aware that arrangements had been made to bring Marie to the scene from Galway, and she probably wasn't far from the scene at that point. He had been told that John was very close to his sister and he had hoped that regular mentions of Marie would help the situation. Peering above the wall however, Jackson could see the impact his words had. Carthy was laughing to himself and smirking. Continuing on, Jackson told Carthy that he knew he was a good plasterer and that everyone said he was a hard worker. He reassured him that nothing bad would happen if he did come out, because nobody had been injured and no real harm had been done.

Carthy didn't want to hear it, and he turned up the volume on the television again to try to drown out the stream of words coming from outside. But that didn't work. He could still hear Jackson, and he wanted him to stop. Again, he walked to the window, aimed his gun and fired a shot. His aim was frighteningly accurate. The bullet hit the cap of the pillar behind which Jackson was sheltering. Shaken by the attack, Jackson pleaded with Carthy to stop shooting.

'No way, no way come on in and get me,' Carthy invited.

Jackson was concerned at this and he sensed an indifference in the way Carthy was behaving. The negotiator began to think seriously that Carthy did not care whether he lived or died that night. It was as if Carthy was planning on sitting back and watching all of it unfold, just like the thousands around the country who were hearing the first news reports of what was happening in Abbeylara. Jackson set him straight and told him the gardaí would not be coming in to get him.

'John, we don't want to hurt anyone, especially you and we don't want you to hurt anyone so please stop shooting and put the gun down.'

With silence reigning in the kitchen, Jackson headed for the deep end and asked Carthy straight out if he was suicidal.

'John, are you thinking of hurting yourself?'

He got no reply.

8.

Marie Carthy was on her way to Abbeylara. She was in the back of a patrol car, along with her friend, Martin Shelly, who was known to both John and herself as 'Pepper'. The trip was proving to be long and awkward. Two gardaí sat in the front, Marie and Pepper in the back. Pleasantries had been exchanged in the beginning, but after that little was said, none of them fully sure of what was going on in Abbeylara. The patrol car was flying down the road towards Longford, and the speed, coupled with her natural anxiety about her brother made Marie feel nauseous. She asked the gardaí to stop the car, so she could go into a hotel to use the bathroom. They obliged.

Back on the road, Marie continued to stare out of the window and to think about John. She had been talking to him only a few hours earlier, when he had phoned her while she was on her lunch break. They called each other every day, often several times a day, because there were just the two of them and they were best friends. In that last phone call his humour had been fine. He was happy to hear that she would be home for the forthcoming Easter weekend and he was full of ideas on what they would do and where they would socialise. Only a year and two months separated them in age, and from childhood through teens and twenties, they had played together, gone out together and supported each other.

Marie knew that John hadn't had it easy over the past few weeks, and that he had been feeling the onset of one of his 'turns'. She thought of the day and date, and remembered that he was due at an appointment with Dr Shanley the very next day, Holy Thursday. He had asked her to make the appointment for him. She was proud of the way he dealt with his manic depression, accepting when a high or a low was on the way, and seeking help. She hoped that he would still be able to make the meeting with his psychiatrist, confident that that would sort him out.

Talking to herself and reasoning with the situation, Marie came to her own conclusions on the journey down. In her mind the situation was simple. John was in the house. He was high. It happens. She would get there; have a word with him and it would all be sorted out. She knew that the gardaí were involved, but she couldn't imagine that it would amount to anything other than a few local members keeping watch on the house, just in case anything happened. She understood they were probably afraid he would commit suicide, and she only hoped they had the good sense to give him the space he needed to come round.

Nothing could have prepared her for what she saw when the patrol car finally swerved off the Granard road into Abbeylara village. The area around the church was taken up with media satellite vans. Cameras were set up; journalists were wandering about, talking on their mobile phones and making notes. She saw the RTÉ van and the TV3 satellite cruiser. They seemed to have set up camp, and for the life of her she could not understand why her brother was of any interest to the media.

But as they moved further up the road and were waved through the outer traffic cordon, Marie began to understand why the country's press had been drawn to the area around her humble home. It was like a movie set. Gardaí were everywhere, some of them dressed up in full ballistics gear. Patrol cars lined the road, armed gardaí were positioned around her neighbours' houses, and they all had their eyes on the faint familiar light she could see in the kitchen of her family home. It was terrifying. She thought of John in the house. He must be scared out of his mind.

The patrol car paused up the road from the cottage, and Marie was vaguely aware of some gardaí having a discussion outside the vehicle. Superintendent Joe Shelly was one of these officers, and their discussion resulted in a decision that Marie and Pepper should be brought around the Ballywillin side of the house where they would be interviewed by Detective Sergeant Sullivan. Before she knew what was happening, Marie was moved into a garda jeep and was being driven away from the scene again. This was the practice over the course of the incident. If someone needed to travel to the area on the opposite side of the house – a short walk – they had to drive back out of Abbeylara village, into Granard and around to the Cavan side of the Toneymore townland.

On their arrival at the far side of the Carthy cottage, Detective Sergeant Sullivan sat into the jeep beside Marie. He could see immediately that she was very distressed, and he tried to broach his questions with as much sensitivity as possible. Clipboard in hand, he asked her why she thought her brother might be acting in this way and if there was anything she could enlighten them on. Still shocked at the scene that was playing out before her, Marie struggled for the words that might explain John's actions. She mentioned the depression and referred to John and her mother's imminent move from the house, which she felt could be bothering him. She also mentioned that tomorrow was their father's anniversary and that John had been very close to his dad. From the back seat, Pepper, who had known John Carthy for a number of months in Galway, contributed what information he thought relevant. He told Garda Sullivan about John losing his job in Galway, and also that he understood him to say that he had been barred from McCormack's pub the previous weekend.

Marie became lost in all the questions and possibilities. She just wanted to sort this out, as she always sorted everything out. Marie was the backbone of the family, holding them together, being sensible, looking out for them. John was a part of her, and she understood him well. She knew how to deal with him, the right things she could say to bring him around when he suffered from one of his bouts. Given a few minutes with him, she knew she would at least give him a lifeline if he had, in fact, reached such an extreme point.

While Marie and Pepper were in the jeep with Detective Sullivan, Tom Walsh was outside speaking to a garda. At one point, Walsh opened the door of the jeep and asked Marie who was the family solicitor. Marie told him it was 'Gearty's'. Later, Tom Walsh could not recollect which officer had asked him for this information, but thought it was Superintendent Shelly. Shelly denies ever discussing the issue of a solicitor with Walsh. The gardaí claim that the only conversation with a member of the Carthy family regarding a solicitor came when Inspector Martin Maguire raised the issue with Walsh hours before. The Inspector claimed Walsh told him that Carthy had no legal representative.

Despite Carthy's request for a solicitor, the officer who was liaising with the family in the Mahon household was never contacted to inquire from the women if they could provide any information in this regard. The family have suggested that the gardaí did not pursue the identity of Carthy's solicitor with them because they did not want to involve such a professional in what was unfolding. The gardaí deny this, and say they would have been happy to accept assistance from anyone.

♎   ♎   ♎

Still sitting in the garda jeep, the shock of what she was seeing was starting to hit Marie hard. None of it made sense. Part of her wanted to just run down the road and into the house to show John she was there with him. But she looked again at the scene before her, and was scared even to move a muscle. Detective Sullivan continued to ask her the same questions, to explain the inexplicable. She did all she could from that distance, and told Sullivan that the gardaí should just 'give him some space'.

Sullivan finished his cycle of questions, and orders were given to get Marie away from the scene. She didn't want to go, but on that night she did what she was told, because there was little else she could do. A junior officer was told to bring both Marie and Pepper to stay with a neighbour; the garda duly dropped the two of them off at the Devine household at around midnight.

The Devine family sat around Marie, saying anything encouraging that came to mind, and making small talk to try and keep her from dwelling on what was going on down the road. It was a cool April evening and Mrs Devine made some hot whiskeys to warm both Marie and Pepper up after their journey and their visit to the scene. Marie wasn't saying much, and after she had finished her drink, she asked if she could bed down for the night.

♎ ♎ ♎

Holy Thursday had arrived, and Jackson and his colleagues were still crouched at the wall. The situation hadn't changed, and no progress had been made. There had been a changing of the guard at the command post. Shelly had clocked off for the night, and he was replaced by Superintendent Michael Byrne who was the district officer for Granard. He had been at the scene since ten o'clock, and had been briefed by Shelly on what he knew of John Carthy and also on the nature of the cordons that were in place to try and contain the situation. Byrne knew the situation was volatile. He had heard a number of shots coming from the house. The last one had been fired just before he took up duty as scene commander at midnight. Carthy didn't seem to be calming down at all.

There were periods when Jackson could pop his head up over the wall and observe Carthy and his behaviour. Apart from when he would come to the window to fire a shot, the young man seemed to be preoccupied within his own world, oblivious to the shouts and movements outside. Now, at midnight, Jackson watched as he paused in one of his laps of the kitchen to eat some bread and drink from a cup. But at all times he kept the gun near at hand.

Picking up the loudhailer again, Jackson decided to take an alternative route, accepting that he might not hold the key to what would crack Carthy. Although he had heard about the bad reception Tom Walsh had received earlier, he still believed there was a possibility that somebody close to Carthy would be able to talk him around. Knowing that Marie and Pepper had arrived at the scene, he mentioned this to Carthy, and there appeared to be a degree of interest. Jackson asked him if he would like to speak with Pepper perhaps, and, mercifully, Carthy threw him a line.

'Get Pepper.'

Jackson sent the request up the line. In the initial stages of the incident, Shelly and Russell had decided to use one of the ERU jeeps as a type of command post. It was parked at the wall outside Burke's house, just up from the ESB pole, and whenever Jackson wanted to get a message to Shelly, he would ask either Russell or Sullivan to go up along the wall, run past the gateway and bring the message to the command post.

It was the same with the instruction that Pepper should be brought to the scene as a matter of urgency. The message was received by officers at the command post and taken as a minor breakthrough after hours of nothing. The order that somebody should go and 'get Pepper' as Carthy had asked was circulated, but it bounced back and forth, and it was eventually conceded that nobody actually knew where Marie and Pepper were. The superintendent's log book placed Carthy's sister and friend opposite an entry which read 'whereabouts unknown'. The garda who had dropped them off at the Devine's house had gone off duty for the night and he had not told anyone else where he had left the two.

This was now a problem – one that should never have arisen. John Carthy had specifically asked for Pepper, and now the gardaí were going to have to start knocking at doors in the middle of the night to try and find him.

♎   ♎   ♎

At the negotiation point, Jackson continued with his assurances, feeling safe in the mistaken assumption that it couldn't take long to get Pepper to the scene. He wanted to speak with Carthy over the phone, but all of his calls went unanswered. Carthy was growing agitated again, mumbling to himself, berating himself one moment and giving himself a pep talk in the next. Jackson kept on calling, until he was silenced by a shot being fired inside the kitchen itself. The target for this bullet was particular and Carthy hit it first time. The landline phone was blown off the wall.

Jackson pleaded with him to stop shooting. He went through his line of reasoning once more, telling Carthy that his mother and his sister and everyone cared for him; that the best course of action was for him to come out unarmed. John Carthy wouldn't listen. He threw Jackson's words back at him, and told him it was 'bullshit'.

Jackson plunged further, and told Carthy that he himself cared for him. He said that all he wanted was for Carthy to come out safely. He could feel his anger and his resentment, but he couldn't understand why he was behaving his way. Carthy responded by telling Jackson that there was no way he could possibly care for him, because he was a garda.

The bitterness in Carthy's voice was clear, and Jackson's efforts to convince him otherwise met with little interest. He shouted into the kitchen that, yes, he was a guard, but that he was there to help and he assured John that despite his encounters with the force before, he would be treated fairly this time. Carthy ignored him, and Jackson went back to the safety of the old script, telling him again that everyone cared and that friends like Pepper had travelled long distances to try and help him.

The mention of Pepper brought Jackson back to glancing at his watch. He should have been brought down to the negotiation post a long time ago. Carthy had asked to see him just before midnight. It was now 2am. Despite the fact that the Devine household where Marie and Pepper were staying that night was just 300 yards away from the scene, it took gardaí two hours to locate them.

Ω   Ω   Ω

Marie wasn't able to sleep. She had never been so afraid or worried in her whole life. She felt sick and confused. She couldn't get John out of her head, and it was torturing her to think of him alone in the house, surrounded by gardaí. That image made her angry.

She thought too of her mother, who was spending the night in her cousin's house. She couldn't imagine how Rose would ever get through this. With her fears growing worse by the minute, Marie was almost relieved to hear a car pulling up outside the Devine house just before two o'clock in the morning. Not knowing and wondering in the dark had been hellish. If this car was bringing news, good or bad, at least it would be something. She heard what she took to be a garda's voice at the door, and was afraid to breathe, waiting to hear what he wanted. He was looking for Pepper. John had asked to speak to him.

It would be much later before Marie would learn of the delay in finding Pepper, and at the point when the garda arrived at the Devine house, she thought her chance had come at last. There was no question but that she would accompany Pepper down to the scene, and she thought that she too would now be given the chance to talk to John and sort the whole misunderstanding out. That was not to be the case.

It was 2.15 am when Marie and Pepper arrived at the cordons on the edges of the scene and met with Superintendent

Byrne and Detective Sergeant Jackson. The two officers had been discussing events and had decided that even though Marie was accompanying Pepper to the scene, only the latter would be allowed down to speak with Carthy at that time. This, they said, was so that they could build up trust with Carthy. They didn't want to surprise him by presenting his sister at the negotiation post without clearing it with him first.

Marie had not been privy to this agreement, and as Pepper was being escorted down to the inner cordon, she attempted to follow him but was stopped in her tracks by Superintendent Byrne, who held out his arms to stop her going by him on the road.

Marie struggled to get past the officer. She tried to move by him again, but was met with more resistance. She could not believe that the gardaí were preventing her from going down her own road towards her own home, and she attempted to argue with the Superintendent. She told him she wanted to go and talk to her brother, but the reply from Byrne was that that could not be arranged 'at the moment'.

'I put out my arm and I blocked her passage and she went to go to the other side of me,' said Byrne. 'She made two attempts and I prevented her from going down because I said it wasn't right at the time. Martin Shelly [Pepper], he wanted Martin and we wanted to bring Martin down to him to resolve the situation.'

The issue of why Marie was kept from the scene has been the subject of much debate. Carthy was obviously open to talking, considering he had asked for Pepper. And for their part, the gardaí were clearly open to allowing third parties to have some involvement in negotiations, having allowed Tom Walsh and now Pepper to attempt some dialogue with Carthy.

The gardaí had another explanation for why they didn't allow Marie down to the post with Pepper at that time, and it was a controversial one. They claimed that Marie was drunk. Both Superintendent Byrne and Detective Garda Jim Campbell, who was in the area when Marie and Pepper arrived at the outskirts of the scene, stated on the record that Marie was under the influence when she arrived at the scene at two o'clock that morning. Byrne described her condition as being that of someone who was 'socially drunk'. She was able to stand up, he said, but her speech was slurred and she was swaying from side to side. Similarly, Detective Garda Jim Campbell stated that he felt Marie smelled strongly of alcohol and said he was '100% sure' that she was under the influence.

Marie has always utterly refuted the claim, and has said time and again that the only alcohol she consumed that night was one hot whisky in Devine's. It is an accusation that she feels places serious question marks on her character, and she worries that those who have never met her will believe the claims.

Having considered the evidence, Justice Robert Barr stated his belief that Marie was telling the truth. While accepting that she may have a 'volatile personality', he ruled that the allegations that she was under the influence were not true. Justice Barr also said that the allegation of drunkenness was just one example of the 'strenuous efforts' the gardaí had gone to in their attempts to 'downgrade Ms Carthy's potential importance as an intermediary with her brother'.

Ω Ω Ω

It was two thirty in the morning when Pepper was finally brought down to the negotiation point to speak with Carthy, but the earlier promise shown in Carthy's desire to speak with him had long since evaporated. Pepper, under some instruction from Jackson, asked John what had happened to him to put him in such a state, and asked him to come out before anybody got hurt. He told him Marie and his mother were up the road, and they loved him and everything would be okay. Carthy showed little interest in Pepper, however, giving no response to anything that was said. The little glimmer of hope that had been Carthy's request to 'get Pepper' was extinguished by stony silence.

When Pepper returned to the outer cordons of the scene, he found that Marie had already gone back to the Devine house. After finally accepting that she would not be allowed down to speak with John, she had been persuaded to go back to bed to try to get some rest. Gardaí assured her that they would allow her to talk to her brother in the morning.

Returning to bed, Marie continued her night of wondering and waiting. She thought back to the last phone call she had shared with John that lunchtime, how his voice had not belied any signs of a severe deterioration in his mood. Like the relative of anyone who suffers from depression, Marie could always tell if he was up or down. It was usually confirmed in the first instants of every conversation, but she hadn't heard any down tones that day. She turned over in her mind what could have been bothering him, and wondered if it was something to do with the job losses he had suffered of late. But that had happened before, and he had bounced back. She wondered if the slagging from locals had finally beaten him, but dismissed that too. John could laugh at himself, and while the slagging might annoy him, he wouldn't let it get the better of him.

Then she thought of Kathleen.

9.

In January 2000, John Carthy met a girl at a party in Galway. Her name was Kathleen, and he liked her. John had never really had a relationship before because he had never given himself that chance, but on that night with this girl, he got brave. He worked hard at impressing her, and at the end of the party she agreed to meet him again. It was the start of something special for the young man, and without doubt the relationship that was to follow was the single most liberating experience in his life. With Kathleen on his arm, he reached the ultimate state of what he believed it felt to be 'normal'. He had a girlfriend, and more than his interest in the football, and the gun club, and his liking a pint at the weekend, this finally made him ordinary, and he loved it.

John had never shared details of his illness with anyone outside of his family or beyond his circle of medical experts before. People generally didn't understand, and he preferred it when he wasn't stamped with the mental illness label. But with Kathleen, he opened up and let himself go, and for a few brief weeks, it was the making of him. In theory at least, she was not put off by the idea of him being manically depressed; she assured him it wouldn't be a problem, and they started out with the same hopes and excitement as every young couple.

But Kathleen had come along at the wrong time. She happened to fall into John's life just when other elements were stretching him and making his battle with his illness all the more difficult. After only a few dates with Kathleen, his happiness was challenged when work problems hit him hard. He began to feel low, and Kathleen was to see him at his worst before she could ever get to know him at his best.

John had been living in Galway for a few months, working as a general labourer at a site at Edward Square in the city. He enjoyed the freedom of being in a place where few people knew him or his past, and he quickly made friends with his colleagues on the site. One of those new friends was Martin 'Pepper' Shelly, and another good mate was a man called Kevin Ireland. They thought John was quirky, and he made them laugh with his antics at work, especially his tendency to strut around, referring to himself as the 'Toneymore Fox'.

On 17 January 2000, John decided to finish up at the Edward Square site. He had been offered some work as a plasterer, and for the sake of his finances he had opted to accept the new job. He gave in his notice and his reasons for leaving, but he wasn't content to leave it at that. He had a few issues with how the site was run, and seeing as he was leaving the job anyway, he decided to get one or two grievances off his chest. He told his boss that the foreman on the site was engaging in improper practices. The allegation was not appreciated, and when John turned up to begin working out his notice the next day, he was sacked.

The job loss was a blow, and the following day it was doubled. He began his new job with the plastering firm, but was let go at the end of his first day due to the quality of his work. His confidence was taking a beating. In that kind of mindset, inadequacies were blown up, and his fledgling relationship with Kathleen suffered.

His lease at 159 Tirellan Heights in Galway ran out at the

end of January 2000, and he asked to stay with Kathleen for a few nights. She could see he wasn't happy in himself, and agreed to allow him room at her house. However, he ended up staying with her for two weeks, and by the end of that fortnight, Kathleen had seen aspects of John that scared her and ultimately led her to end the relationship.

John didn't like being out of work because it gave him too much time to think. In the weeks while he was staying with Kathleen, he spent his days obsessing over what had happened at the Edward Square site, and he took the view that he had been unfairly dismissed. He got in contact with SIPTU in the hope of taking an action against the building contractors, but they just asked a lot of questions and put him off with promises to get back to him. The red tape was frustrating him, and by the start of February 2000 John eventually decided to take the matter in his own hands, by placing a picket at the site.

He had continued to meet up with his friends from the site after he had been fired. He would preach to them about the injustice of his sacking, they would listen, and after a few drinks they would agree to support him in any industrial action he wanted to take. John was relying on them, and when he arrived to set up his picket that morning, he waited for the familiar faces to join his protest. But, one by one, his old colleagues walked by him into work, crossing his picket. The protest became a one-man operation.

He was a pathetic sight, standing alone at the entrance to the work yard and he was mortified by it. The minutes dragged by, and he could hear the laughter that was going on behind his back. His protest ended at 9.40 am that same morning, after some SIPTU officials came along and offered him some friendly advice. He skulked away from the site, embarrassed in the extreme. While he did eventually receive a payout of £1,140 from his previous employers, his solitary picket continued to haunt him. In the following days of unemployment, his demeanour drastically changed, to the detriment of his personality and his relationship.

Kathleen now began to see a side of John that was utterly different to the man she had first met. He was always in her house, and he was beginning to feel like a burden. She began to see the practicalities, realising that this was a man she barely knew, and wondering why she was putting up with it. 'John's friendly, caring, affectionate personality changed to be domineering, possessive, jealous, argumentative and demanding of my time,' she said.

Her doubts were confirmed on a night out in Athenry that February. John's mood was grim and he lashed out verbally at the new woman in his life. He threw insults at her, looking for a fight and acting out of character. On the drive home his mood worsened, and he asked her to stop the car and let him out. Kathleen was afraid for herself, but she refused to stop the car because she was more afraid of what might happen to him if he was let loose in such a dangerous state. Instead, when they arrived back in Galway, she gathered John's belongings and threw him out of her home.

In the following days John continued to behave erratically, setting ultimatums and starting arguments for no reason. His mental state was getting worse, and Kathleen was finding it difficult to see anything familiar or warm in him. She wanted out, and by the end of February she finally brought the relationship to an end.

Their final argument, the one that led to the break up, was

the worst. John said some horrible things, and she began to feel threatened by him. A basic fear for her safety finally convinced her she had to walk away.

'John raised his hand, making me believe he was about to hit me, but he stopped. I was afraid. He said he couldn't believe that I thought he would do such a thing. I remained calm and passed it off. I was afraid and didn't know what was going to happen,' she said.

The whole relationship had been a struggle for John. He tried to make it work, but his attempts were foiled again and again by the depths of his mental problems. Much as he wanted to keep Kathleen in his life, his over-anxious demands drove her away. The break-up was a huge disappointment, and the nature of his illness meant that from the moment Kathleen closed the door he sank to a low level of depression.

He turned to alcohol. On the night after Kathleen told him it was over, he went straight to the pub to drink himself into a state where the whole trauma would be at least manageable. Marie and Pepper went to meet him, and saw immediately that he was in a bad state. He sat on his bar stool and said little, all his energies concentrated on getting the drink down as quickly as possible. He was in the mood for a fight, and eventually got into an altercation with another man in the pub. They were pushing each other, and John was asked to leave.

Marie and Pepper decided to bring him for food, and steered him towards Supermacs on Eyre Square. Marie was very worried about him, so worried that once her brother was settled in the restaurant, she went and sought out the help of two passing gardaí, Garda Mary Ann O'Boyle, and Garda Oliver White of Galway Garda Station.

The account of what was said in this encounter differs between Marie and Garda O'Boyle. The garda claims that Marie told her that John was depressed and suicidal, and that she was extremely worried about him to the point that she said she would have him certified if necessary. She asked the gardaí if they would be able to get a doctor for him.

Garda O'Boyle claims that she explained to Marie that they could arrest her brother under the Mental Treatment Act 1945, that she explained the implications of this and warned Marie to think carefully before having her brother committed. She says that Marie said she was afraid Carthy 'might be found in the river in the morning'. Marie denies ever expressing such a fear, repeatedly saying that she did feel her brother needed help at that time, but did not believe him to be suicidal.

The gardaí went to Supermacs with Marie, and John was quick to realise what was going on. Marie saw it register on his face, a feeling that she had betrayed him. In a resigned tone of voice, he asked her, 'What have you gone and done?' However, he knew better than to fight it, and he voluntarily left the premises with the gardaí. He was put in the back of the patrol car, from where he complained to his arresting officers about his being taken into custody in such a manner. He asked Garda O'Boyle why she wasn't out arresting a real criminal instead of someone like him.

In the garda station, however, Carthy showed no hostility towards the officers, and he complied with all their requests. He gave them the full details of his medical history, and the names of the doctors he had been attending in the recent past. A local practitioner, Dr Dympna Horgan, came to the station to examine him, and she found some symptoms of elation. She advised him to go to the hospital, but he refused, and at that stage Marie said she did not feel comfortable with signing a committal form.

He was released from custody in the early hours of the morning. He shook hands with the officers and thanked them before leaving, and his only annoyance seemed to be with Marie. It is unclear where he actually stayed that night. While Marie claims he came home to her house, other evidence suggests that he actually hitched lifts during the night to get back to Abbeylara. His cousin, Tom Walsh, recalled meeting John at home the next day. He was in bad form and giving out about Marie. He told Tom Walsh about his arrest on the previous night. Walsh recalled that the incident seemed to have scared John, and remembered his cousin saying that when he saw a cell in the station he could picture himself 'inside for years' because he thought he was going to be committed.

His arrest in Galway that night has been inextricably linked to what had happened with Kathleen earlier that same day. He was driven to the refuge of drink, and his sister recognised the familiar symptoms of an oncoming low. Whether or not she expressed a fear that he was suicidal is almost irrelevant now, and what remains is only a what-if clause. Had he been hospitalised that night, would treatment have helped stop the spiral into the nightmare that was to unfold at Abbeylara a few weeks later?

With no job and no girlfriend, there was nothing keeping John in Galway, and he returned home again to live with Rose in the cottage in Abbeylara. He had a lot of time on his hands and he dwelt constantly on the ending of the relationship. He didn't blame Kathleen for finishing it, but it tortured him to know it was beyond his control. He was well aware that he was a burden and annoyance when he was in a period of mania or depression, but he gradually managed to convince himself that he could win her back.

He poured his heart out to Kathleen in two separate letters, which reveal him to be a sensitive but assertive young man, with a keen knowledge of how his illness affected him and those around him.

On 26 February, he wrote his first letter, expressing his sadness at how the relationship ended and trying and succeeding to put his manic depression into words that she could understand.

Toneymore,
Abbeylara,
Co. Longford

26.02.00

Dear Kathleen,
I do not want to get you into trouble with your boss, by phoning you at work, I just want to let you know that I am missing you and let you know how I feel about you.

You know that I believe that a person should not be with someone unless they love them, as I do you. I hope you feel the same. Furthermore, whatever decision you make, I will respect it and will not be pestering you. I think too much of you to upset you any further. I give you my deepest apology for the upset and annoyance I have put you through.

I haven't told you this before, but due to the fact that from time to time I get elated (high) has caused me not to get deeply involved with someone until I met you. You were the first I told about the problem I have. I have been perfect for quite some time and am fine again thank God. I am sure you can understand somewhat, ... The way I have been acting in the last few weeks has put a lot of strain both on you and those closest to me. Marie in particular has been upset and my friendship with Pepper has been put under strain. To them I owe a lot. But it is you Kathleen, I have hurt most and it is this that upsets me most.

I do not wish to use this problem as an excuse for my behaviour, but it is this that has made me so impatient and argumentative and so overbearing over the last while. I admire you for your honesty and you should always be in the future, as trust is always best, in the long run.

I am sure we would be still together were it not for me being elated and my mood swings.

Being elated has never got me in trouble really, but if it means that I have lost you, it has been very costly and ruined my happiness.

When I am 'high' everything, must in my mind, be instant. Although it is usually a pleasurable experience being elated causes a lot of frustration for loved one. As for my feelings at the moment, I have never been as happy with anyone before and I hope all is not lost.

It seemed to me, to be the real thing, 'I never thought love could feel so good'. I told you on numerous occasions that I would be honest with you and I mean every word I say.

I feel something this good, only comes along once in a lifetime and I hope all is not lost. My friends could not understand why I was so happy when I met you, they didn't realise how much you meant to me and you still do. With the elation goes big ideas, racing thoughts that has left me impatient. I hope you understand. My mood is fine now other than the emptiness and sadness due to missing you.

Maybe I don't deserve a second bite at the cherry but I believe everyone deserves a second chance. The way I have been acting irrationally over the past few weeks hasn't happened for five years up until now. So while it has caused a lot of hassle to both you and Marie, it is not a persistent problem and I hope you can take this into consideration.

Maybe we could meet to have a chat. I think we owe that to each other. I will be in Galway probably next Wednesday or Thursday. Maybe we could meet then 'hopefully'.

I hope this letter gives you some idea of how I still feel about you. I hope it also gives you some explanation of the reason for my out of character behaviour which led to this situation.

No matter what has happened you still mean everything to me and I hope we can sort things out. By the way, I hope you had a good weekend.

Your happiness is most important to me and I mean that. I could write all night, but what I have written, means something to you, hopefully. It's now 1.50am. I should go to bed.

Missing you more than words can say.

Love, John xxx

John waited for a reply from Kathleen, but weeks passed and nothing arrived. Growing impatient, in the first week of March 2000, he phoned Kathleen at her work place on two occasions. He wanted explanations. Why she had ended it, why had she ignored his letter, why wouldn't she agree to meet with him one last time? When she didn't respond as he would have liked, he shouted abuse down the line until she finally hung up. Kathleen was tiring of John. She contacted Marie, and made it clear she did not want to see or hear from him ever again. Despite this, another letter arrived through her door at the end of March.

It would appear from the letter that Kathleen had told him in one of the phone calls that she was going to see a fortune-teller for advice on her future. John was keen to know what she had been told, and felt it had influenced her decision to stay away from him.

Dear Kathleen,

Hoping to find you in good form as I find myself. I am working in Longford now, plastering for the moment. The money is pretty good, £60 a day plus overtime, but I would rather be back in Galway. I will probably move back permanently soon.

The main reason I am writing to you is that I think I deserve an explanation on why you would not meet me, and you told me on the phone that you would tell me what the fortune teller said about [words unclear], and the next day you had changed your mind and bluntly refused to meet me.

I have told you on numerous occasions how I feel about you and what you mean to me. I have feelings too, you know. I am the first to admit I was out of order, and didn't give you the attention you deserve, but I was very hurt that you wouldn't even meet to finish things. You know I wouldn't treat you that way. In your heart, you know this.

I still can't believe you were so cruel to me by doing this, after all we have been through why did you refuse to meet me? Some say fortune tellers do the devil's work and I now believe them. In my mind, it is unrealistic to believe that they can tell your future. How would they know who was the right person for you, only you know this. It has ruined my happiness for definite.

I believe that you will never have a truly lasting relationship with someone if you continue to believe in fortune tellers. A relationship is based between two people and their love for each other. You are a brilliant person and don't need fortune tellers – don't put your future in their hands. Make your own decisions. I have a simple request to make of you. I will be in Galway next Saturday 25th and Sunday 26th. I would appreciate an explanation if you would see it in your heart to meet me, it would be nice. You name the place. I think this request is not a lot to ask of you, please be reasonable.

Tell your mother and father I said hello, and also to *** and ***, he is lovely. I believe that life is short, we are only here for a good time, not a long time. I believe we could be good together, as we were. I am missing you more than ever.

I would appreciate if you could meet me. I see no reason why not. I don't think it is too much to ask. If, for some reason you will not meet me please write to me at my home address with a full explanation of your actions.

I hope you are happy, take care of yourself.

Love, John

PS I have the money I owe you to give to you soon.

Kathleen did not respond to this letter either and John gave up writing to her. The rejection continued to play on his mind, exacerbating an already fragile mental state.

10.

The night-time hours seemed to pass reluctantly in Abbeylara. Endless cups of tea were being made in the Mahon household. Nobody felt like sleeping. The women sat in silence most of the time as they waited for news, but they heard little news of what was going on at the scene. Garda Sinead Cunniffe was keeping them company and trying her best to comfort Rose in particular, but it was difficult to know what to say. She had little communication from her colleagues at the scene, so could tell them nothing to help calm them down. Occasionally, someone would switch on the news or check Aertel to see if there were any developments, but for the most part they kept the TV and the radio switched off so as not to upset Rose further. They knew Marie was down in Devine's, and they worried about how she was getting through the longest night of their lives.

At the scene, little had changed. It was a cold night, and the men who were still standing in ditches and behind trees were feeling the drop in temperature. All eyes were kept on the allotted points of the Carthy house. For the ERU men, there came a break in the silence every fifteen minutes, when their radios would crackle to life and Russell would check in with them, to make sure they were okay. The local men did not have the same luxury of regular communication from the command post, and they were left to strain their ears for clues as to what was going on. They became accustomed to the silence, and were thankful for the light that came from the full moon that hung over them that night.

At the front wall, Jackson continued to sneak glances around the pillar, so that he could watch the now familiar figure of Carthy and his movements across the kitchen. The negotiator marvelled at his endless pilgrimage around the small room. He just paced back and over, back and over, hanging on to the gun, occasionally muttering to himself. The negotiator hoped he would eventually tire himself out and choose to sleep for a while. Jackson was sure a period of rest would help calm Carthy's nerves and clear his mind, and that maybe things would look brighter for him in the morning.

But for as long as Carthy was awake and alert, Jackson had to continue in his attempts at communication. He tried phoning Carthy again, and receiving no answer he went back to shouting over the wall. He returned to the basics, the same promises he had repeated over and over again since he had first arrived at the scene. No response from inside.

Attempting instead to win some form of trust from Carthy, Jackson decided to offer him some simple provisions that might form an olive branch. He asked Carthy if he had enough food to eat, but was told to 'fuck off'. He brought up the solicitor again, but got no reply. Finally leaving the question open-ended, he asked if there was anything at all Carthy needed, and the response came from the kitchen, an order for cigarettes.

'Fags. Twenty Major,' was all Carthy said.

The request received different reactions from the gardai who were at the negotiation post. While Jackson was pleased with it, Russell immediately knew the request was going to provide his men with a dilemma. He hadn't known Carthy was a smoker – Shelly's intelligence gathering had not uncovered that detail – and as tactical commander it would be up to him to devise a way in which any delivery could take place. He looked towards the kitchen. The lights were still ablaze and Carthy's shadow lined the walls. Getting cigarettes in there would be difficult and dangerous. With the glass of the gable window almost entirely shattered, the electric light would illuminate anyone who approached, and there was a real fear of what Carthy would do if he came face to face with a garda. He could see that Jackson was pleased with the request, and he knew that from a negotiating point of view it could mark a step forwards towards some sort of rapport building. He told Jackson to try to encourage Carthy to agree to some form of safe delivery.

Jackson knew that Russell was right. They couldn't order any of their men to risk their lives by making such an approach to the house. Some cooperation from Carthy would be required, and the gun would have to be out of the equation for at least a short period of time.

Inside the house, John waited for a response. He smoked between twenty and thirty cigarettes a day, and he needed a nicotine boost. He could only hope the gardaí would grant him that much. The moonlight outside allowed him at times to get a glimpse of the officers at the wall, at least when they raised their heads up. There was no sign of them now. He waited.

Jackson eventually reappeared at the pillar, and what he had to say was not pleasing to Carthy. He told him the cigarettes could be provided – but it came with conditions attached. He told Carthy he would have to grant a safe passage for the fags to be delivered. The conditions were complicating things for Carthy, he was suspicious of what the guards wanted, and he eventually told Jackson to forget about his request.

'Fuck off and don't bother'.

But Jackson was not going to let go that easily. He continued to explain what his idea of a safe method of delivery was, to outline it again and again. If Carthy just put the gun where they could see it, if he could stay where they could keep an eye on him for an agreed period of time, somebody would deliver the cigarettes to a position around the house. The monologue seemed to be bothering Carthy, it was if they were teasing him, and he became extremely irate. At 3.25am he let off two rounds in quick succession, both of them aimed at Jackson's position at the wall. The pellets struck the concrete, but Jackson was getting used to it now. He told Carthy the gun was not going to solve anything. Carthy smiled and shook the gun in defiance. The gun was going to solve everything.

Ω   Ω   Ω

Jackson was concerned that little progress had been made in terms of any real dialogue with Carthy. His attempts at negotiations had been ongoing for a number of hours now, and he worried that there might be something else in Carthy's medical history that he should know about. He sent word up to the command post, requesting that two gardaí be sent to pay a late night visit to Dr Cullen at home in Coole. The negotiator wanted details of the medication Carthy was on and the possible effects of his tablets. He also asked that the officers ask the doctor to provide them with any medical records or additional information he had that might be helpful.

When the gardaí arrived at the Cullen home that night, the

doctor rose from his bed to go and speak with them. It was 4am. The doctor was told that the negotiator, Detective Sergeant Michael Jackson, was looking for any extra medical information he might have on Carthy. Dr Cullen had not been kept informed of the ongoing situation and this was the first time he became aware that a negotiator was at the scene.

In relation to medication, Dr Cullen told the gardaí that John Carthy was on lithium, and also said that he might be experiencing highs and lows. Dr Cullen then went to retrieve Carthy's file from his clinic and photocopied a number of medical reports concerning Carthy's first admission to St Loman's in 1992, and some records on Carthy's admissions to University College Hospital, Galway. He also handed over a copy of a report from Dr David Shanley, dated 12 April 1995.

When the two gardaí arrived back at the scene, they delivered the reports straight to the command post. There they found both Jackson and Superintendent Byrne waiting to hear what the doctor had said. Of all the information contained in those reports, the mention of Dr Shanley struck both Byrne and Jackson as being very important. Up to that point, the night-time scene commander had been unaware that the manically depressed young man firing shots at the ring of gardaí outside his house was under specialist psychiatric care.

Byrne discussed the issue with Jackson, and they decided they would try to get in touch with the psychiatrist in the morning, to see if he could help them out. Although the report from Dr Shanley was five years old, they were hopeful that the psychiatrist could still be in touch with Carthy. Neither Byrne nor Jackson suggested they should go back to Dr Cullen to seek confirmation that this was the case.

Ω   Ω   Ω

Russell had felt the impact of the last bullets hitting the wall, and wondered how Carthy could expect them to deliver anything to him when he was firing off rounds like that. He felt things were spiralling, and he and his team needed time to rest and think. He looked at Jackson, well aware that he had already been on duty for twenty hours. The negotiator needed some sleep, and they all needed time to regroup and think about their next moves.

To his relief, the house went suddenly quiet after the last burst of fire. He glanced around the pillar a few times, and when several minutes passed without any sighting of Carthy, he became certain that the young man in the house had finally become tired. It was a welcome reprieve for all the front-line officers, and they immediately set about taking advantage of the break. Jackson headed straight for one of the garda jeeps for a much-needed rest. On his way there, he met with Superintendent Byrne who asked the negotiator how he was doing. Jackson told him he was 'holding up'. Sullivan was left at the wall, to keep an eye on the window and to watch for any movement. For Russell however, the quiet time was his chance to clear up some loose ends.

Russell met with Byrne at the command post, and learned that Byrne had some concerns. The unmarked garda car was still in the driveway, and the keys that remained in the ignition were a worry. There were still hours to go before sunrise would make the area secure again, and he was afraid that Carthy would try to creep out of the house and take the car. The quiet in the kitchen was disconcerting. It allowed every garda at the scene to think and to imagine what could happen and what might go wrong. This was Byrne's worst-case scenario.

Russell knew what was being asked of him, and he prepared himself for a quick approach up the driveway. He radioed his men to warn them of what he was about to do, and to ask them for cover. The yards between the gate and the car were minimal, but he would still be left totally open to fire for at least a few steps. He took a final glance at the kitchen window, and moved swiftly up along the hedge, thankful when he finally reached the cover of the unmarked car. It had been simple really, and slipping the car keys into his pocket, he considered what else he might get done while Carthy was sleeping.

He had been thinking about an intervention in the past few hours, wondering if it might be possible for his men to enter the house somehow, and he decided to try circling the house to learn as much as he could about the layout, the windows and doors, and the state of the locks on all the possible entry points.

Byrne watched him from the road, trying to understand why Russell was delaying at the car for so long. He had seen him put the keys in his pocket, and he wanted him to get back to the safety of the road as quickly as possible. He watched in disbelief as Russell began to move further up the driveway. And then he disappeared from sight.

Russell crept around the back of the house, memorising the layout, moving quickly past every window, fearful that Carthy may be lurking in the dark rooms at the rear of the house. With fear like that forcing him onward, it didn't take him long to reach the front door at that side of the house that looked into the hedge on the right hand side of the property.

He paused at the door, this being the most obvious means of anyone making a surprise entry into Carthy's stronghold. He tried to gently push it open, but it had been locked on the inside. Figuring there was nothing else to do but turn back, Russell went to retrace his steps around the back of the house, but something stopped him. He could see a crack of light, and it was coming through the bottom sash of the window at the right of the front door, a window that looked into the kitchen where he presumed Carthy was still resting.

Inching closer to the window, Russell could see the source of the light was a hole in the wooden frame surrounding the glass. It was only the size of a ten pence coin, but Russell saw his chance to sneak a look inside. Controlling his breathing, he paused for a second, and then swung his body round to peek through the hole. Inside he saw the big picture, the full view of what they could only catch glimpses of from the road. He put the poor quality of the kitchen, the run-down and unacceptable conditions that the Carthys lived in to the back of his mind. He would think about that again days and months down the line, the sad surroundings of this sick young man. At that moment, gripping his gun, alarmed by the slightest sound, Russell had to concern himself only with where Carthy was and where his gun lay.

Carthy was stretched out on a couch at the far side of the kitchen. His eyes were closed and he had a blanket over him. Darting his eyes around the messy room, Russell could not see the gun, leading him to believe the weapon must still be in Carthy's hands, concealed under the blanket, just in case. His eye searched the area again, and scanned anything else of interest in the kitchen. The place was a mess, furniture had been kicked around, scraps of bread lay on the kitchen counter; the small room was without any kind of order.

Having taken his eye off the couch for a second, Russell sensed movement from Carthy. He didn't dare move a muscle, but allowed his eye to flick back to the figure huddled on the couch. Carthy moved again. It was a shuffle, an attempt by Carthy to get comfortable, but it was enough for Russell and he began to worry that Carthy might not be fully asleep. Sliding himself away from the window, he moved as quickly as he could back down the side of the house, re-tracing his route, round the back, down by the hedge and on to the road.

If only the gun wasn't under the blanket. Russell was adamant afterwards that if he could have given one of his men a running chance of getting to the gun before Carthy, he would have tried it. But with the gun firmly in Carthy's hands, any attempt at going in would have been 'reckless' he said. No matter how deep a sleep Carthy was in, it wouldn't take a marksman like him long to take aim and fire.

Back on the road, Russell met again with Byrne. He told him what he had seen, still shaken from his reconnaissance. Byrne appreciated the extra information – and then he asked Russell to do it all over again. The night-time commander had been thinking that they should try to cut the TV cables on the house at some stage, but had not mentioned it to Russell before he set off on his first mission. Byrne felt Carthy's insistence on turning up the volume on the television when Jackson was trying to talk to him was hampering negotiations. He also pointed out to Russell the potential negative implications of Carthy hearing about himself on the news reports that were going out on the TV channels. Russell felt it was a sensible request, and he agreed to make the second trip.

He knew where the TV cables were, but he would have to think about his approach and work out the best route to them. It was now approaching 6 am and the first flickers of sunlight were starting to break through the darkness. He did not want to have to linger around the house in daylight, so he hurried to where the TV cables were clearly visible on the gable end of the house, just beside Carthy's shooting window. As he crept past his peephole at the front of the house, he glanced inside, saw that Carthy was still resting and quickly and quietly edged forward to slash the wires.

When he returned to the comfort zone on the road, Russell decided to take the opportunity to have a rest himself. He had done all he could under the cover of darkness, and he wanted to have some sleep before Carthy came round again. He thought of the cigarettes, and wondered how they would tackle that issue. Senior officers who would visit the scene the next day would ask why the cigarettes couldn't have been delivered on either of his two trips around the house. They could have been left on a windowsill or the doorstep, but that hadn't occurred to Russell or to Byrne. Indeed, they didn't actually have any cigarettes to give him. Despite the request that had been made hours previously, nobody had actually been sent to buy them yet.

Jackson was sleeping in the garda jeep, so Russell had to go elsewhere for his nap. Flaherty told him the new Carthy house was empty. There was no furniture in it, but he would be able to make some sort of a bed for himself with his sleeping bag. Russell did just that, and he settled down in the new home, the one that Rose had been so proud of. Little did she know that the first person to enjoy a nap in it would be a total stranger, an armed garda who had come to Abbeylara to deal with her son.

11.

Russell didn't manage to sleep for long. By seven that morning, he was up again, worrying about the hours ahead, planning for another potential full day at Abbeylara. The scene was still quiet, and he wanted to have some plans in place before Carthy woke up. Foremost in his mind was the need for reserves. His men would be getting tired, and they couldn't withstand endless hours of shifting from one knee to another, concentrating their eyes and their nerves on the windows and doors of the Carthy cottage. He was thinking mainly of the three officers he had brought with him. They were his responsibility and he placed an early morning call through to the Garda HQ in Dublin asking for relief ERU members to be sent to the scene. What Jackson and Sullivan wanted to do was up to them, but he felt sure Jackson would not leave this scene until the job was done.

Russell was right. When Jackson awoke in the garda jeep that morning, he was determined and his confidence had been revived. He had dozed off from time to time in the hours since he had left the negotiating post for a rest, but his mind was too active to facilitate real sleep. Adrenaline was driving him onward and his thoughts continued to circle around other plans and other negotiating possibilities that might just work. Stretching out stiff limbs, he was ready to try it all again. He had now been on duty for twenty-four hours.

As he set into his work that Holy Thursday, Jackson decided

it might be time to get the expert opinion from somebody who knew the minute intricacies of the mind. Dr Cullen was there as an option, an experienced doctor who knew Carthy well, just minutes down the road. But Jackson didn't consider talking to him. Instead he made contact with a clinical psychiatrist at the Department of Justice, Mr Colm Regan.

In the late eighties, Regan's predecessor at the Department of Justice, Desmond O'Mahony, took part in a course being run by the gardaí and the psychological services attached to the Department. The course was run with a view to helping the gardaí deal with the exact situation that they were facing in Abbeylara, stand-off incidents where persuasive talking and finely tuned people skills were needed. At the course, Mr O'Mahony provided information to gardaí about mental illness and suicidal behaviour, while the gardaí shared with him their expertise on hostage situations and negotiating techniques. Mr O'Mahony took part in a similar course a few years later, and considered himself to be part of the national hostage negotiating team. This was seen as a new direction for the gardaí, whereby they were accepting the valuable contribution that psychological experts could make to their work. It was a step in the right direction, but the theory never became practice.

Mr O'Mahony found as time went on that he wasn't being called into action in any situations. While he was ready and willing to be dispatched to the scenes of stand-offs and hostage situations any day and any time, O'Mahony instead found himself reading about such incidents in the papers the day after they happened, and wondering why he had been left out. As the years passed by, O'Mahony came to regard his involvement with the hostage negotiation team as a 'dead letter'.

Mr Regan had not been involved in any of those courses – they came and went before his time – and he was unaware that any such link had ever existed between armed gardaí and his own section of the department. In his phone call with Jackson that morning, Regan felt there was little advice he could offer because of his remove from the scene and also because it would be difficult for him to make judgements on the condition and behaviour of a man he had never met. He gave the negotiator some common-sense advice, and told him to talk to someone who actually knew Carthy's history.

☊ ☊ ☊

When Russell had sorted out the replacements for his officers, he made his way carefully to the front wall and found that Carthy too was up early that morning, and his mood had not been lightened by his period of rest. Having already smashed out most of the glass in the kitchen window, Carthy was now using the butt of the gun to break the wooden bars of the window frame. Russell considered that there was a possibility Carthy would attempt to escape by jumping through the window.

Superintendent Shelly resumed duty as scene commander just after eight o'clock that morning, and he too quickly discerned that there was something different in Carthy's demeanour. From the noise that was coming from the house, he sensed the aggression in the cottage had reached a new frenzied state. On account of this, he ordered one of his men to arrange for an ambulance to be put on standby at Granard Garda Station, and he also asked an officer to arrange for Dr Cullen to be brought to the scene. The superintendent did not want to speak with the doctor, but wanted him to be present in a purely medical capacity, in case the worst happened and Carthy needed immediate medical attention.

Bringing himself up to date on what had occurred in his absence from the scene, Shelly discussed the most recent happenings with Byrne. He was informed that the TV cable had been cut, that Carthy had requested a packet of cigarettes, and that Dr Cullen had provided them with some reports that indicated that Carthy might have a psychiatrist, Dr Shanley.

At nine o'clock, Assistant Commissioner Hickey arrived on the scene and he was keen to get to grips with everything that was unfolding in the immediate area. He met with Byrne as he walked around the scene, taking in the visual details of everything and marrying them with the information he already had. Byrne filled him in on what had unfolded on his watch the night before, including the fact that Carthy had requested a packet of '20 Major', but that they had not yet been delivered. As a smoker, Hickey could sympathise with Carthy's cravings.

'Why didn't you throw them into him?', asked Hickey. Byrne told his superior that he and Detective Sergeant Jackson had discussed the issue, and had decided that they wanted to use the cigarettes 'as a vehicle to get a rapport with John', and to this end Jackson was still trying to interact with Carthy on the issue. While Hickey said he appreciated this tactic, he admitted his initial feeling was that it was 'a pity' Russell had not delivered the cigarettes during one of his trips around the house in the early hours of that morning.

As he continued his scout around the scene, Hickey met with Inspector Martin Maguire. Hickey had by this time been made aware that there was a psychiatrist in the equation, and he asked Maguire to phone St Patrick's Hospital to speak with

Dr Shanley. The psychiatrist however was not available at the time, and his secretary said Dr Shanley would phone back as soon as possible.

♎   ♎   ♎

Settled back at the negotiation post, Jackson immediately sensed that the mood inside the kitchen was still angry; if anything Carthy had woken up in even more defiant form. There was no suggestion of a weakening in Carthy's resolve. This was just a continuation, day two of the battle.

Jackson began the day with a summary of all that had been said the night before. The same assurances were uttered, revived by the unfounded hope that Carthy might be more open to listening on a new day. Jackson told Carthy that the previous day had been a black one, but that things could improve with the new morning. Carthy walked to the window, made sure he had Jackson's eye, stuck out his chest and dared Jackson again.

Carthy: 'Come on, shoot me, come on.'

It was more self-destructive talk, and Jackson took it head on.

Jackson: 'John, we don't want to shoot you. Are you thinking of hurting yourself? Are you thinking of suicide?'

There was no reply from Carthy.

Jackson: 'Think about what will happen if you are dead, think about your family and friends and how they will feel, think about Marie, your mother and Pepper, think about how they would feel if you got hurt or hurt yourself, think about how badly they are feeling at the moment because of what you are doing. Think about how good you would make them feel if you put the gun down and talked. If you won't come out for yourself John, then come out for them. Come out John, come on out.'

This was promising. Carthy had never allowed Jackson to get so far into his monologue, and from glances over the wall, the negotiator could see that he was finally hitting a nerve; Carthy looked confused and anxious, as if he was trying not to listen, but was hearing the words and letting them sink in. He put his head in his hands, looking for once like the broken man that he was. His air of defiance had evaporated. For just a few moments, it looked like Jackson had won him over.

But Carthy didn't want to be beaten. He shook the logic away and cleared his head. Jackson could see he was losing him again, Carthy muttered to himself 'No, no!' and he took his head from his hands. Standing straight at the window, he shook the gun defiantly out at Jackson, leaving no mistake that it was still there and it was still the prime factor in this equation.

Ω   Ω   Ω

Abbeylara was buzzing from an early hour, now populated by hordes of reporters and media people who had traced the back roads on their maps to find their way to the tiny village. They had descended en masse; they hung around in packs, warily bartering their information, conversations being interrupted constantly by calls on their mobile phones. Altogether, there were now about twenty-five different news organisations represented at the media camp in front of St Bernard's Church.

They had to operate from a distance, leaving them at a loss when it came to painting their word pictures of the scene. No one was allowed beyond the church, keeping them almost half a mile from the cottage. The newspapers were there in force, but the whole event was ideal material for TV and radio, as the drama unfolded hour after hour. While the papers would reflect on it the following day, radio and television could bring live updates to the listeners and viewers around the country.

The RTÉ satellite van was there, and crime correspondent Paul Reynolds was the reporter who would feed the latest updates to the television news, RTÉ Radio 1 and also 2FM. TV3 was also represented. There was no question that Abbeylara was going to be the top story of the day on every news bulletin. It had everything: armed gardaí, a volatile young man and the potential for bloodshed. It was a rare opportunity for the Irish stations, allowing them to follow a perfectly scripted real-life drama from start to finish, and they were going to do their best to depict the story in full-blown technicolour.

There were obstacles, however. There was little new information emanating from the cottage. They were being told nothing about the ongoing negotiations. The basics of the operation were not being embellished, and the story was in danger of dying from repetition.

With the pressure from their editors growing, the reporters at the scene determined to find out more and to get something more. That morning, the Garda Press Officer Superintendent John Farrelly became a wanted man.

☊ ☊ ☊

It was ten o'clock in the morning, almost seven hours after Carthy made his request, when a garda was sent to the local shop to bring back three packets of cigarettes and some matches. He had been told that Carthy had asked for 'Majors'.

As the garda went down to the village, a shout came from

Carthy's house; he was still waiting for his 'fags'. Jackson gave Carthy the same response as the night before. He told Carthy he wanted to deliver the cigarettes to him, but that he was concerned about the presence of the gun. He asked Carthy to cooperate, and work with him on a safe delivery. He got no reply from the kitchen.

Jackson instructed his assistant negotiator Michael Sullivan to go to the command post to see if the cigarettes had been purchased, and to bring them down to the negotiation point, just in case he managed to make some progress with Carthy. Sullivan obliged. On arrival at the post, he found that the local officer had returned from the shop with three packets of Benson & Hedges, rather than the Majors Carthy had requested.The shopkeeper, who knew Carthy well, had assured him that it was this brand, rather than Major that Carthy actually smoked.

☊   ☊   ☊

An hour after placing his call to Dr Shanley, Inspector Maguire received a return phone call. Shanley was stunned to hear what was happening with his patient. He recalled the last meeting they had; it had been months ago, and nothing in Carthy's demeanour at that time had given him cause for concern. Maguire asked Shanley for any assistance he could give the gardaí, and the psychiatrist went through a run-down of the day ahead. He was due to finish up for the Easter break that afternoon, and he had planned to travel to the west to spend the long weekend with some friends. He glanced at his diary to see what time he had scheduled his last appointment. There it was, '2pm– John Carthy'. He presumed Carthy wouldn't be making that appointment.

Unprompted by Maguire, Dr Shanley said that he would be travelling west later that day, and offered to come to the scene en route if the incident was still ongoing at that time. Maguire agreed to this. Before ringing off, Dr Shanley informed Maguire that Carthy had a dislike for St Loman's and told the inspector that it might be helpful if someone could let Carthy know there was a bed for him at St Patrick's if he wanted it. Inspector Maguire thanked Dr Shanley for his help and said they would be in contact again later that day.

Ω   Ω   Ω

At the negotiation post, word came through to Jackson that now, fourteen hours after Carthy had dismissed him, Tom Walsh was anxious to make another attempt at getting through to Johnny. The negotiator, concerned by Carthy's increased aggression, agreed that another intervention by his cousin might be useful. He put the idea to Carthy, asking if he would speak to Tom. Carthy didn't seem all that interested, but he mumbled an agreement, and arrangements were made for Tom to make his way to the wall.

Once at the wall, Walsh crouched down behind it and had a short conversation with Jackson about what was left to say to convince his cousin to leave the gun behind and come out. Walsh had not heard at that point that Carthy had asked for cigarettes, but it was something that had occurred to him overnight. He told Jackson his cousin was a very heavy smoker and they should try to get some cigarettes into him. Walsh claims the negotiator told him it was 'a negotiating practice' to look for something in return before they would give him the cigarettes. Jackson denies this.

A night of worrying and feeling helpless had convinced

Walsh that he could turn this around. He had had time to think now, and he had formulated a list of ideas that would bring Johnny back to some straight thinking. Picking up the loudhailer, he spoke to him on a personal level about the people they knew and the people they were descended from. He spoke to him about their uncles and their grandfather, saying they were all tough men, but they knew when it was time to give up. He told John he had won, nobody had been hurt, but he had made his point. He asked him to answer his phone so that they could talk privately, but while John picked up the receiver a few times, he hung up again almost immediately. He never said anything.

Walsh felt uncomfortable speaking on the loudhailer, and he asked Jackson would it be okay for him to put his head over the wall and ask John to come to the window so they could talk properly. Having watched his family spend a sleepless night in absolute distress over what was going on, Walsh was desperate and felt an obligation to save the day.

But when he put his head over the wall, Walsh wasn't prepared for what he saw. John Carthy walked to the window, holding the gun across his body. He looked sick, and the image of him at that moment would remain with Walsh forever. 'I was shocked when I saw him,' he said. 'His eyes looked very black to me and his skin looked very yellow. His mouth looked very tight and his cheeks looked pulled in. He did not look to me like the John Carthy that I knew.'

Gathering his nerve, and trying his best to sound relaxed, Walsh attempted to catch John's eye. He offered everything he could to his cousin, and tried to allay any fears he might have about the consequences he would suffer for his actions. He then told him if he didn't trust the guards, then he would meet him out in the garden if he just left the gun behind and came out.

'I said he wouldn't be locked up and wouldn't do time. I said they knew he was in Loman's and couldn't be prosecuted for this and he was intelligent enough himself to know this. I said he could trust me and receive treatment from his own doctor and we'd be having a pint and a fag and laughing at this in a few weeks. I said if he came out he wouldn't be hurt and if anybody tried to hurt him, they'd have to hurt me as well.'

Walsh had done all he could and Jackson put his head over the wall to watch for Carthy's reaction. When it came it shocked him, because it was cold beyond belief. Carthy took up his gun, and keeping one eye on the cousin he had played with and socialised with and had known all his life, he picked a spot on Walsh's head, and aimed the gun squarely at it. Walsh slumped behind the wall, shaking, frightened and crying. At that moment, he knew yesterday had been bad, but today was going to get a lot worse.

Ω   Ω   Ω

Walsh claims that as he was walking away from the scene, he met with Inspector Maguire and again raised the issue of why the guards would not give his cousin the cigarettes he had asked for. According to Walsh, Maguire dismissed the question.

'No, he's acting the bollocks, he's not getting his own way anymore.'

Inspector Maguire has totally denied the accusation.

Ω   Ω   Ω

As the morning wore on, the occasional quiet time allowed Jackson to continue his negotiations with Carthy. He asked him if he was worried about the consequences of his actions and what might happen to him when all this ended. He asked him twice, and Carthy replied the second time, voicing one of his fears.

'I'll have to go back to the hospital', he said.

It was a step forward, an important indication that Carthy was seeing life after the incident, and it gave Jackson hope that Carthy was not suicidal. Jackson replied that he didn't know the full details of how he would be dealt with, but he mentioned Dr Shanley and the offer of a bed in Dublin rather than at St Loman's.

'I told John I didn't know what was happening about the hospital but Dr Shanley was willing to come and speak to him and Dr Shanley also said that if had to go to hospital, he could go to St Patrick's.'

Carthy made no reply, other than to grunt the 'yeah, right' laugh of a man who felt let down by every authority he had ever known.

Jackson told Carthy that everyone was trying to help him and was willing to do anything to make life better for him. He seized on the moment of weakness in Carthy and launched into one of his monologues. Carthy put his head in his hands, as if trying to fight his logical thoughts.

Jackson: 'John, the right decision and the best way out for you is not to hurt yourself or anyone else but to put the gun down and come out, the right decision now makes up for all the bad things that happened yesterday and all the bad things that happened in your life. The right decision now is what is important, it can change everything. Come on John, come out. It's the right thing to do. It's the best way out. John, everyone out here is on your side, your family, friends and me. Come on out and I'll meet you half way. Come on out, I'll meet you half way. Come on, John, it's the right thing to do and it's the only thing to do.'

Carthy: 'No, you won't break me, no way.'

Jackson: 'John, I am not trying to break you, I just want you to come out safely, come on, don't worry about yesterday, come on out and we can work this out together.'

Carthy did not reply, and Jackson was discouraged by the last message that came from the kitchen. To Carthy, this was a battle of wills, a struggle between the logic put forward by the negotiator and whatever demons were tearing his thoughts apart and slowly destroying him.

12.

Occasionally, Carthy would move out of the kitchen. He would take a walk down the short hall, into the bedrooms, so that he could glance out of the windows around the house and keep an eye on what was going on. He knew there were about three gardaí at the wall in front of the house, but he suspected there were many more lurking where he couldn't see them. Out of the corner of his eye he would sometimes catch glimpses of hedges being disturbed and figures scurrying, and he started to imagine there were dozens and dozens of guards out there, waiting to pounce on him and to catch him unawares.

As it would turn out, Carthy wasn't far out in his estimations. At that particular time, mid-morning on Holy Thursday, there were thirty-three gardaí in and around the area surrounding his home. They had come from all around, some on traffic duty, others standing in the fields on either side of the road, and some were just hanging around the command post in case they were needed. No real account was kept of what officers were there at any given time. Gardaí have denied the suggestion of counsel for the Carthy family that 'every garda in the county' was free to stroll past the cordons and into the scene for a look at what was going on, but at one point in the incident there were as many as forty-five officers at the scene.

Many of these officers occupied what was technically referred to as the sterile area that existed between the inner and outer cordons of gardaí. That area was the stretch of road between the ESB pole at the edge of the Carthy property and the traffic cordons further up the road. In practice both armed and unarmed gardaí from the local divisions were free to roam in this area just outside the boundary of the Carthy property throughout the incident.

Ω   Ω   Ω

Jackson had the cigarettes with him at the negotiation post, and despite the fact that they were not the brand Carthy had requested, he waved them over the front wall to show Carthy they were there. His assistant, Sullivan, had placed a concrete block on the wall to afford additional protection for Jackson when he stood up to look into the kitchen. The uncertainty of Carthy's behaviour had also meant that the negotiator had put back on his ballistics helmet for the sake of his own safety.

When Carthy saw the negotiator's hand waving a packet of cigarettes at him, he became excited and he beckoned to Jackson to bring them into him.

'Bring them into me, come on.'

But while he was prepared to show Carthy the cigarettes, Jackson still wanted to come to some arrangement for their delivery. He went back to his conditions, laying down the rules for the delivery

Jackson: 'John, I want to give you the cigarettes but I am worried about the gun you are firing at us. Can we agree a safe way of getting the cigarettes in to you or can you suggest a safe way of getting them in to you?'

Carthy became agitated.

Carthy: 'Fuck off and don't bother.'

Jackson: 'All we want is for you to come out without the gun.'

Carthy: 'Why?'

Jackson: 'Because I want you and everyone else to be safe.'

Carthy: 'Why?'

Jackson: 'Because your family, friends and us all care about you.'

Carthy: 'Why?'

Jackson: 'I know you are doing this because you are angry and not because you are a bad guy.'

Carthy: 'Why?'

Jackson left it at that. While he was happy that Carthy was at least responding to what he was saying, little was going to be gained by allowing Carthy to wind himself up by repeatedly shouting 'Why?' After a few moments, Jackson tried phoning Carthy, but each time the phone was answered, Carthy shouted 'fuck off' down the line. The negotiator went back to calling in at Carthy over the loudhailer, once more asking him to give them some indication of how they could get him to leave the house peacefully.

Jackson: 'John, you do not seem to trust me, but we will get anyone you want – a solicitor, a priest, your family, friends or anyone else.'

Carthy: 'No, nobody. I'm not coming out, no way. You come in and get me, shoot me, come on.'

Jackson: 'John, we don't want to shoot you. We want to help you. John, are you thinking of hurting yourself, are you thinking of suicide?'

There was no reply from Carthy.

Jackson: 'John, think about what will happen if you are dead. That is not the best way out. The best way out is to put the gun down and come on out and we can talk. The right thing to do is to leave the gun in the house and come on out, come on out John, please.'

The negotiator then beckoned to Carthy with his left hand, willing him to go along with what he was saying.

Carthy: 'No, it's not the right thing to do.' He picked up the gun and pointed to it. 'This is the right thing to do.'

Jackson: 'No, John, that is not the right thing to do. That only hurts people and the best thing to do is to leave the gun behind you and come out. That's the important thing. It doesn't matter how all this started, what is important is that you leave the gun behind and come out to meet me. Come on, John, I'll meet you half way, if you meet me half way. Come on, John, just me and you. The right decision here changes everything.'

No reply.

Jackson: 'Everyone out here, your mother, Marie, Pepper, Tom and all your friends, that's what they want you to do, so come out and leave that gun behind.'

Carthy: 'No way.'

Carthy levelled his gun at Jackson and tracked him with it until the detective sergeant ducked down behind the wall again.

Ω   Ω   Ω

Beyond the negotiating post, cajoling and persuading of another kind was ongoing, as Superintendent John Farrelly tried to contain the impatience of the swarming reporters at the outskirts of the scene. Things were getting out of hand. Some reporters had taken to speaking with locals to find out information, others had been driving around the by-roads trying to find an alternative route that would get them closer to the cottage. The cameramen and photographers were getting desperate for some footage and some action shots of the garda operation. Their patience was growing thin, and Farrelly was under pressure to give them something.

For the duration of the incident, Farrelly carried out his role with a view to containing the assembled media's curiosity, and ensuring that they would not be giving a running commentary on the progress of the negotiator. He himself only had brief meetings with the senior officers at the scene, and did not ask too many questions about how Detective Sergeant Jackson was faring with his attempts at dialogue. Aware that John Carthy did have access to a radio in the house, he felt his duty was to ensure that nothing was broadcast on the airwaves that would inflame the situation further.

Of course, Sergeant Farrelly wasn't the only source of information for the reporters gathered at the scene that morning. There was much more to be gleaned through the rumours and hearsay flying around Abbeylara. Off-the-record chats with local people who knew Carthy, who knew the area, and who had their own ways of getting the latest from the scene were much more valuable. As Day Two at the scene wore on, the reporters gradually built up a store of knowledge that had not been delivered to them via the garda press officer. Under these circumstances, the flow of information was warped and made complicated, and this placed extra pressure on Farrelly. On a number of occasions, the first the garda press officer came to hear about an issue in the negotiations was when a reporter asked him about it. The first he heard of the request for cigarettes, for example, was when a journalist enquired if they were going to be delivered. Farrelly was also totally unaware of the request for a solicitor.

Farrelly appreciated the time pressures that were driving the reporters at the scene to be more specific in their questions. He understood that they had deadlines to meet.

The most familiar face in the press pack that day was RTÉ's crime correspondent, Paul Reynolds, a reporter that Farrelly knew very well due to his brief. They had built up a good working relationship down through the years. Farrelly respected Reynolds' knowledge of garda operations and his respect for the work they did. He trusted Reynolds' ability to know what he should and shouldn't reveal in his reports, and on this basis, he would often give the RTÉ man off-the-record information to help him have a better understanding of a case.

Reynolds was one of those reporters who had been driving around the area that morning trying to get a better look at the scene. Farrelly had given him all he could in terms of information, but it was useless to him without pictures to accompany the story. They needed footage, and he was anxious to see for himself what was going on.

Eventually, he managed to take Farrelly aside to convince him it was time the media were given a glimpse of the scene and the garda operation. Reynolds said that there was a chance that some faction of the media would eventually try to get pictures of the scene on their own initiative, perhaps by hiring a helicopter to take photographs from above the cottage. He admitted to Farrelly that he himself had tried to get closer to the scene, and suggested that it would better for the press officer to work with the media rather than against them.

Farrelly took the idea on board and considered the potential advantages to be gained by giving the media this leeway. It would certainly take the pressure off both himself and the reporters, and a few minutes at the scene could surely do no harm. He had been told when he had arrived at the scene that morning that the TV cables to the cottage had been cut by the gardaí during the night, so he knew that any pictures broadcast would not be seen by Carthy.

He decided to confer with the chief officers at the scene. He brought the proposal to Shelly, explaining how it would work. The journalists and cameramen would be driven down to the scene in groups, they would have a few minutes to get what they wanted and then they would be taken away again. Shelly wasn't against the idea, agreeing with Farrelly's view that it was probably best to control the media rather than to leave them to their own devices. He told Farrelly he would discuss the idea with the ERU men and give him a verdict as soon as possible. The reporters awaited the decision, conscious of the fact that midday was approaching, and time was against them if they were to have their pictures for the lunchtime news.

In a discussion at the command post, Shelly broached the idea of the media visit with Russell, and was met with an unfavourable response. Russell told the scene commander that he 'certainly wasn't happy' about the proposal, that he had enough to deal with at the time, and that he would be concerned that his officers might be distracted by the presence of a press pack up the road. While he could recall the ERU being filmed on various duties in the past, he had never heard of the media being invited to film the unit while they were in the middle of this type of a dangerous and live situation.

But Shelly managed to convince him of the benefits of a brief media visit. He told Russell it was becoming more and more difficult to control the large media presence at the edge of the scene, and it was felt there was a real possibility that the reporters and cameramen and photographers would take their own steps to learn more about the garda operation. Russell acknowledged this, and agreed that the last thing the gardaí needed were straying journalists. With reluctance, he told Shelly to go ahead and arrange for the media visit, but his unhappiness with the proposal remained.

'I wouldn't have been happy being photographed trying to do a particular thing like this at that time. I wasn't entirely happy about it; that's being perfectly honest.'

Word was sent back down the line to Farrelly, instructing him to arrange for journalists and cameramen to be brought to the scene in as orderly a manner as was possible. A point on the Abbeylara side of the Carthy house, just behind the garda jeep that was acting as command post, was chosen as the spot where the reporters and cameramen would congregate. No safety plan was discussed to deal with the possibility of Carthy emerging while the press people were at the scene.

Despite the fact that it was just a short walk, the cameramen and journalists were driven down to the newly established media cordon in patrol cars. Farrelly took some of them himself, amongst them Paul Reynolds and another RTÉ reporter who had just arrived at the scene. His name was Niall O'Flynn, and he was to compile an extensive report for that evening's Five-Seven-Live broadcast on Radio 1.

When they got to their designated point, the reporters took notes on what they saw and asked questions of any gardaí they could find. The photographers zoomed in and snapped shots, most of them centred on the gardaí in their ballistics gear. The cameramen panned their lenses to every corner of the area, taking clips of the local gardaí who were scattered around the road, the head bosses like Shelly and Hickey who were talking and discussing what was going on, but again most of their footage focused on the police force as Irish people had rarely seen them – dressed in padded bullet-proof vests and protected by ballistics helmets.

Russell was down at the negotiation post when the cavalcade of reporters arrived. For the twenty-five minutes they remained on that stretch of the Abbeylara road, he was conscious of their presence, and concerned that they wouldn't delay for too long.

The decision to allow the media access to the scene was certain to draw criticism as a PR stunt, but expert views from around the world also applauded Shelly and Farrelly's decision. It is common practice at the FBI academy to train students in giving the media a view of the scene. They firmly believe that it is best to work with the media rather than facing a situation where they may go off and do their own thing, to the detriment of the operation, a policy also pursued in New Zealand and Australia.

After the media had been driven back from the scene, the frantic gathering of information continued away from the cottage. Shortly after the media visit, Superintendent Farrelly received word that Carthy's cousin, Ann Walsh, wished to speak with him. Ann Walsh was sitting in a car near the checkpoint at the church when Farrelly arrived to greet her. She was annoyed at the number of media people in the area, and commented to the Superintendent that the place was 'full of press'. She told the garda press officer that the media coverage would be very bad for John, and she asked him to 'call a media blackout'. Farrelly told her this wasn't an option.

Ω   Ω   Ω

Inside the house, Carthy was unaware that the cameras were rolling and that footage of his home and his road were being recorded for the purpose of feeding the curiosity of viewers around the country. He had said little to Jackson in the last while, still apparently annoyed that the cigarettes were so close but he couldn't get to them.

From time to time, he would hear Jackson tell him again that the cigarettes were there if he wanted them, but the offer was always superseded by that condition of a 'safe method of delivery'. The safe method, as proposed by Jackson, involved Carthy putting his gun where they could see it, and then staying in a position where they could see him. Then somebody would approach the house and drop the boxes. The reply from Carthy to this list of conditions was always simple.

'Fuck off.'

Jackson tried to bring up the issue of the solicitor again, but he was ignored. He then told Carthy that his mother, Rose, was very worried about him, but that only got a laugh out of the kitchen.

'You haven't lived with her for ten fucking years.'

The negotiator ignored the retort and went on with another monologue, telling Carthy how easy it would be for him to bring all of this to an end. He laid it out in clear language, giving Carthy a step-by-step guide to what he needed to do.

Jackson: 'Think about this, John, think about everyone out here wanting you to put the gun down and coming out. Think about how you are going to do this. Think about putting that gun on the floor, walking out of the room, opening the front door and coming out to meet me, please think about it.'

Carthy again ignored the invitation.

13.

When Kevin Ireland's mobile phone started ringing around midday that Holy Thursday, it wasn't a good time for him. He was driving down the docks in Galway, there was a lot to be done before the Easter weekend, and he really didn't have a minute to spare. But he answered the call anyway, and on the other end of the line he heard a familiar voice. It was John Carthy.

The two young men had become friendly during Carthy's stint as a labourer on the Hegarty site in Galway. Ireland was a Longford man as well, and the two struck up a casual friendship. They shared pints and laughs together from time to time, and they knew a lot of the same people back home. That was the extent of their friendship, but, for some reason, Carthy decided that the one phone call he was going to make in all the lonely hours he spent in the house was to be to his old workmate.

Ireland had been listening to the radio that morning, intrigued, as anyone would be, to hear what was going on in a village he knew well. Considering the size and population of Abbeylara, it did cross his mind that there was a possibility that the man everyone was talking about that day was John Carthy. He had always found John to be a fairly normal young man, and he had no knowledge whatsoever of his medical background, but he knew that John could sometimes get into bad form. He picked up his mobile, and in a conversation that lasted just 1min 52 seconds, his suspicions were confirmed.

Ireland: 'Hello.'

Carthy: 'Howaya, Kevin, any craic?'

Ireland: 'Not a bit, what about yourself?'

Carthy: 'Nothing much. I've a bunch of guards out here – nearly sixty of them, with guns and everything, and I'm shooting out at them and making them duck down. I've nearly every window in the house broken out.'

The reply threw Ireland for a second. If it had been any of his other friends he would have thought they were joking, but it didn't occur to him for a second that John was just having a laugh. It was his tone. It was eerily calm and deadly serious. Ireland said the only thing that came to mind.

Ireland: 'Don't do anything stupid, John. Don't shoot yourself or anyone else.'

Carthy: 'I haven't a notion of it. I'm just trying to keep them away from the house.'

Ireland: 'Would you not just give yourself up?'

Carthy: 'I will, I will, if you can get me a solicitor. You get me one; my own family haven't even got me one. You get me Mick Finucane.'

Ireland: 'I'll get you a solicitor, John, just don't do anything stupid.'

The phone went dead, and attempts by Ireland to phone John back reached only his message minder. It seemed that John had switched off his mobile, happy that contact had been made, and that he had sent the word out that he wanted this solicitor by the name of Finucane.

Giving up on his efforts to phone John back, Ireland thought again about what had been said. But more about how it had been said.

'I just couldn't believe how calm he was,' Ireland said. 'I

couldn't believe it was him in the house. He just sounded like he didn't care.'

But at the moment when he lifted the phone to call Ireland, John Carthy apparently did care, and he had his reasons for getting in contact specifically with this former colleague. When Ireland got to thinking about it, the name Finucane was familiar. He remembered an evening out in Galway with John a few months previously. It was around the time that John was in dispute with the bosses at the Edward Square site. He was worried how things would go, and on that evening he passed Ireland a note. There was nothing on the piece of paper except the name 'Mick Finucane', along with a Dublin address and a phone number. He told Ireland that this man was a solicitor and he asked his friend to get in touch with him if he got into serious trouble with his unfair dismissal claim. When the issue at the site was resolved, Ireland returned the piece of paper and never thought about it again until he was recruited as John Carthy's messenger that day.

Ireland told some of his work colleagues about the phone call, and they advised him to go to the gardaí and give them the information. But it was two hours before Ireland actually made his way to his local garda station. He went to collect his wages, went to the bank, met his girlfriend for lunch at Supermac's, did 'a few other bits and pieces', and then turned his attention back to the situation in Abbeylara. Asked after the event why it had taken him so long to go to the gardaí, Ireland could only say, 'I didn't think it would end like that'.

$$\Omega \quad \Omega \quad \Omega$$

Phone records show that shortly after he hung up from Kevin Ireland, John Carthy made an attempt to phone Marie. She had recently changed phones, however, and it would appear that John dialled her old mobile number by mistake.

At this point, Marie had joined her mother and her other relations in the Mahon household. She was still hoping to be brought down the scene to speak with John, but so far the gardaí had not made any attempt to involve her in negotiations. Neither had any garda carried out an in-depth interview with her to canvass her opinion on what was unfolding and what they could possibly do to defuse her brother's anger.

Marie continued to wait her turn at the negotiation post.

Ω   Ω   Ω

RTÉ's Five-Seven-Live reporter Niall O'Flynn was out and about around Abbeylara. After he and Paul Reynolds had returned from the media visit to the scene, they had decided between them that Reynolds would remain around the church, while O'Flynn would go further afield and compile some background information for his evening report. Reynolds loaned O'Flynn a camera and a microphone from the RTÉ van, on the understanding that whatever footage he got for his radio piece Reynolds could also use for his TV reports if he so wished.

The first O'Flynn had heard of the unfolding events in Abbeylara came on the morning of Holy Thursday, when he was making his way back to Dublin from a family gathering in the northwest. He hadn't tuned in to any news bulletins the night before, and it was only when he started flicking through stations on his car radio that morning that the garda operation in Longford first came to his attention. It sounded serious, and when he came upon an RTÉ interview between Rodney Rice and Superintendent John Farrelly, he pulled over to get the full gist.

The interview was long and comprehensive. But both presenter and garda press officer were cautious in what they said. At no time did they use John Carthy's name, only ever referring to him as 'the man'. Emphasis was on the sensitivity of the situation. Rice repeatedly said that negotiations were ongoing and that concern first and foremost was for 'the man' in the house.

Rice: 'Obviously, you are in a situation where the man may well have a radio on in the house and be monitoring what is going on in so far as he can from the radio, and that makes it an increasingly, potentially an increasingly sensitive situation for all to deal with ...'

Farrelly: '...We are trying to assure the man inside to come out, that there is no major problem here, that if help is required we will get it for him.'

From snippets like these, there was a suggestion in the interview that 'the man' was perhaps not in the best mental health. There was also the possibility that 'the man' had a radio and could be listening to news reports.

Being right on the edge of the Longford border at the time, O'Flynn put a call through to the studio in Dublin, and it was agreed that he should travel to Abbeylara and provide an extensive report for the Five-Seven-Live programme that evening.

He went to a shop en route to buy the national and local papers in order to familiarise himself with the events he had missed out on the night before. Reading the papers, he found two national titles that went further than the radio and named 'the man' as John Carthy. He did not hear any other reports on the airwaves, and arrived at the scene at 11am.

After the media visit to the scene, O'Flynn set off on his task to find some locals who would be willing to speak with him. It didn't take him long to find a wide range of people who agreed to give him some information. He gathered short interviews, vox pops, with more than a dozen locals, each of them speaking about the type of man John Carthy was, their last meetings with him and their hopes that all this would come to a peaceful conclusion. O'Flynn felt that the material for a fantastic package was coming together nicely – the insider accounts of this young man in crisis were pure gold.

♌ ♌ ♌

At lunchtime, the three back-up ERU officers arrived: Detective Garda William Sisk, Detective Garda Joseph Finnegan and Detective Garda Aidan McCabe. Russell was pleased to see them, but was reluctant to let his other officers go. He worried that what the new boys had in energy and physical alertness, they might lack in a true appreciation of the dynamics of the incident. They had not yet heard the crack of the shotgun from the cottage, or heard Carthy shout insults out through the kitchen window, and Russell brought them up to the new house for a thorough briefing on what was going on.

The tactical commander explained all he knew about John Carthy's background and the events of the first hours at the scene. He also told the officers about the plan to try and contain Carthy in the house in the hope that through negotiations he would eventually be persuaded to emerge without the shotgun. If Carthy came out of his own accord, there would be two likely scenarios.

'If the subject exited the building unarmed, we could conduct a controlled exit and enable his arrest to be conducted in a safe manner when he would be handed over to local gardaí.

If he exited the house in an uncontrolled manner with a fire-arm, their objective would be to disarm him and to use whatever reasonable means at their disposal to achieve this purpose – to enable them to make an arrest.'

The 'reasonable means' that Russell referred to encompassed a range of options that would be open to his officers in the event that Carthy emerged to face their inner cordon. Russell told them that if the situation spiralled out of control and it came to a situation where any person present was in danger of losing their life, then they must use as much force as necessary to stop Carthy in his tracks. This included shooting Carthy, but only as a last resort.

'(I told them) that every other avenue should be exhausted; that it was incumbent on them to offer any other possible tactical initiative before they would resort to firearms and in that, as I said, you are relying on the initiative of the particular members who are in the situation. I can only set the scene and the plan, it is up to them to actually deal with the situation as they found it at that particular time themselves. It is impossible to legislate for his demeanour at the time.'

After their talk, Detective Garda Finnegan crept to the mound of clay behind the house to relieve Ryan. He was armed with his Uzi sub-machine gun, and he settled down, familiarising himself with the territory around him. Sisk went to relieve Carey towards the side of the house, one of the few points where they could safely keep an eye on the front door. He was armed with a Hechler and Koch rifle. McCabe picked up another Uzi and remained in the vicinity of the new house.

Russell needn't have worried about the officers' ability to appreciate quickly the climate at the scene. Even from where they had gathered in the new home, they could hear shouts and the sound of breaking furniture coming from the cottage. Carthy was becoming increasingly aggressive, shouting various insults out at the gardaí. He told them they were 'Free State bastards' and accused them of being 'just like the Black and Tans'. He could be heard smashing furniture at various points around the old house, tearing the place apart bit by bit.

Done with demolishing the place for a while, Carthy again turned his attention to the gun and to the front wall outside. He seemed to be concentrating on something. Steadying himself at the kitchen window, he made a determined effort to aim the barrels of the gun at one object in particular. With a steady hand, he applied the pressure on the trigger and watched the shot go. Got it! The loudhailer went spinning off the wall. It wouldn't be bothering him again.

Ω   Ω   Ω

An hour after the loudhailer was put out of action, Kevin Ireland arrived at Mill Street garda station in Galway city. He told the garda on the desk that he had some information on what was going on in Longford. The Galway gardaí immediately put a call through to Granard station, and, handing the phone to Ireland, they allowed him to tell his story straight to the local officer, Sergeant Daniel Monahan. Sergeant Monahan made the following note of what was told to him by Kevin Ireland.

'12.00 midday received a call from John Carthy on his mobile. Appeared calm and relaxed; advised to give himself up. Mentioned a solicitor by the name of Mick or John Finucane from Dublin. His mobile phone went dead. Worked on a building site with him in Galway. Worked as a labourer. Does not know the mobile number for John Carthy. Not to inform the gardaí that he had rang. Not to inform John Carthy that he had rang gardaí.'

With his duty done, Ireland left the garda station and went back to his normal life, keen to hear what would unfold with John Carthy. Leaving the station, he made a call to his mother to fill her in on how he had become a part of the story that was at the top of every news bulletin.

Mary Ireland worked at Shannonside Radio at the time of the incident, and her first thought after hearing from her son was to ring Noeleen Leddy, the Shannonside reporter who was at the scene in Abbeylara. Mrs Ireland told Leddy that John Carthy had rung her son. When Leddy asked her what Carthy had said to Ireland on the phone, all Mrs Ireland could remember was that he had mentioned he wanted a solicitor and that he said something about making the guards duck down. Kevin would often talk to his mother about lads he worked with that she might know and she remembered from those conversations hearing that Carthy had said to some friends two weeks previously that he was going to do 'something big' because life was tough. In her evidence to the Tribunal, Noeleen Leddy claimed that she was also told that John had said to Kevin to 'watch this space'.

Noeleen Leddy was at the church with all the other reporters when she got the call from Mary Ireland. She sensed she had stumbled on some crucial information, and headed for the garda cordon. She told them she had details about a phone call John Carthy had made to a friend. Arrangements were made for her to be brought closer to the scene so that she could meet with Shelly and Sullivan and pass on all she had been told by Mary Ireland.

The gardaí took it all in, the mesh of details partly made up of hearsay and rumour, and partly what John Carthy had actually said, but some of Carthy's statements to Ireland were lost. So, rather than hearing that Carthy 'hadn't a notion' of doing anything stupid, the negotiating team were told that Carthy had told his friend to 'watch this space' and that he intended to do 'something big'.

Sullivan returned to the negotiation point to inform Jackson of what he had learned. The information was accepted by the negotiator. Neither he, nor any of the other senior members at the scene, ever contacted Kevin Ireland directly to hear from him what exactly was said in that short phone conversation. The original message from Carthy had now been substantially distorted.

'It is evident that Mr Ireland was not adequately interrogated about Mr Carthy's phone call. If that had happened, the scene commander and the negotiator would have learned that the subject had assured his friend that he had no intention of shooting himself or anyone else and that his purpose in firing shots was to keep the gardaí away from his house.' (Justice Robert Barr)

At the negotiation point, Jackson took in the information that Sullivan had gathered, and, hearing that Carthy had mentioned his wish to get a solicitor to the scene, he decided to broach the subject again. The negotiating team had not been told at this point that Carthy had actually specifically made mention of a solicitor by the name of Finucane, so Jackson pressed Carthy to give them a name.

Carthy: 'The republican solicitor, the republican one.'

Jackson: 'What is his number? Where can we contact him? We will ensure you are okay when you come out.'

Carthy: 'No fucking way, I want him in here.'

Jackson: 'John, we are worried about letting (a) solicitor in there with you because of the gun you have, but we will get him to meet you outside if that is what you want. John, please tell me who he is and where he can be contacted.'

Carthy: 'Don't bother, don't bother.'

With no further assistance from Carthy, the gardaí were left to their own devices when it came to finding Mick Finucane. Back at Granard station, Sergeant Daniel Monahan and some other officers were tasked with finding out who this solicitor was and where they could find him. Their efforts, however, were minimal.

'Garda Oliver Cassidy checked Golden Pages and myself checked Directory Enquiries,' noted Monahan. 'John Cunningham, district clerk, checked 01 Directory ... Sergeant J Folan was present at that time. I could find no name of a solicitor by the name Finucane.'

The gardaí did not get in contact with the Carthy family to ask them if they had ever heard of this particular solicitor; they did not get in touch with any local solicitors to inquire if any of them were aware of the name Finucane. Neither did they did get in touch with the Law Society. If they had, they would quickly have found the answer they were looking for. Any legal person in the capital, and possibly even closer to home in Longford, would have been aware that Michael Finucane, son of slain human rights lawyer, Pat Finucane, was an apprentice solicitor in Dublin at the time. This was the man Carthy was referring to. He was easily traceable, but never found.

Why Carthy had a fascination with Michael Finucane is not known. The young solicitor has said he never had anything to do with John Carthy, and he has been unable to shed any light on Carthy's knowledge of him. Presumably, Carthy had read about the Finucane case in the papers and was impressed by Michael Finucane's efforts to get justice for his father.

14.

Time was moving on, and as evening drew in, the pessimists and realists started to foresee a second night spent in this surreal setting. Initial flows of conversation from Carthy had dried up, and the only communications from him now were sporadic verbal assaults on Jackson and his colleagues. He invited them again and again to go in and take him out, he continued to break things inside the house and he gave up asking for the cigarettes.

But it was the periods between bouts of destruction and abuse that were starting to worry Jackson. They had become used to hearing glass being smashed and furniture being broken, but Carthy had now started a new practice that caught the attention of the gardaí. Now, when he passed the kitchen window, they could see him looking at his watch in an obsessive manner. He would pace a bit, check the time and continue on. Occasionally he would smile, and it was a knowing type of grin that was starting to make the rational Jackson feel a hint of paranoia. It was as if Carthy knew something he didn't.

Jackson wanted to get his attention and to try to bring him back to some communication, if only to settle his own nerves. The smashed loudhailer lay on the ground. The bullet that went through it had done the desired damage, but it didn't take long to replace one garda megaphone with another, and within half an hour of Carthy's perfect shot, Jackson was back in contact with him again. He understood however that the loudhailer was obviously annoying Carthy, so he asked him to answer the phone so they could talk more easily. Carthy obliged, and in a short conversation on his mobile, he queried the garda presence around his home.

Carthy: 'What's with the hundred guards outside and only one of me?'

Jackson: 'John, there's only a few guards here and the only reason they are here is that you have that gun and you are firing at us. If you put the gun down and come out the guards will go away. I'm out here to help you to come out of the house.'

Carthy: 'You're not going to come in and take the gun off me again.'

Carthy then hung up, but when Jackson attempted another call two minutes later, he answered again.

Jackson: 'John, please tell me what has happened to make you do all this, tell me about it and I can help.'

Carthy: 'I'm going to do ten years for all of this, ten fucking years.'

Jackson: 'John, you won't get ten years. Nobody has been hurt and that is good. We understand what happened yesterday was because you were angry, so come on out and it will be okay.'

The line went dead again and Jackson was left to think about the latest expressions of fear from inside. Carthy thought there were a hundred guards outside, and he was afraid he would be sent to jail when all this ended. Again, the latter fear was promising to some degree, indicating that Carthy was hoping to live through this, but Jackson also worried that the fear might push Carthy to do something reckless. If Carthy thought a long prison stint was all that lay ahead for him, he might be driven to extremes. Jackson knew he couldn't let it come to that.

♎ ♎ ♎

Niall O'Flynn was still away from the scene, continuing to seek out more willing interviewees who would tell him what they knew about John Carthy. He hadn't been in contact with Paul Reynolds since he left the scene that morning, and he had been too busy to listen to any of the news bulletins that were continuing to focus on Abbeylara every hour. Consumed by his own work, he had no idea of what was happening at the hub of the incident, but he assumed he would hear if something drastic happened.

It had already been arranged that Superintendent Farrelly would grant an interview to Five- Seven-Live if the incident was still going on that evening. O'Flynn only spoke with the press officer on two occasions throughout the day – one of those meetings was when Farrelly drove him and Paul Reynolds down to the scene for the media visit, and another was a few brief words in the afternoon. Farrelly could not remember whether or not he had definitely informed O'Flynn of the request that the media not name Carthy, but this policy was being followed by every other broadcast reporter at the scene.

♎ ♎ ♎

Various members of Carthy's extended family and other community figures had offered their assistance to the gardaí, and in particular had volunteered to try and talk some sense to the man in the house. Local county councillor, Brian Lynch, had been in touch with the guards twice to suggest that as a pillar of the community, he might have some luck in talking Carthy round. Rosaleen Mahon, John Carthy's cousin, had also left her number with the gardaí, as had a neighbour from down the road, Michael Heaney.

But Jackson had to be careful about who he allowed down to the negotiation post. He had heard horror stories from other negotiating teams in other countries who told of instances where a third party would be introduced, it would turn out they were hated by the subject of the siege and that would be the end of it.

But when he was told that Sean Farrell, a friend of the family, was at the scene and willing to try speaking to Carthy, Jackson appreciated the offer. Tom Walsh had told them earlier that Farrell was a man much respected by Carthy, and he was hopeful that Carthy would feel almost obliged to speak to him. When Jackson shouted in to Carthy, suggesting that perhaps he would like to speak with Farrell, those hopes were boosted. Carthy shouted out, 'Bring him down'.

But when Farrell arrived at the post, Carthy was unresponsive. For half an hour, Farrell spoke over the loudhailer, asking Carthy what had happened to make him act like this. He said that everybody, including the guards, was there to help. He told Carthy that he would give him work and keep him in a job if that was what was worrying him. Carthy stood at the window, appearing to listen to what Farrell was saying, but he never replied to anything that was said. When Farrell tried phoning his mobile on six different occasions, Carthy answered, but said nothing and then hung up. For all Farrell's attempts to crack Carthy, nothing was uncovered to help explain why Carthy was doing this.

♎   ♎   ♎

After Sean Farrell left the negotiation post, Carthy's anxiety levels increased once more. He continued to call the gardaí 'Free State bastards', and continued looking at his watch. Jackson asked him why he kept checking the time. No verbal response came from the kitchen, but Carthy glanced out at him with what the negotiator described as a 'wry or a sarcastic' smirk.

At this point, word was finally sent up the line to inform Jackson that in his phone call to Kevin Ireland, Carthy had asked for a solicitor by the name of Finucane. Armed with this extra information, Jackson shouted in to the kitchen, telling Carthy they knew his solicitor was a Mr Finucane, but they didn't know where to find him. The negotiator asked Carthy to help them out, but received no reply. During this period, the only time Carthy came near the kitchen window was when he walked across the room and threw the landline phone out into the garden.

When most people hear the name Finucane and a reference to the 'republican solicitor', their thoughts would immediately turn to the murdered human rights lawyer in Northern Ireland, Pat Finucane. But despite the fact that many of the ERU men had worked in the area of terrorism and security issues with the North, none of them made the connection.

At around this time, Carthy received a call on his mobile from his old workmate Kieran Lennon. A short conversation ensued. Mr Lennon asked Carthy if he had 'any craic?' Carthy said no, and asked his old workmate what he wanted. Lennon said he was just ringing to see how he was. Everything about the conversation was calm but Carthy told Lennon he was very busy and he had to go, and with that he hung up. While on the phone to Carthy, Lennon could hear a radio playing in the background.

At twenty past three, Jackson decided to take another rest break. He told Carthy that he would be gone for a while, but that Michael Sullivan would be there if he needed anything. He had now been on duty for thirty-two hours. He went to the garda jeep again, to try to relax for at least a while.

Russell also decided it was time for him to have a break. He retired again to the new house where Carey and Finnegan were resting. The ERU men had opted to remain at the scene after they were relieved in case the incident went into a second night and they were needed again. The three officers tried to get comfortable on the concrete floors of the new building, constructing beds out of sleeping bags and shifting around on the hard floor. Russell found it hard to switch off, but sleep came easier when he realised he might be spending a second dark night huddled at that wall. He had now been on duty for twenty-four hours.

At the wall, Sullivan continued on with Jackson's lines. He may not have had any formal negotiations training, but he had heard it all so many times now that he was able to put some of the more basic skills into practice. During this period, Carthy regularly levelled the gun at Sullivan by pointing it through the broken kitchen window, forcing Sullivan to duck down behind the wall. Sullivan said he got the impression Carthy was enjoying this, and said he could see Carthy smiling in a 'knowing way', as if to say 'he was in control'.

Continuing on undeterred, Sullivan went back over all the issues again. He was interrupted mid-flow by a question from Carthy. The shout came through the kitchen window, a query about why his solicitor had not been brought to speak with him. For the first time, he used the name 'Finucane' himself. Sullivan asked Carthy for more information on the solicitor, but all that came from the kitchen was a renewed torrent of abuse.

He taunted Sullivan. At one stage he came to the window, with his arms outstretched, saying, 'shoot me, shoot me'.

♎   ♎   ♎

It was around this time that Dr Shanley was met by a patrol car on the outskirts of Edgeworthstown. True to his word, the psychiatrist had made contact with the gardaí that afternoon and it was decided that he would meet some gardaí on his way to the west and be guided to Abbeylara. Arriving in the village, he went first to the Mahon home to speak with Rose and the rest of the family, anxious to hear the details of how John had been in the run-up to this day. The arrangement was that he would then be taken to the scene, with a view to speaking with John.

♎   ♎   ♎

Niall O'Flynn returned to the scene and hopped into the RTÉ satellite van to begin work on editing his package. He had collected fifteen vox pop interviews in all, and with time ticking down to the start of Five- Seven- Live, he was under pressure to edit them down and choose the best snippets for broadcast. He was pleased with the content of the interviews, feeling they gave a rounded view of John Carthy and the people of Abbeylara. From what he could gather, little had changed at the scene. Carthy was still inside, the negotiations were still going on and he hadn't missed anything.

The area around the church was still packed with journalists, photographers and cameramen, but Niall O'Flynn didn't really engage with them. It was within minutes of airtime, he was under much more pressure to get his package ready. Abbeylara was to be the top story on Five-Seven-Live, and he knew at least twenty minutes of the first hour of the show would be devoted to the stand-off.

Niall O'Flynn would later claim that he had never heard any reference to the fact that John Carthy suffered from a mental illness. He would also claim that he never heard any mention of the fact that Carthy had a radio in the house, which various gardaí had heard playing over the course of the incident. And he claimed he never learned there was a policy amongst the media of not naming John Carthy.

15.

Paul Reynolds hovered outside the RTÉ van, listening to the vox pop interviews that O'Flynn was editing inside. The content concerned him; John Carthy's name was being bounced around freely and details of his life were being discussed. There were only minutes to go before Five-Seven-Live went on air, and he couldn't believe that O'Flynn was planning on broadcasting this material.

He beckoned O'Flynn away from his work for a moment, to discuss the content of the vox pops he had just heard. He asked him straight out if it was his intention to name John Carthy. O'Flynn replied, 'Yes, why not?' and told Reynolds that it was too late to change his report anyway.

Reynolds left it at that. It was not his responsibility to dictate what another reporter should do, but he knew that O'Flynn's package would create problems for the gardaí. There is an unwritten rule in journalism that once one publication or station crosses the line, everyone is free to follow suit. If the same were to happen at Abbeylara, the floodgates on Carthy's life and identity would be whipped open as soon as O'Flynn aired his package. And if Carthy was being named on every station and channel, the worry was that eventually he would tune in to a news bulletin that was laying his life out for the world to hear.

Two minutes after Reynolds left the satellite van, Superintendent Farrelly arrived to honour the commitment he had given O'Flynn to doing an interview with Five-Seven-Live.

Now aware that the media had not been naming Carthy up to this point, O'Flynn decided it was probably best that he let the garda press officer know what was contained in his report before they went on air. When they were settled at the microphones in the satellite van, with just seconds to go before they went on air, he told Farrelly it was his intention to name Carthy and that a vox pop of local opinion would also be broadcast.

The way O'Flynn remembers it, Farrelly did little to object to the broadcast. He said that apart from 'a grunt or a groan,' the garda press officer said little and made no real protest about the forthcoming package. The RTÉ man was adamant that the broadcast could have been stopped, and he claims if Farrelly had voiced serious concerns even at that late stage, he would have pulled the plug on the entire report. For his part, Farrelly says he was 'very annoyed', but he felt there was nothing he could do due to the lateness of the hour and the fact that they were going on air in seconds.

'(I was) caught in a trap,' said Farrelly. 'Either I could walk away and leave it or continue on in the vein that I was doing the interviews, in the hope that it would not be a significant departure from what was happening, but then when I heard the vox pops afterwards I was quite annoyed then, on top of that.'

Ω   Ω   Ω

By five o'clock, Jackson had returned from his second rest break. He hadn't slept at all in the hour he spent in the garda jeep, and he had a bad feeling he might have another long night ahead of him. There was nothing he hadn't said to Carthy. He had tried absolutely everything, and none of his words were getting through or making their mark. He could only hope that if he said them often enough, the logic might eventually ring true to John Carthy.

But when he arrived back at his spot at the front wall, he saw that things had changed dramatically in the hour he had been away. There was an urgency about Carthy, his movements were almost frantic, and his expressions and gestures were in a state of torrential flux. The furniture and glass inside was being broken systematically now, as though he was just trying to get it all done within a certain time frame. The negotiator could only catch glimpses of Carthy as he walked rapidly around the kitchen. He continued to look at his watch obsessively. He continued to smile knowingly.

Dr Shanley had arrived at the scene at this stage, and he and Marie were sitting in a car up the road. Marie was still waiting to be allowed to speak with her brother. Dr Shanley was ready whenever they needed him to go down and use his expertise in trying to talk Carthy down.

Jackson knew he had the two third-party options up the road, and in an attempt to distract Carthy from his manic movements around the house, he offered them both to him. He first offered Marie, but the offer was ignored. Dr Shanley? Carthy had no interest. It was impossible for Jackson to catch a sufficient few seconds of Carthy's attention. He was a live wire, and wound up to an extent that could only spell danger.

Again and again Jackson told Carthy that Marie was there and that she was worried. The negotiator claims Carthy smirked when he heard this. He then picked up the gun and fired a shot aimed at the block on the negotiation pillar. The block fell on Jackson's head, but by then Jackson had replaced his helmet. That was shot number thirty since the incident began.

Ω   Ω   Ω

The five o'clock news on RTÉ Radio 1 that evening was read by Anne Doyle. She summed up the latest from the scene, and then passed over to the presenter of Five-Seven-Live, Myles Dungan. Dungan had heard snippets of O'Flynn's vox pop interviews when they were fed up to the main studios in Donnybrook a few minutes before they went on air. He was not aware that the newsroom weren't naming Carthy, and he had no way of knowing either that as the programme began their reporter in Abbeylara was sitting in stony silence with a garda press officer who was unhappy with the piece of journalism that was about to be aired.

The familiar Five-Seven-Live theme tune came on, and in cars and houses around the country the programme laid bare the life of John Carthy from Abbeylara. Eighteen minutes were devoted to the story, and a good portion of that was taken up by the journalism of Niall O'Flynn. To pacify Farrelly, he did his best to refer to Carthy only as 'the man', but Dungan did not pick up on his attempt at discretion and freely used the name in the questions he put to both the reporter and the garda press officer. But apart from mentioning Carthy's name, the content of O'Flynn's own comments heightened the sense of melodrama. His description of the scene painted a picture of a house under siege by lines of armed officers, weighed down by bullet-proof vests and sub-machine guns. Abbeylara was a village surrounded by a ring of steel.

Myles Dungan: 'Thank you very much, Anne, and we're going live now to the small town, small village indeed of Abbeylara where a gunman has been involved in a siege at his home all day. He's opened fire on gardaí several times today, as you heard in the news there. The area around the house has been sealed off and local people have been evacuated from their homes. The incident began yesterday evening in fact when the man forced his mother out of the house. Our reporter at the scene in Abbeylara is Niall O'Flynn.

Niall, describe to us where you are first of all, because I imagine you're not that close to the scene. You probably wouldn't be allowed that close.'

Niall O'Flynn:' Not too close, Myles, but not too far away either. This is a quiet country village, population probably less than eighty souls, many of whom are elderly, many of whom live alone. The biggest excitement in recent years here has been the success of the local Abbeylara football team. But the house in question, the family home, is actually two houses on the same site, one old and one new. The family, that's the family of this 27-year-old man, are living in the older, run-down cottage. They are waiting for their new home on the same site to be finished. The only other member of the immediate family we know is a younger sister, but she doesn't live in the village and the father died some years ago. ...

And as you know, this man has fired off some twenty shots in the past twenty-four hours. I have been down, the guards have allowed us down to the edge of the house, but very warily, I can assure you.

There are about thirty-two houses on the road, it's a very long road, gardaí have evacuated the nearest five families, there is an ambulance at the scene and a doctor has been around during the day. But it's quite tense here, I can tell you.'

MD: 'Tell us about the security response so far, Niall.'

NO'F: 'Well, this man is armed, as I say, and he has a supply of shotgun ammunition. Hunting and fishing are very popular recreational pastimes in Abbeylara, and it's quite usual for families to own a legally-held firearm. Nevertheless, the gardaí, as they must, are treating this very seriously. Upwards of sixty gardaí have been moved into the area, and about three dozen are on duty at any one time. There are trained negotiators at the scene, but what really strikes you when you see the house is the number of armed officers there are here, members of the Garda Emergency Response Unit, there are also local detectives armed with Uzi sub-machine guns. When you look at the house and the area, helmeted figures in bullet-proof vests hug the wall outside the house, the hedges above and around the site and the hills and valleys all around, and yet what they want, what they all want is a peaceful resolution to this tragic story.'

MD: 'What do we know about the man inside the house, John Carthy?'

NO'F: 'Well, he's been named locally as John Carthy, we haven't got that officially just yet. We do know he's twenty-seven, a single man, he's in the building trade, I think a plasterer, certainly a labourer, and he's very well liked by all accounts locally.

The background to the incident, as you know, is that about five thirty yesterday, that's twenty-four hours ago now, he ordered his mother out of the house, she called the police, a uniformed officer and a plain clothes policeman arrived. They spoke briefly to John Carthy, he produced a shotgun and they were forced to flee the site. A shotgun blast hit the garda car they had with them, they were forced to abandon it and it remains at the scene. Currently officers are continuing to communicate with him through a loudhailer, and also by phone, but he's saying very little. As Paul Reynolds said, there on the news, he's been playing loud music during the day, he doesn't seem to want to talk, and all he's asked for so far is a packet of cigarettes.'

MD: 'Okay, Superintendent John Farrelly of the garda press office is with you at the moment, Niall. John Farrelly, what is the latest?'

John Farrelly: 'Well, the latest Myles is that we are now just twenty-four hours into this situation. The negotiations are still going on, the gardaí are down there trying to make contact by different means, by loudhailer, by mobile phone and indeed by the house phone as well. This has been very protracted, one of the same negotiators has been busy doing this from nine o'clock last night, right up to this particular point without a break, and we will continue to do this approach in the hope that he will eventually come out, because we are more than interested in safety here, because the threat is to himself, by himself, and not by ourselves and we have insisted on that all day, that we want him out there as safely as possible and as quickly as possible.'

MD: 'But he's obviously a threat to the gardaí, we're talking about somebody who obviously is having problems, but who is nonetheless armed and dangerous because he has been taking shots at gardaí all day?'

JF: 'Well, certainly that is true and quite a number of shots over the past twenty-four hours have been shot from inside the house out on to the grounds themselves. But we have taken measures ourselves for our own self-protection, and of course, we have plenty of time on our hands, in so far as he is in the house, we are outside, the public aren't allowed around the vicinity, we have cordoned off the area about half a mile each side of the actual house itself. Five families, as was said in the earlier report, have been evacuated for their own safety out of the area, and we want to contain the situation there in the hope that it will be peacefully resolved in time.'

MD: 'Okay, other than cigarettes, has he made many or any demands and what have you given him?'

JF:' Ah, in fact the only demand was for the cigarettes, which were brought to the scene. They have not gone in there yet, we are obviously working out a formula for that, but no other demands have been made. It's a sporadic sort of communication, it's very much on our side trying to make communications, to keep it fixed and to try to build up a relationship with him inside the house. This is a difficult process, we know that our negotiators are trained for this long process, but eventually we hope that it will yield a result for us.'

MD: 'And I gather that a psychiatrist who is known to John Carthy is on the way?'

JF: 'Yes, I believe actually he may have just arrived here in the last five minutes, and he's gone to the scene, and obviously measures will be taken for him to communicate with the man in the house at this time, but we'll await further developments on that.'

MD: 'John Farrelly, thank you very much for talking to us. Niall, just back to you – you've spoken to a number of local people haven't you?'

NO'F: 'Yes, Myles, and I would stress that people here are very positive about John Carthy, they say he's a very nice young man, he was heavily involved in handball here and in the rebuilding of the handball alley which has been here since 1924, quite a fixture in the town. He worked in Galway until recently, he has recently been working in Longford and he walked into Granard, which is about three miles away every day. People, including the local priest, quite often picked him up, drove him into town, he chatted with them, he's very friendly, as I say he's very well got in the area.'

The report then cut to the three vox pop interviews O'Flynn had selected for broadcast. The first of those was with the parish priest of Abbeylara, Fr PJ Fitzpatrick, who spoke in a prayerful way about his wish for a peaceful ending. There was nothing inflammatory in what he said, and had John Carthy been listening, he would have heard nothing that would further frighten or anger him.

But the second and third clips were of a more personal brand, both revealing details of Carthy's life and his problems and informing the listening public of the type of man he was and the family he came from. The interviewees in both cases certainly had good intentions in providing the information to O'Flynn, but not all of what they said was accurate. The first of these interviews was with a local woman, Mary McDowell. She would sometimes give Carthy a lift into town, and the information she gave to O'Flynn that day was based upon recollections of the conversations she had with Carthy over the previous months. Mary McDowell later said she could not remember O'Flynn introducing himself or identifying himself as a reporter from RTÉ.

Mary McDowell: 'Well, actually John Carthy, he's a really nice bloke and I've picked him up a couple of times from Longford, you know, he was hitch-hiking a lift and I picked him up.'

NO'F: 'He works in Longford, isn't that right?'

MMcD: 'Yeah, he works in Longford, he's a very, very easy-going lad, he's a smashing person.'

NO'F: ' So, no doubt you're surprised to hear about all this?'

MMcD: 'I'm very, very shocked actually, because John, you know, he's so easy going, it's unbelievable, you know.'

NO'F: 'And did he have any problems in his life?'

MMcD: 'No, no, he was always laughing and joking and that's really...'

NO'F: 'What did he do for a living?'

MMcD: 'Well, when I spoke to him, I picked him up last week, on the way from Longford, and he was telling me that he's working on a building site or something, you know. And he was up in Mayo and he was going out with a girl in Mayo, and he split up from the girl or something, because the girl – he smokes and he has a drink – and the girl says if he packed in the drinking and packed in the smoking they'd get back together again.'

NO'F: 'Right, so it's still on maybe?'

MMcD: 'Yeah, it's still on, but he was going to go back up, this week actually, he was going to go back up.'

NO'F: 'And if you could talk to John now, have you a message for him?'

MMcD: 'Well, John, John, if I was you John, I'd come out. Everybody loves you, and everybody is thinking about you and worrying about you and you're a good friend and you've lots of friends out here, so please, John, please come out.'

O'Flynn's report concluded with a snippet from Michael Heaney, and prompted by the reporter, he gave details on the Carthy family and the type of person John Carthy was. References were also made again to the huge garda presence lurking outside the cottage. Michael Heaney claimed afterwards that O'Flynn did not tell him that the interview would be broadcast, and he believed he was just giving some background information to the reporter.

NO'F: 'Can you tell us a little bit about the Carthy family?'

Michael Heaney: 'They're a very respectable family, a very decent family, very well liked in the neighbourhood, there wouldn't be anything that anyone could say wrong about them in the number of years that I've known them, very, very highly respected in the area.'

NO'F: 'And what about John, what do you know about him?'

MH: 'I've known John from his school days in Abbeylara here, and he was always a very nice-mannered young fella, nobody could say anything about him in that respect. And he played with the local football team for a number of years. He was a great handball player, and when we renovated the handball alley down here, he worked very hard at it, and he spent a lot of time there with all the other lads that were there. And he was a very good handballer, a very keen handballer, very respectable in the area.'

NO'F: 'He's a plasterer by trade, is that right?'

MH:' He does a lot of work, plastering, block-laying, he's very good.'

NO'F: 'I understand he's been working in Galway for the last while?'

MH:' I believe so, I believe he was, yes.'

NO'F: 'And tell us, how do people feel about all this, it must have come out of the blue?'

MH: 'It certainly has. As I said, everyone is very shocked and very saddened by the whole situation at the moment, and with all the media that are here and all the television cameras, it hasn't happened in the village of Abbeylara that I've known, so obviously people are very annoyed about all that, and we would hope that it would come to a satisfactory ending.'

NO'F: 'And, of course there are armed guards around the house and in the fields at the back – it must be completely unusual to you?'

MH: 'Oh, as I said, it's never happened in the village of Abbeylara, so it's unusual, and as I said, we hope it comes to a satisfactory end.'

NO'F: 'If you had a chance to talk to John, what would you say to him?'

MH: 'I would talk to him about the good times we had with the handball, and I'd get him out to have a game of handball and a game of football and get the good times back again, and hopefully that would help him. And that we'd see him back down at the alley again, playing handball. And I'm sure all his friends, and all his mates he went to school with would say the same as I'm saying about him.'

NO'F: 'Would you expect it all to be over by Easter Sunday?'

MH: 'Oh, I hope so, I hope it's over this afternoon or this evening, I hope so.'

♎   ♎   ♎

Back at the negotiation post, Jackson was still trying his best, but it was getting more and more difficult. The situation had reached a difficult point, everything was starting to feel jaded and uncertain. Sullivan was still beside him at the wall, dutifully logging most of what happened on a clipboard. Further down the wall, he could see one of the newly-arrived ERU men, Detective Sergeant Aidan McCabe. Russell, Ryan Finnegan and Carey were still in the new house on a break and the whole thing was starting to wane and drag.

All the officers at the front wall had observed the increased agitation inside the house. At one stage Carthy closed the curtains across the kitchen window for a few minutes, leaving them to wonder what he was doing inside the house. The only glimpses they had of him in this time was when he would point the gun out through a hole in the curtain every so often. When he opened the curtains again, Jackson could see him moving quickly from room to room, while Detective Garda McCabe saw him knock the television set on to the floor.

While Jackson did not feel Carthy would speak to anyone at that stage, arrangements had been made to bring Marie as far as the command post, and from there she was instructed to try phoning her brother. Jackson shouted in to Carthy, telling him to pick up the phone, his sister was on the line. All he heard from the kitchen was a bout of laughter. Shanley was offered again, and another smile was raised.

What Jackson couldn't have known was that Carthy had come to a decision. It was time.

16.

He unlocked the door, and he walked outside. After twenty-four hours, it was that simple. He was spotted first by Detective Garda Finnegan, who was located at the mound of clay at the rear of the house. He hadn't heard Carthy unlock and open the door, and it was only when he saw the slight figure step out of the porch that he became aware that the situation had escalated to a new level. Finnegan watched as Carthy turned in the direction of the front of the house and began walking at a determined pace. Finding his voice, Finnegan grabbed his radio and sent the word down the line.

'He's out.'

On hearing the message, Jackson rose to his full height at the front wall and first saw Carthy as he was making his way past the window at the gable end of the house. He was walking quickly, and yes, he had the gun. It was broken open, [i.e. incapable of being fired immediately] and that was some relief. If he wasn't going to leave the weapon behind, this was the preferred second best. If he would keep the gun like that, they could buy themselves some time.

The negotiator kept his eyes on Carthy all the way, following him as he moved at pace across the front of the house and down on to the driveway. He watched as Detective Garda Carey, who had emerged from the new house, ran to a spot between the abandoned patrol car and the sheds and almost came face to face with Carthy as he made his way out on to the drive. Carey shouted at Carthy to drop his weapon. Carthy paused and glanced his direction. Then he kept on walking.

Jackson had now stepped out from the front wall, his Sig Sauer pistol was in his hand, trained on the moving target. Gardaí all around him were doing the same. Detective Garda McCabe, also at the front wall, cocked his Uzi sub-machine gun and selected the repetition mode of firing. Further up the road, he could hear footsteps fleeing as the uniformed and un-armed men who had been caught by bad timing ran to find cover. The combined noise of their flights to safety formed an apt backdrop to the shouts that were being directed at Carthy from all angles.

'Armed gardaí. Drop your weapon!'

John Carthy seemed oblivious to it all. He just kept on walk-ing. When another armed garda would appear close by, he might cast a glance in their direction, but his eyes never lin-gered on any one person. The Uzi sub-machine guns and the pistols and revolvers that were all singling him out for a shot didn't unnerve him for a second. He held on to his own gun, and he walked with purpose, looking like he knew exactly where he was going.

He got as far as the gateway, and one quick movement of his hands later, the gun was closed and ready for action. They all saw it, and their thoughts progressed to a heightened sense of danger. He could now fire the gun at any time. Jackson, McCabe and Sisk spanned out across the road to form a hu-man cordon to the right of the Carthy gateway. Now facing directly up the road, looking towards Abbeylara, Jackson took in the scene that lay before them. Local officers were still des-perately trying to get as far away as possible. Jackson willed them to run faster and to get to safety before Carthy turned in their direction. He could see some men sheltering behind the garda jeep that was still serving as a command post, but he knew they were armed members who could defend themselves if necessary.

To the left of his peripheral vision, Jackson could see Russell running down the patch in front of the new Carthy home. He was flanked by the other ERU men who had been resting in the new house when the message came through on their radios. They were running for the new wall, hoping Carthy was not moving in their direction and that they would get to cover before the inevitable happened.

Russell willed his legs to keep him moving as he sprinted over the uneven ground, struggling to get his pistol from his holster. Searching the area for a glimpse of where Carthy was, he finally caught sight of him walking through the gateway. Russell couldn't see the gun, but the shouts of the men on the road told him it was still there in his hands. Above all the voices, Russell singled out the familiar tones of Jackson and he was struck by the calm demeanour he was still managing to maintain. There was nothing excitable or anxious in his voice. He didn't sound forceful or threatening in his final pleas to Carthy.

'John, this is Mick, it's over, please drop the gun.'

Russell made it to the wall, and without thinking twice, he jumped up on to it. He respected all those who wanted to remain behind hedges and walls, but he wanted to see this through to the end. It was when he had steadied himself on the wall that he became aware for the first time of the panic that was going on up the road, as unarmed personnel ran for cover.

Looking down on the road, Russell watched Carthy walk

from the gateway, straight across the road towards the hedge. All eyes were on him, waiting for his next move, and when he paused in the middle of the road, he had an attentive audience. The ERU men stopped shouting for a moment, the sound of footsteps finally ceased, and there was a moment of nothing while they let Carthy dictate what would happen next.

He broke open the gun again. Promising. The gardaí closest to him managed to catch a glimpse of what was inside. They saw two cartridges, one in each of the barrels. Carthy reached inside and pulled one of the cartridges out. He threw it into the hedge and closed the gun again. Whatever he intended to do in the next few minutes, he would need just one bullet to do it.

Still standing on the wall, Russell watched as Carthy turned to his left and began heading up the Abbeylara road. It was a route that was laced with the potential for danger, walking as he was towards the command post jeep where local members had taken cover, towards the car further up the road where Dr Shanley, Marie, Tom Walsh and Pepper had been waiting, towards the garda cordon which marked the scene off from the outside world, and beyond that towards the media at the church and the village beyond.

Russell had his first good look at Carthy. He was very thin, dressed in old jeans, a rugby shirt and a padded jacket. He was bent forward a few centimetres to keep a good grip on his gun. He held the weapon at waist level, and as he strode up the slight incline in the road, the barrels of the shotgun bobbed up and down in tandem with his movements.

In his exposed position up on the wall, Russell was standing in full view of Carthy. He was an easy target, but Carthy never noticed. His mission, whatever it was, continued, unhindered by the guns and the gardaí all around him. All kinds of theories circulated in garda minds as to where he was going. Some wondered if he had perhaps decided to go and get the cigarettes himself. There was also a possibility that he might have wanted to go and talk to Marie in private, and there was also a theory that on the day that was in it, he might have been heading to the graveyard and the final resting place of his father.

But the reasons for his exit would be hypothesised at another time. For Russell, Jackson and the other members of the ERU, the reality of the scene before them was their immediate concern: they were watching an armed man, who had already fired thirty shots, walk up a road that was lined by unarmed police sheltering in hedges and behind walls. As they saw it, the possibility for disaster was very real.

♎   ♎   ♎

Sergeant Alan Murray had gone up to the ESB pole at the border of the Carthy property at around half past five in the evening. He wanted to speak with Detective Sergeant Aidan Foley about when he and some of the other officers could take their next break for food and rest, and despite the fact that he was not armed he felt he was in no danger so close to the Carthy house. They had become used to the tense atmosphere around the scene and an unreal sense of security prevailed so that they were happy to hang around and wait for what would happen next. Murray had been at the scene almost from the start, and his job was to be responsible for the gardaí who were at the command post.

The ESB pole was his own personal cordon. He could go no further than that point, because across that line was ERU territory, and Murray was happy to leave the danger to the professionals. He had been told by both Shelly and Foley that he and the rest of the local officers were there as back-up to the specialist force, but that was a back-up that all were hoping would not come into play. It was getting to a stage when it looked like this could go on forever.

While he was standing at the ESB pole, Detective Sergeant Sullivan passed by. The ERU man was on his way up the road to bring Dr Shanley down to the negotiation post. Moments later, however, Sullivan came running back down the road again, summoned by the message that Carthy was out. The ERU men were the only gardaí who were in possession of a radio, and therefore they were the only ones to receive the initial message that Carthy had emerged. Aware of this, Sullivan spread the word. Standing at the ESB pole, he shouted at the officers in the vicinity, 'He's out, get back, get into cover.'

Hearing this, Murray did what other unarmed officers in the vicinity did – he jumped over the nearest wall and ran for his life. His nearest escape route was over the Burke wall, but he still felt too close to the thick of the action, so he skirted along the wall to the garden gate and out on to the road to sprint further away from the danger. Without a gun, he had no intention of placing himself in the line of fire. He was fully aware of the danger that Carthy posed, and he believed without doubt that somebody would have to stop him. Still running up the road, desperately seeking cover, he willed the ERU men to act quickly and he waited to hear the shots go off.

'I knew the lads didn't want to do it,' Murray said. 'You would want to give the person as many chances as you can and I was afraid they would give John Carthy one chance too many and that someone would be shot.'

☖ ☖ ☖

Detective Sergeant Aidan Foley was an armed garda; this was what he was trained to do, and he had to stay put and act in accordance with the plan. To afford himself some cover, he retreated from the ESB pole, hurrying backwards, aiming to get behind the command post jeep before Carthy moved too far. He reached the cover of the vehicle and moved round to the rear left wing, keeping his eyes on Carthy the whole time, waiting for something to happen.

He could see the ERU were following Carthy, keeping a few steps behind him, and they were all taking aim. Jackson was still shouting out commands in his calm voice, while Sisk, McCabe and Carey flanked him on all sides. But Carthy didn't seem interested in the gardaí who were surrounding him. Foley watched him come closer and closer. In his mind, Carthy had just one target and that was him.

Foley could see his face now. It seemed yellow to him, the colour of a man who was very sick. Foley's eyes darted from the gun to Carthy's face, and as the distance between them lessened, Foley became convinced that Carthy was looking at him, was 'fixated' by him, was penetrating through any remaining bits of bravery with what he described as a 'dead stare'.

Crouched behind the command post jeep along with Foley was Garda Eugene Boland. The scene that lay before him was terrifying. And he was aware of what was happening further up the Abbeylara Road, where there was 'a big rush of members going up the road, running for their lives'. Like Foley, at that moment, Boland tried to curb the thoughts racing through his mind and to focus on the reality of the situation.

This was an armed man who wasn't afraid to use his gun. He had fired at gardaí already, and now he was just yards away, and he was staring at them. Although Carthy had already walked past several other gardaí without a second glance, who was to say which one his disturbed mind might single out as a target? Fear had brought them to the conclusion that this armed man was headed straight for them and nobody else.

Foley made up his mind. Regardless of what the ERU men were planning, he was now in the line of fire. His life was in danger. He was the one who was going to have to shoot John Carthy.

'I felt I was going to be shot, that was my belief. When John Carthy came towards us, I told Boland to move in. When he walked towards us, I had made up my mind that I was going to have to fire at John Carthy and I said to Boland, "We are going to have to do it ourselves".'

Boland agreed. With every step Carthy took, Boland felt closer to death. He put his hand on the cocking mechanism of the Uzi sub-machine gun. Foley had his gun aimed at John Carthy, his finger on the trigger .

☊ ☊ ☊

Jackson was following Carthy, keeping about four and a half metres of road between them. Sisk and McCabe were with him, walking gingerly and slowly, guns at shoulder height, tracking every move he made. Carthy had now travelled a distance of forty-one metres from the front door of his home; he was just eight and a half metres away from the command post. After twenty-four hours of attempted negotiation, Jackson was left with no more bright ideas and no words that were going to help the situation. He had been the negotiator for long enough; setting that role aside, he concentrated his aim and told himself he had to do it.

When the first bullet rang out, it echoed around Abbeylara and sounded like a death knell. Marie heard it and knew it was the end. The local gardaí heard it and felt relief that it was all over. But the bullet had found Carthy's upper right leg and passed right through it. Contrary to all his training, Jackson had fired a bullet with a view to injuring Carthy rather than killing him. It was his first departure from the rulebook, an action that went against best police practice in almost every country in the western world. Recruits are trained to aim for the central body mass so as to leave little chance for the subject of your fire to recover. But this was Jackson's first case as a negotiator, and he felt sympathy for Carthy. He didn't want to kill him.

Sitting in the car up the road, Marie hoped and prayed that they had missed; that it had just been a warning shot.

Then the first shot was followed by a second one.

And a third.

And a fourth.

There were perhaps seconds between each of the bursts of fire, but it was slow motion living for the gardaí who watched Carthy's death. They weren't the only witnesses. When he had heard the shots being fired, Tom Walsh jumped from the car where he had been waiting with Dr Shanley, Pepper and Marie. He began to run against the flow of the unarmed men who were trying to get away from Carthy and his gun. When he reached the brow of the hill, he saw Johnny starting to fall.

From his perch on the wall, Russell had heard all the shots, and when the fourth bullet struck, he watched Carthy's body finally surrender. It was an image that would never leave him, the sight of this young man dying before his eyes. He heard Carthy groan as the pain overtook him. With death almost upon him, Carthy paused on the road; he turned around to his left, and looked directly into the face of Russell.

' … at the fourth shot, he almost paused and turned around in my direction, almost opposite … and that is the first time I got a good look at his face. I remember him groaning.'

Russell kept his eyes on Carthy's as the young man began to fall, his body unable to hold him up any longer. He collapsed onto his back, 'almost facing me as if I was the last person he had eye contact with' fifteen feet away from the wall where Russell remained frozen in shock. The colour drained from Carthy's face, he rolled on to his side. Russell shouted at nobody in particular, 'Get an ambulance'.

The ERU men were around Carthy in seconds, still holding their weapons at the ready, barrels trained on the body until they were sure he wouldn't be getting up again. When they reached the bloodied spot on the road, one officer put a foot on Carthy's leg while another kicked the shotgun away and removed an ammunition belt from around his waist. Detective Gardaí Oliver Flaherty and Michael Sullivan knelt beside John Carthy. His eyes were fixed; they checked his pulse and found none; they listened for any breath coming from his lungs and heard nothing.

They could hear Marie screaming from somewhere up the road. Gardaí restrained her as she repeated the same request she had been making since her first arrival at the scene: she wanted to talk to her brother, but this time all she wanted was to say goodbye.

Sullivan and Flaherty were applying CPR to try to revive his heart and lungs. The ambulance that had been on standby was called, and it wasn't long before its sirens wailed through the village up to the scene. The paramedics used all their expertise and equipment to shock Carthy back to life, but his vital signs were not even registering.

John Carthy was pronounced dead at eleven minutes past six on 20 April 2000.

17.

The confrontation was over. John Carthy was dead. Now the gardaí circled, lost for words. They walked the length of the road and back again, trying not to stare at the body still slumped on the opposite side of the road, but unable to keep their eyes off him. He lay there, bloodied and still, awaiting some dignity in death. But until the scene had been preserved, he could not be moved, and the people who loved him could not see him or touch him or cry over him. Russell did the circuit many times. He met Shelly on one of his rounds, and told him, 'we had no other option'. He phoned his boss in the ERU, Detective Inspector Patrick Hogan, and told him the news. He passed his colleagues on the road, and they agreed: they had had no other option.

The exit, the shouting, the shooting and the death had all come and gone in thirty seconds that seemed to have passed in slow motion. That was the time it took for Carthy to make it from his front door to the point on the road where garda bullets took him down. While the shooting was going on, it had all been confusing and bewildering, but in the minutes after he was declared dead, it became clear what had happened.

There had been four bullets, all coming from behind John Carthy. Jackson had fired the first one at Carthy's leg. He had then fired a second shot at the same spot. McCabe took up where Jackson left off. He played by the rule of aiming for the central body mass, and fired a shot at Carthy's lower back. He then fired a second bullet a little higher up his torso. And that was it. John Carthy fell to the ground, and now he was dead.

The gardaí who had shot John Carthy were certain that within seconds Carthy would have discharged his own weapon at one of their colleagues behind the command post jeep. That was their stated primary concern: they had to protect the lives of those members, and at that point, they felt lethal force was their only option.

They had fired four times because they were convinced that Carthy had kept on walking – kept moving forward – after Jackson hit his leg with the first bullet. That he kept on walking when Jackson fired a second bullet at the exact same area. And that he kept on walking after McCabe took aim and fired a bullet that would travel through Carthy's bladder and exit through his scrotum. The gardaí maintained that, despite his injuries, Carthy continued taking steps in the direction of the command post and the cordon further up the Abbeylara road.

McCabe remembered hearing the two cracks from Jackson's gun. His eyes detected a movement in Carthy's jeans, but he wasn't certain that the bullets had actually hit because Carthy was still moving. Peering over his own weapon, he made up his mind to fire. He let off one bullet, and then another and he killed Carthy. It was the first time McCabe had ever shot a man.

When John Carthy had emerged suddenly from his home, there were twenty gardaí and other personnel in and around the house and out on the roadway just above the entrance to the Carthy driveway. A further seventeen officers, including Shelly, Inspector Maguire, and Chief Superintendent Tansey were also present further up the road and in the vicinity of the neighbouring houses.

Of the nine ERU men at the scene, eight of them had witnessed the shooting, and they concurred that the actions that had been taken had been unavoidable. The ninth ERU man was Detective Garda Sullivan. He did not see what happened. Sullivan had been standing at the ESB pole when Carthy emerged on to the road, and while he contemplated taking action against Carthy, he reconsidered when he took in the exact positions of his colleagues on the road and the possibility of 'a crossfire situation'. John Carthy was placed between him and his other ERU colleagues. If Sullivan had fired and missed, there was a chance that his bullet would hit a fellow garda. Because of this, Sullivan decided he had to move away from the immediacy of the scene. As he jumped the wall into Burke's garden, the first shot rang out. Three shots later, he lifted his head above the wall to find that Carthy was on his back, dead on the road.

The claim that Carthy continued walking despite being penetrated by a number of bullets drew queries when the details leaked outside of garda quarters. People talk, and in the hours after Carthy's death, neighbours and friends would reach their own conclusions. They gathered for Mass in St Bernard's Church that evening, distraught at the tragic end that John Carthy had come to. Many had known him since he was a boy. They had known John Senior and the rest of the family. They couldn't imagine how those closest to John would cope with this ordeal, and all they could do was join in the prayers that were said that evening for the repose of the soul of their twenty-seven-year-old neighbour.

Ω   Ω   Ω

Rose was inconsolable and couldn't believe what they were

telling her. John was dead. He had been shot by the guards. There was nothing they could do. Four bullets had hit, but it had been quick and he didn't suffer. She cried and cried, feeling sick to her stomach at the thought of John lying dead on the Abbeylara road. The thought of that was the worst part of it.

The extended family in the Mahon house talked to each other in hushed tones and cried together. It was impossible for them to comprehend what had happened. There had been such an enormous upheaval in all their lives in the last twenty-four hours. Illness, accidents, those things could take a life on any day, but to think that their John had just been shot dead by the gardaí was beyond them. They had never heard of such a tragedy before – the gardaí shooting a civilian like that – and it wasn't long before the grieving of the Carthy family turned to a feeling of bitterness towards the officers who had policed the scene. It was an inevitable outlet for their trauma; it was much easier to get angry at the gardaí than to deal with the awful reality that John was dead.

Marie embraced the anger. She was still trying to purge the memory of those gunshots from her brain, wishing she could forget everything that had happened in the last horrible day. She questioned every detail of what had gone on since Rose made that call to Granard station. She was still adamant that she could have talked her brother round, and her family agreed. They couldn't understand why John was never given the cigarettes. They couldn't understand why four bullets had been necessary, and it was some kind of comfort to them that even after the first and second and third shots, John himself had never discharged his own weapon or retaliated in any way.

That would be their focus in the weeks and months to come. In their own time and in their own way they would grieve for John, but they had something else to be getting on with. They wanted justice and they wanted answers for why their son and brother had been shot dead by the very force that is meant to protect civilian life.

Ω   Ω   Ω

The ERU men gradually drove away from the scene. They were brought to Granard Garda Station for a debriefing. Assistant Commissioner Hickey spoke to them as a group. He had been away from the scene when the actual shooting happened, but Shelly had filled him in, telling him that Carthy had been shot by two ERU men. Hickey told the men that counselling was on offer if they needed some help in dealing with the trauma of what had just happened. He also told them that a formal internal garda inquiry was to be launched into the shooting and the events leading up to it.

In a matter of hours, a senior officer who had no involvement in the incident had been chosen to carry out the investigation, to question everyone involved, to learn more about the circumstances of John Carthy, and to present his findings to the Oireachtas. The officer chosen was Superintendent Adrian Culligan from Cork.

It came as a surprise to none of them that in the coming weeks they would each be visited by detectives and asked to make statements on their actions during the incident. That was the least they expected, fully aware that their superiors in the force would have to be able to provide some answer to the Carthy family for why John had been killed.

When I spoke with Marie Carthy she queried the length of

time that had elapsed between the shooting and the interviews with the gardaí involved; she felt that these should have taken place much earlier and pointed out that her family had been interviewed much sooner.

♎︎   ♎︎   ♎︎

Once news of the fatal shooting reached Dublin, specialist officers from the Ballistics section at the Garda Technical Bureau were ordered to head for Abbeylara.They weren't going to a crime scene as such, but a man had been killed and due process had to be followed. Sergeant Seamus Quinn and Sergeant Patrick Ennis left Dublin immediately to drive to Longford.

On the way down, they listened to the reports on the radio; the story of the shooting had taken over the broadcasts. John Carthy's identity was now being revealed by all the stations; the details of his life being opened up to public scrutiny. The peculiar form of privacy that had been afforded him during the incident was gone, with reporters vying for interviews with anyone who claimed to have known Carthy. They were starting to refer to it as 'The Abbeylara Siege'.

The scene had to be preserved, and, while awaiting the arrival of the chief ballistics people from Dublin, Shelly took preliminary steps to protect the scene. The body needed to be covered up to spare it from prying eyes. The scene commander called in some temporary aid to cordon off the area of the shooting and erect a tent around the body.

Sergeant Sean Leydon from the Athlone station was an experienced crime scene examiner, and he was the officer tasked with protecting the vital stretch of road where Carthy met his maker. When Leydon arrived at the scene, tapes had already been put in place by local officers to prevent unauthorised access. Leydon walked around the body. Scattered around Carthy were the shotgun, his ammunition belt and spent cartridges. He looked around the immediate area for the bullets that had hit Carthy, but couldn't find them. The bullets were never recovered.

Leydon had a plastic covering put over the shotgun and cartridges that were lying on the road. He had no conversation with any of the officers at the scene as to what had happened, and his information on the shooting was derived only from the news reports he had heard that evening. He assumed as he walked the scene in the aftermath of the shooting that everything was as it had been in that moment when Carthy was shot dead. But he would later learn that something vital was missing from that small area between Carthy's cottage and the neighbouring houses. The garda jeep that had acted as a command post for the duration of the incident had been driven away.

Shelly would later be questioned about this again and again. The jeep was central to the garda operations that day; it was the haven for the local gardaí and the meeting point where the ERU men would keep in contact with the management at the scene. But more than that, its position was the reason that McCabe and Jackson gave for firing at Carthy when they did. Because local officers were sheltering behind it, and Carthy seemed to be heading straight for it, the ERU men saw Carthy as an immediate threat to them and they killed John Carthy.

The Carthy family would be told that John was shot because he put the lives of the gardaí at the jeep in danger. But the actual proximity of Carthy to the jeep, and the real danger those men were in, could not be definitively determined because the jeep had been moved. Any future investigations would have to rely on photographs from the media visit to gauge where the vehicle was, an imperfect method by any standard.

Shelly felt that the jeep was only an accessory to the real centrality of the scene. Because the vehicle hadn't been hit by any bullets, and because no shots had apparently been fired from the vicinity of the jeep, the scene commander did not deem it necessary to keep it at the scene.

☊ ☊ ☊

Sergeants Quinn and Ennis from the Ballistics Section arrived in Abbeylara at nine o'clock that evening. Things had started to quieten down; the ERU men were gone for their debriefing and most of the local men had gone back to their homes to reflect on a night they didn't want to remember. It had been a long day. Some food had been brought to the scene after Carthy had been shot, but that was the first bite they had been given since breakfast early that morning.

The two ballistics officers met with Shelly on their arrival, and were joined soon after by Assistant Commissioner Hickey. The senior officers who had been in command of the scene told Quinn and Ennis that when Carthy emerged from the house, he had started walking towards Abbeylara; that he was called upon to stop, but failed to do so, and he was then shot by the ERU. At this point, the ballistics officers were not made aware that there had been other local armed gardaí at the scene in close proximity to Carthy.

Quinn and Ennis went to carry out the essential ballistics duties that had to be completed as soon as possible. Passing through the garda tapes, they began their work. The most important task was first to photograph and outline Carthy's body, so that it could be moved away from the scene for formal identification and a postmortem at Mullingar General Hospital. Quinn set to work.

'On the opposite side of the road to the Carthy house and at a point near the end of the garden wall, beside the Burke property, a crime scene tent had been erected. Near the garden wall a plastic sheet covered some object on the road. At a point opposite the Carthy entrance on the road, two pieces of red plastic covered other objects. Having had this scene photographed, I entered the crime scene tent and saw a body covered with a red blanket. I removed this blanket for photographic purposes.

'The body was that of a male, lying on his back with the feet on the road and the head on the road edge nearest the ditch. The body was dressed in a jacket, tee-shirt, vest, jeans, underpants, socks and shoes. The belt and fly of the jeans were open and the vest and tee-shirt pushed up, revealing a bare mid-area.

'The left arm was outstretched from the body at an angle of approximately 30 degrees and the right hand was resting on the right hip area. The legs were outstretched and the heels were six inches apart. Eight feet away from the right hand side of the body lay an empty leather shotgun cartridge belt. I then marked out the outline of the body with crayon together with the shotgun cartridge belt.'

Shortly after ten o'clock that night, a hearse appeared over the brow of the hill up from the Carthy house. It was time for the body to be moved. Quinn and a number of other officers helped to lift the body carefully from its position on the road into a coffin, and it was decided that Sergeant Leydon would travel with the corpse to Mullingar General Hospital.

☊   ☊   ☊

In the coming days, Quinn and Ennis, along with an experienced team, would carefully tread every inch of the road to gather the scientific evidence that would be required by the investigations that were in the pipeline. They would also search through the Carthy cottage. Inside, they found the results of Carthy's destructive efforts in his last hours. There was broken furniture everywhere. The television had been knocked off its stand. Bits of the phone he had shot off the wall lay on the ground.

The ballistics officers searched through the cupboards and wardrobes in the house, and found seven remaining live cartridges. On closer inspection, however, it was found that these cartridges were not in good condition. It seemed that Carthy had exhausted his supply of good rounds in the shots he had fired from the kitchen. The only remaining cartridges he had were the two that were in the gun when he emerged, one of which ended up in the hedge opposite the house, the other of which was still in the barrel of his gun when he was shot dead.

☊   ☊   ☊

The gathering of details and evidence in the aftermath of the shooting at Abbeylara brought with it its own problems and its own areas of controversy. What should have been a basic preservation of the scene was questioned and probed because the command post jeep had been moved. But the issue that prompted most questions was the manner in which the garda weapons were collected and inspected after the shooting.

Sergeant Sean Leydon was the officer tasked with collecting the arms. He claimed that the only instruction he received on the guns that were to be collected was from Shelly and came just before he got into the hearse to travel to Mullingar that evening. Leydon claims that the order he got from Shelly was to collect the ERU arms and ammunition, and he obeyed this order. After he left the hospital, he travelled to Mullingar station where the ERU had gathered following their debriefing at Granard. He asked the officers to hand over their weapons. None of the ERU men objected to the procedure, fully aware that the garda code states that any weapon discharged must be handed in for examination. As the frontline men at the incident, they had all been capable of firing, and the accepted account of the shooting, which was that just Jackson and McCabe had discharged two shots each, had to be verified. Leydon collected thirteen weapons in all.

But those thirteen guns were not the only weapons at the scene that evening, and the ERU were not the only armed men waiting for John Carthy to emerge. There were others, like Aidan Foley and Eugene Boland, who had been preparing to fire. Theoretically, any of the local officers could have fired their guns and said nothing about it. In the confusion that came after the event, the local men were all presumed not to have been involved in the shooting, but later investigations would bring this into question. Without examination of their weapons, there was no evidence to discount the possibility that other officers could also have fired at John Carthy.

Leydon's account of what he was instructed to collect and by whom differs from that of Sergeant Quinn. As the ballistics officer who would be responsible for the actual examination of weapons, Quinn claims that on his arrival at the scene that Thursday evening, he instructed Leydon to 'acquire for me all garda firearms which had been at the scene since the incident commenced'. He said that it was only on the following Sunday night that he told Leydon he would be examining only ERU weapons because the examination of the scene and the postmortem had tallied with the account of the shooting. Leydon denies this.

Shelly has said there was never any talk of bringing in anything other than the ERU weapons for examination, and he didn't even seem to think there should be any question of collecting the local arms. He was there, he heard the shots, he was running towards Carthy's body in a matter of seconds after he fell. There was no question about what had happened. He spoke to all the officers present about what they had seen and heard and what they had done, and in the honest raw emotion of those upsetting moments after the shooting, he believed they all told the absolute truth. Two officers had fired four bullets in all.

But the conflicting accounts of who instructed whom to collect which weapons would come to be a significant element years later when Justice Robert Barr came to examine what he called 'the disaster at Abbeylara'. The possibility that a local armed garda might have fired his gun and not declared it was revisited on numerous occasions, casting suspicion on those members and creating concern for the force as a whole.

18.

The task of identifying John Carthy's body fell to his cousin, Tom Walsh. Shortly after midnight in the early hours of Good Friday he was escorted to Mullingar General Hospital morgue. John's face was undamaged, peaceful, despite the trauma that had been suffered by the rest of his body. Tom confirmed to gardaí that it was Johnny, and left quickly.

The State Pathologist, Professor John Harbison, had arrived at the hospital, and he ordered that x-rays be taken of Carthy's body to detect if the bullets that had hit him had caused any fractures to any bones. He spoke to some members of the gardaí, and at some point was told that Carthy had been hit by four bullets and had died almost instantly.

The pathologist began his examination in the usual way, by trying first to understand how Carthy was in life. It was a simple task, requiring nothing but a glance at the clothing, a touch of the skin and an examination of the teeth to piece together the practices of a lifetime. Looking at Carthy that evening, Professor Harbison found a body that had been neglected in its short life. The skin was yellowed from smoking, and the teeth had not been adequately cared for.

Professor Harbison carefully removed Carthy's clothing and laid the jeans, the football shirt, the padded jacket and the underwear aside. All the items were covered in blood from the injuries Carthy had sustained, and more importantly in terms of the pathologist's examination, they were bored by holes from the bullets that hit Carthy's body. A brief inspection of the clothes and a glance at the body was enough for the pathologist to confirm in his own mind that there were four definite gunshot wounds: two on the leg, one that had been aimed at the lower back and a fourth further up the spine.

When it comes to bullets and the harm they inflict, pathologists talk in terms of entry and exit wounds. Their job, in its most basic terms, is to find where a bullet first pierces the body, follow its path and find the damage done in its wake. Harbison set about tracking each of the bullets and examining the body for other marks and injuries. He spoke into a dictaphone as he worked, outlining his findings so that he could put it all down on paper at a later stage.

The least damaging of the wounds on Carthy's body were the two entry and exit wounds on his left thigh, caused by the first bullets fired by Jackson. Both bullets had skimmed past Carthy's thighbone, leaving it intact with no sign of a fracture. Examining the depth and severity of the wounds, Harbison felt it would have been physically possible, if extremely painful, for Carthy to continue walking after being struck by these two bullets that came from Jackson's Sig Sauer pistol.

Moving up the body, Harbison turned his attention to the entry wound in Carthy's lower back, and the corresponding mark where the third bullet had exited. This wound was far more serious than the first two, and the path the bullet took was destructive in the extreme. Tracking its route, Harbison could see that the bullet went through Carthy's sacrum, it penetrated his bladder, and exited through the area around his penis and scrotum.

The pain from those injuries would have been excruciating, but Harbison could not say that the third bullet would have prevented Carthy from walking. People who are in a severe state of shock can sometimes be immune to pain. They can walk into casualty departments on two broken legs after an accident, not feeling the agony of their injuries due to the shock that can overpower a person after a traumatic experience. A person like Carthy, in a severe state of mania, could have had a similar immunity to pain.

Harbison examined the spinal cord around the area where the third bullet had passed through Carthy's body. It was intact, meaning that Carthy's lower limbs would still have been capable of movement in spite of such serious injuries – a fact that would grant weight to the garda claim that he was still walking up to the time the fourth bullet hit.

But the wounds from the fourth bullet were different, and their location bothered the pathologist. Following the track of this fatal shot, Professor Harbison looked at it again and again, and always came to the same conclusion: that John Carthy had either been falling forward or stooping when he was shot for the final time.

The path of the fourth bullet was different to all the rest, in that its journey through Carthy's body was vertical rather than horizontal. The first three bullets had all been concentrated on Carthy's lower body. They had all exited at a spot that was almost in direct line with their entry points. This was not the case with the fatal wound. The final bullet, fired by Detective Garda Aidan McCabe, entered Carthy's body at a spot nine inches above the entry point of the third bullet. It travelled upwards and towards the left of Carthy's body until it exited in the area around Carthy's left nipple. It punctured Carthy's stomach, hit off his left kidney, travelled through his diaphragm and shot through the left ventricle of his heart.

Measuring the distances, Harbison found that the exit point of the fatal bullet was about nine and a half inches above the entry wound. This, he felt could only have been possible if Carthy was bending or falling forward at the time he was struck by the last garda shot. He summed it up in his notes after the postmortem was completed.

'Certainly the trajectory of the bullet deriving from wound number one in his back was in such an upward trajectory, unlike all the others, that he must have been falling forward or stooping low to avoid being hit by more shots,' he wrote.

A second opinion was needed. If Dr Harbison was correct in his analysis of the final bullet, it effectively inferred that there was no justification for firing a fourth and fatal shot at Carthy. The details of the postmortem were shared with a British Professor of Forensic Pathology, Christopher Milroy, who was asked to provide his opinion on the track of the fourth bullet. His answer was in agreement with the conclusion of Dr Harbison, stating as he did that Carthy's body must have been angled forward when he was shot for the last time.

The finding brought added pressure on the gardaí, who were already under public scrutiny for their handling of the episode. But members of the force provided their own explanations for the trajectory of the fatal bullet. A number of those who were on the road when Carthy emerged described him walking in a stooped position, leaning forward slightly as if to get a good grip on the gun. The gardaí also measured the gradient in the slight hill outside Carthy's house, which would have put the ERU at a lower position than Carthy when he was shot for the last time.

Shelly's description of the way Carthy walked was that of somebody who was bent forward in the usual manner when walking up an incline, and this was his explanation for the trajectory of the final shot.

'There was a rise in the road and if you can envisage somebody who is walking against a hill or walking forward a little bit – it wasn't that he was stooped down or anything like that, but that he was stooped and leaning forward in his gait when he walked,' he said.

Gardaí also pointed out that while McCabe didn't change his position between firing the third and fourth shots, he did aim his gun higher for the fatal shot, firing upwards, and they say this could also explain the path of the bullet up through Carthy's body.

There is also the evidence – which could not be disputed by the pathologists – that no mark was found on Carthy's face. If he had been falling forward when the final bullet was discharged, why was it that he ended up lying on his back on the Abbeylara Road? Those officers who had witnessed his death could vividly recall the moment when Carthy registered that death was upon him, the way he almost paused on the road, spun around and collapsed on to his back. That image was etched in their minds, and it was a sequence of events that haunted them.

The pathologists were united in their view that Carthy was leaning forward. They applied the various circumstances of the shooting to the wounds, but still believed that the trajectory of the bullet would have to infer that Carthy's body was leaning forward when he was struck for the last time.

This was not to say, however, that they were accusing the gardaí of not telling the truth. Professor Milroy accepted that those officers, and particularly Detective Garda McCabe, could well have believed that Carthy was still walking up to the time he felt the deadly force of the fourth bullet. The problem was that because the two bullets had been fired in such quick succession, there was very little time for the gardaí to detect the change in Carthy's body position.

All of the shots that were fired at Carthy that evening came within seconds of each other. Garda senses had been heightened following twenty-five hours of watching and waiting, and their reactions were rapid. Taking this into account, Professor Milroy contended that had there been a few more seconds left between the third and fourth shots, Carthy would have fallen to the ground from the pain of the third bullet that had left his lower organs in pieces. Had that been allowed to happen, a fourth and fatal shot would have been unnecessary.

♎   ♎   ♎

Professor Harbison's postmortem on the body also caused controversy for the gardaí on another key issue, bringing the focus back to why all of the weapons at the scene were not examined. He found an inexplicable wound on Carthy's right rear calf, which raised the possibility that a local armed officer had fired a fifth bullet at Carthy, but had never declared it.

For a long time, the inexplicable wound remained a minor point in Harbison's notes as nothing more than an aside to the accepted version of events. The pathologist didn't dwell on it. He knew which shot had killed Carthy and he knew his own professional opinion on the justification for that fatal bullet. A graze on Carthy's calf was almost irrelevant in the grand scheme of things.

But years down the line, that mystery wound would be headline news, casting suspicion on the local men who had been at Abbeylara, and causing serious insult to the most senior quarters of the gardaí.

♎ ♎ ♎

In the days after the shooting, the garda cordon remained in place, making the cottage off-bounds for Rose and Marie and their relatives and friends. The gaudy garda tapes fluttered in the April winds. The funeral was arranged for the Easter weekend. The family went through the motions, accepting the condolences and barely taking heed of the TDs and top gardaí who attended the removal and the burial. The shooting had become a political issue, and the funeral was a chance for the politicians to show solidarity with the Carthy family.

Tom Walsh remained at home for a time after the funerals to look after his mother, his aunt and his cousin. He often walked down as far as the cordon to look at the cottage again, to count the panes of glass that had been broken out by Johnny and to convince himself that it had really happened. Marie and Rose were still staying with relatives, and that would be the case even after the gardaí had taken down their yellow tapes and opened it up to them again. They were not ready to visit John's final hours.

In the absence of Rose and Marie, Tom Walsh and his family and neighbours took it upon themselves to keep an eye on the cottage and to make sure nobody was interfering with it. They became accustomed to hearing cars slow down as they passed up the road, accepting that people were curious and that some would come from miles around to have a look at the site of the stand-off.

But on Easter Monday, Ann Walsh noticed a different type of vehicle standing on the road outside the Carthy site. It was an unmarked garda car. She phoned her brother, Tom and told him to go down to the cottage and find out what was going on. Approaching the house, Walsh saw a few familiar faces. The ERU men had come back to the scene.

Russell, Jackson and their boss Superintendent Patrick Hogan had travelled from Dublin back to Abbeylara. Hogan had not been at the scene at all for the duration of the operation, and he thought it would be necessary for him to get an idea of what exactly had happened. As the two main ERU men at the incident, he had asked Russell and Jackson to accompany him on the trip.

Russell drove the car, and when they arrived at the Carthy house, he chose to remain in the vehicle while Jackson and Hogan got out and had a walk around. He saw Tom Walsh approach the men, and while Hogan skirted the boundary of the property, Walsh and Jackson appeared to have a brief conversation.

The recollection of what was said in this exchange between Carthy's cousin and the man who had shot him differs entirely between the two. Jackson claimed afterwards that Walsh was perfectly friendly, that he accepted his condolences, and had said he felt the gardaí had 'done all they could'. Walsh, on the other hand, tells a different story. He said he was angry to find the gardaí there, 'wandering around'. The way he remembers it, there weren't any friendly exchanges. He went up to them, and demanded they explain what had gone wrong. He claims Jackson replied, 'Between you and me, we fucked it up'. Walsh said it looked to him like Jackson hadn't slept in days.

The ERU men involved were asked repeatedly why they had decided to return to the scene that day and why it never occurred to them that it might cause further upset to the Carthy family. They claimed it was for therapeutic reasons, to face their demons in a sense and try and come to terms with what had happened. It was an unofficial visit, they said, a mutual decision between a few of them to go back and deal with it. The visit was kept quiet, and even the senior officer in charge of the ERU admitted he never heard anything of the visit until years later.

Prior to giving evidence at the Tribunal, Tom Walsh did not reveal the full details of what he claimed was said between himself and Jackson, leading gardaí to question the veracity of what he was suggesting. Walsh is adamant that the only reason he didn't reveal what Jackson said to him at the time was because Jackson was one of the gardaí who he felt had done their best at the scene. The family knew Jackson had only fired at John's leg, and that put him marginally ahead of the others. He said Jackson had said those things to him in a 'man to man' fashion, and he did not like betraying that.

♎ ♎ ♎

Had the ERU officers postponed their visit for a few weeks, they would have found an entirely different scene in Abbeylara. By the middle of May, the scene of the incident had undergone a transformation; in spite of everything that had just happened – or maybe it was because of everything that had just happened – Longford County Council had gone ahead with the planned demolition of the old Carthy cottage. By 11 May a local builder had finished the job. The cottage was levelled to the ground.

After all that had happened the Carthys felt nothing as the old home was knocked to rubble. What was it to them now only the scene of John's last battle, a battle he had lost? The last footsteps that had tread through it were those of the forensics people who had ripped it apart in their search for clues. The last memories made there were horrible ones, and they ended in death. They thought again of some of John's last words to Rose that day:

'Nobody is going to put me out of my house.'

Both the house and John were gone now.

19.

'On the subject of the loss of civilian life at the hands of the armed forces of the State, the law has to be very exact, and justice very exacting.'

(Mr Justice Hanna in Lynch V Fitzgerald & Others, 1938)

Weeks passed. Months passed. Years passed. Questions remained and accusations were frequent. The calls for an independent inquiry into the shooting came with increasing force and regularity from the family and those they had employed to help them in their quest. John was dead, and nobody had really explained to them why.

The newspapers occasionally carried reports that added weight to the call for an inquiry. Stories appeared, alleging that members of the ERU had failed the firearms module of their training. These stories were untrue but they created in the public mindset a suggestion that it was a lack of training on the part of the gardaí rather than the behaviour of John Carthy that had been the main cause of the tragedy.

There were other occasions when unfavourable publicity attached to the ERU, the worst of these being a bank raid in Abbeyleix in 2001. In this case, the ERU had received a tip-off about the planned raid, and were standing by waiting to foil the attempt. But the operation went badly wrong. Shots were fired; one officer was wounded and a member of the ERU ended up accidentally killing Detective Sergeant John Eiffe, another officer at the scene.

Most recently, the ERU were in the news for their handling of an attempted post office robbery in Lusk, Co Dublin in May 2005. Armed officers shot dead two raiders, and they came in for criticism when it emerged that while one of the robbers was armed, the other was not carrying a weapon.

The inquest into the shooting of John Carthy yielded a largely unsatisfactory result for the family. It took place over the course of four days in the Longford County Buildings and Rose, Marie, Tom Walsh and various members of the extended family attended in the hope that this would be the forum where answers would be provided. But while Professor Harbison took the stand and expressed his view that John Carthy 'must have been falling forward or stooping low to avoid more shots' when he was hit by the fourth bullet, the twelve-member inquest jury chose to decline their right to return an open verdict or to provide any recommendations that might prevent such a tragedy from ever occurring again. The jury simply returned the obvious verdict that John Carthy had died from gunshot wounds, and they offered their sympathies to the Carthy family. For the family, sympathy was not enough.

Superintendent Adrian Culligan had completed his investigation into the shooting just two months after the siege, but his findings were also something of a disappointment to the family. An in-house garda probe was seen by the family as an inappropriate means of uncovering the truth of what had happened at Abbeylara, and again the need for an independent inquiry became evident.

Marie became the unofficial spokesperson for the family,

making herself available for meetings with politicians and interviews with local and national journalists.

An introvert by nature, it took her some time to get used to the cameras and the questions, but she was well aware that without regular publicity, the death of her brother could easily be shifted off the agenda. The family had arranged their own legal representatives to help them campaign for a proper investigation into the shooting.

The government was aware of the increasing pressure for an independent inquiry into the shooting and, as a type of compromise, they established an Oireachtas sub-committee to carry out an investigation. Neither the representatives of the Carthy family nor the gardaí were pleased with the planned investigation by the Joint Oireachtas Committee on Justice, Equality, Defence and Women's Rights. All sides felt the committee was limited in what it could do and was too constrained by unreasonable limits. They were given only nine days of hearings to get through all the evidence and they were only allowed to call sixty witnesses. The committee hearing was to take place in April 2001, a year on from the incident, but the lack of faith in its ability to uncover what happened at Abbeylara meant it never really got off the ground. There was an intervention by the legal representative of the gardaí, John Rogers SC. He was unhappy with the hearing from the beginning, feeling that a tribunal with full judicial status was the fairest way by which the incident could be examined. This view was shared by the representative for the Carthy family, Michael O'Higgins, SC, and when the issue was brought before the highest courts in the land, it was ruled that the Oireachtas sub-committee was unconstitutional.

On 17 and 18 April 2002, a motion was proposed and passed

in Dáil Éireann and seconded in Seanad Éireann that a tribunal of inquiry should be established to inquire into the facts and circumstances surrounding the fatal shooting of John Carthy at Abbeylara. As is the common practice, the government looked to a group of recently retired judges to find a suitable candidate who would become the sole member of the inquiry, and the man they chose was retired High Court judge Justice Robert Barr.

Having only retired in June 2002, Justice Barr hardly had time to get on the retirement trail before being called back for the Abbeylara inquiry. The majority of his experience had been at the Special Criminal Court, where he presided over some of the landmark trials of the past two decades. He was one of the key members of the judiciary faced with trying those accused of some form of involvement in the Omagh bombing and the murder of Veronica Guerin.

At various points during his career on the bench, Justice Barr was faced with situations that brought the integrity of the gardaí into question, and on more than one occasion he threw out a case on the basis of falsified evidence by members of the force. Coming to the Abbeylara inquiry, he seemed to regard his forthcoming task as a huge challenge, and he approached the whole process with an enthusiasm that belied his age. When the first public hearing began on 31 March 2003 he was seventy-three years old.

Ω   Ω   Ω

In the first days of the Barr Tribunal, the strong character of Justice Barr became quickly apparent. He spoke without haste and in a genial and welcoming manner. The overriding feeling he gave on the first day of the Tribunal was that it would not be a lengthy process and should be wrapped up within a few short months. Unlike the other inquiries which were rife with complexities and which concerned events over a number of years, the Barr Tribunal would be dealing with twenty-four hours in the life of a man who had only lived twenty-seven years. Justice Barr himself, in a letter to the Clerk of the Dáil in May 2003, predicted that the proceedings would run off without difficulty and he would have completed his report within the year.

'I hope that the tribunal will complete its work and that I shall be in a position to furnish my report to the Oireachtas in the early months of 2004,' he wrote.

The optimism on the time frame proved to be way off the mark. After eighteen months and a cost of 18m, the whole process finally worked itself through, and in the end, Justice Barr was left with a mountain of evidence gathered from witnesses who came from all corners of the world. Twenty thousand pages of typed transcripts were the result of two hundred and eight days of questions and answers. One hundred and sixty-four witnesses were sworn in at the inquiry, and gave their account of John Carthy, his last hours, his medical history and their opinion of what had unfolded at Abbeylara.

Ω   Ω   Ω

Once the first days of the inquiry had come and gone, the media interest in the country's latest tribunal largely died down and the attendance at each day's hearings was streamlined to include only those who had to be there. Beyond the benches that held Justice Barr and the legal people, the public area to the rear of the chamber was usually dotted with faces that quickly became familiar. The main gardaí involved in the incident were there almost every day. Jackson, Russell, Shelly and their colleagues from Abbeylara lined out to hear almost all of the evidence, and to await their turn in the stand. They sat together. They had lunch together. They left together.

Occasionally, a new face would appear in the public seats. Members of support groups for people suffering from depression occasionally dropped by to keep up with what was going on and to show solidarity with the Carthy family. Interested members of the public would also call in from time to time, to see where their taxes were going and to check that the inquiry was running as it should. There is a small group of people who are part of a weekly tribunal circuit; once a week they pop into any ongoing tribunals in the capital, they take notes, they chat to interested parties, exercising their right to watch a public process in operation.

The hearings at the inquiry generally took the same route. Once a witness took the stand, questioning would begin with a counsel for the tribunal going through their particular involvement with the incident or their knowledge of John Carthy. That would take some time, and then the other legal teams would have their chance to pose questions before the witness would be relieved. Justice Barr himself would also intervene with queries if he was unclear on something or if he felt a witness was trying to avoid giving a concise answer.

The first modules of the inquiry dealt with the actual incident itself, how it started, who was there, and what went on. Intertwined with these first weeks of evidence, there came the first details about the person John Carthy actually was. After years of being known only as the manic-depressive who was shot dead at Abbeylara, for the first time the public heard details of his ordinary life. The letters to Kathleen were read out, and they were devoured by the media. His day-to-day living was dissected and again there came a realisation that Carthy was a normal young man.

Locals from Abbeylara were summoned to the inquiry to give their account of John Carthy and their last conversations with him. They were uncomfortable and nervous in the stand, afraid to say the wrong thing. Here they were, up in Dublin, in the dock, swearing to tell the truth, the whole truth and nothing but the truth. They were all there: Mary McDowell, the woman who gave the vox pop interview, Tom Walsh, Pepper, Dr Patrick Cullen, Kevin Ireland and many more.

Rose Carthy was called as a witness in the tribunal's early weeks, and her attendance and evidence was a reminder of the sad reality behind all the expense and hype of the tribunal. She was a humble figure, hunched in the stand. Marie perched on the step of the witness box to give her mother some encouragement, while barristers, journalists and gardaí alike had to strain to hear her soft-spoken and brief answers to the sensitive questions posed. She cried a lot, especially when she was asked about her decision that evening to phone the gardaí. The answer, when it came was poignant,

'I wanted them to help him, not to kill him,' she said.

On that note, she was let go, and despite the fact that the inquiry would go on for several more months, Rose left the chamber that evening and she never came back.

Marie would travel up to Dublin and attend the tribunal when she had a day off work, and sometimes when certain witnesses were in the box she would make it her business to be there.

When her opportunity to take the stand came along, she was

more than ready for it, and she had a lot to say. Having lived with what happened for more than three years, her initial angry and emotional thoughts had been developed into assertive criticisms. Her demeanour in the box was never challenged, in spite of forthright questioning by Senior Counsel for the gardaí, John Rogers.

'I had assumed the guards were properly trained, but if they had been properly trained, if they had done their job properly, my brother would be alive today,' she said.

Marie was still preoccupied with the fact that she was not given the chance to speak with her brother during the stand-off. At the inquiry, she shrugged off the suggestion that she had been drunk, suggesting that this was a story created by the gardaí in the aftermath to justify their reluctance to allow her to the negotiation point. She testified that none of the gardaí she spoke to that night said anything to her about being drunk, and said again that the only alcohol she had that night was one hot whisky when she got to Devine's. She also scorned the suggestion that it wasn't safe for her to go down to the wall in front of her house, referring to the various third party civilians that had been allowed down to that point.

'If it was safe for Martin Shelly, if it was safe for unarmed gardaí, surely it was safe for his sister to be there: a member of his family and the closest person to him. The gardaí had two hours to arrange it, they knew I was coming from Galway, they brought me there for nothing. What was the point of bringing me there and not letting me talk to him? They had no notion of ever letting me talk to him, that's obvious.'

The gardaí were poker-faced listening to these accusations. They sat at the back of the room, listening but never reacting to what was said by even the most bitter of witnesses. They would have their chance to answer their critics.

When their time did come, it was a marathon. Jackson and Shelly spent weeks in the stand, going over the tiniest detail again and again. The legal representatives of the Carthy family grilled them and accused them. Jackson in particular was dealt several verbal blows, most of them claiming that he was an inexperienced negotiator who was so pedantic in his methods that he could not even agree to grant John Carthy a packet of cigarettes. Counsel for the family, Michael O'Higgins, would regularly stand just two feet away from where Jackson sat in the witness box. He would fold his arms, look Jackson straight in the eye and tell him he had been an 'inflexible' and 'rigid' negotiator, that some of his tactics had aggravated the situation and that it was only because of tiredness and lack of foresight on his part and on the part of his ERU colleagues that Carthy had been shot.

Jackson never once rose to the accusations, again finding and keeping the cool demeanour that had seen him through the hours at Abbeylara. His every answer was well thought-out. The following is an example of an exchange that was typical of the encounter between O'Higgins and Jackson, with the barrister laying down the accusations, and the latter unfazed by them.

O'Higgins: 'John Carthy was shot because in twenty-five seconds of the ERU being aware that he was out of the house, he was walking towards an area where there were unarmed people, he had his back to you and you shot him because you didn't have any other ideas of what to do. You panicked.'

Jackson: 'I don't accept that. I think the facts display otherwise in relation to our reactions to Mr Carthy when he emerged. We attempted to give John a real opportunity to lay the weapon down. It was only when the immediate threat arose, the threat that existed, a live threat, that action had to be taken, so they're the circumstances under which, unfortunately, Mr Carthy was fatally wounded.'

On another key occasion O'Higgins asked Jackson a simple question – if he had to do it all again, would he do anything differently. Jackson said he had never thought about it, a reply that O'Higgins found very hard to believe.

Jackson: 'That's a question I have not contemplated to any huge degree. I find it impossible to answer. I don't think I would do myself justice or your good self justice or the tribunal justice without putting long hard thought into it.'

At one stage in the proceedings Justice Barr demanded that the Abbeylara negotiator just give 'yes' or 'no' answers.

But these were altercations that arose during Jackson's lengthy period in the stand. He spent days answering questions, and never once faltered in his version of events. He was by far the most impressive of the garda witnesses at the tribunal.

His colleagues too were well-prepared to deal with the onslaught of criticism when they took the stand. They all spoke in technical mode, dotting their testimonies with phrases like 'moving containment' and generally dealing with the shooting on a detached level. The lack of personal input in the monologues again left a feeling that the gardaí had reached the point where they could speak about what happened as though they were describing a film they had once seen. They were composed and clear about everything they said.

When Garda McCabe was sworn in, he was ready for the question that would be put to him again and again. As the officer who had actually killed Carthy, his time on the stand was spent explaining his reasons for discharging the fatal shot.

Professor Harbison's findings on the final bullet were read to him repeatedly, and he was asked to explain himself. In response, McCabe kept it simple and said he could only tell the tribunal what he saw that day. He persisted in keeping his evidence to his belief that Carthy was still walking and was moving closer to the garda jeep when he shot him for the last time.

'I believed John Carthy was about to pull the trigger and possibly kill or injure some of those people [at the jeep]. I decided that in order to achieve my legal objective of saving the lives of those people, I prepared myself to discharge a shot from my firearm as I believed that all other means of stopping John Carthy from killing those people had been exhausted,' he said.

Justice Barr himself often questioned the gardaí – a fact that would eventually lead to severe criticism from counsels for the force. With McCabe, he brought the issue down to its core.

Barr: 'But was it your intention to kill him in order to prevent him killing others?'

McCabe: 'No, Mr Chairman, definitely not.'

20.

'Commissioner to Chief Superintendent, Inspector,
Sergeants and Gardaí, there was such a large deployment
of human intelligence, experience and training and for all
that they still succeeded in doing one thing well, and that
was killing John Carthy.'

(Patrick Gageby, SC for the Carthy family).

The early weeks of the inquiry set the precedent for how Justice Barr was going to handle the proceedings. His was a hands-on approach. He would ask for clarification on the issues he didn't understand. He would request that witnesses expand on their evidence and at times he expressed his dissatisfaction with the answers that were being provided, particularly by garda witnesses. This practice was not received well by the gardaí or their legal representatives, and it wasn't long before objections were being made against the chairman's forthright method of questioning. As early as Day 40 of the inquiry, the clashes began, with the chairman being accused of having already come to his own conclusions on the death of John Carthy.

One particularly heated exchange occurred as Superintendent Joe Shelly, the scene commander at Abbeylara, was giving evidence. Shelly was being questioned as to why it took the gardaí so long to locate Marie Carthy and Pepper on the first night of the siege. He said that they had been located as soon as possible, a suggestion which roused Barr to interject and query how the scene commander could make such a claim.

Barr: 'Two hours is not as soon as you could. Are you standing over that, Superintendent? There is no harm in admitting garda fault sometimes.'

Shelly tried to defend himself, refusing to admit the delay had been a problem.

Barr: 'Do garda officers ever admit fault, ever, ever, ever?'

Shelly continued to attempt some explanation.

Barr: 'Alright, I know gardaí never admit fault. Let's move on.'

In the course of this tense exchange, Justice Barr banged his fist off the bench, and his tone and actions drew objections from the legal counsels for the gardaí. Diarmuid McGuinness, Senior Counsel for the Garda Commissioner, accused the chairman of bullying Superintendent Shelly, and said this was not helpful to the work of the inquiry.

McGuinness: 'It won't assist the fact-finding process if you react in the way you reacted with the apparent banging of the desk and the slightly heated temperature.'

Barr: 'I am entitled to say there was fault there. The evidence is irritating in the extreme, so don't be surprised that I reacted in the way I did.'

Ω Ω Ω

But Barr's most heated exchanges occurred when he locked horns with the Senior Counsel for the ERU, John Rogers, renowned as one of the top barristers in the Irish legal practice. His commanding physical presence was much in evidence on the frequent occasions when he rose to challenge Barr.

Rogers didn't like the methods that were being employed by Barr. He claimed that his clients were beginning to feel as though they were being threatened and bullied by the chairman. Because of this, he had to make a stand. Rogers said the conduct of the chairman was 'quite unbecoming'of a member of the judiciary, and he accused Barr of treating him with 'disdain and contempt'. He also told the chairman there was a growing 'perception that you tend to bully witnesses.'

Barr had little patience for such accusations. He would shake his pen at Rogers and tell him to sit down and stop wasting his time 'flogging a dead horse' on issues that arose again and again. There was a constant unease between the two men, and every time a garda took the stand, everyone anticipated the eruption of another argument between chairman and counsel.

The tension between Rogers and Barr reached its peak during the evidence of Professor John Harbison. The pathologist had already detailed his belief that Carthy was falling forward or stooping when hit by the fourth bullet, and while many expected that to be the most controversial element of his evidence, his testimony took an unexpected turn. Almost in passing, Professor Harbison referred to the wound he had found on Carthy's calf at the postmortem. It was a minor wound and a minor issue that had been buried in his notes for the past four years, and he probably didn't actually intend to open a can of worms with his musing on this wound, but it was an issue that was taken up by the chairman and dominated proceedings at the inquiry for some time.

Justice Barr had questioned various officers again and again as to why the arms of the local gardaí had not been collected for examination after the shooting. He did not understand why this hadn't happened; why the local officers were not cleared from any suspicion through a simple checking of their weapons. When Harbison brought this inexplicable wound to the attention of the inquiry, it was enough to re-ignite the issue. Barr suggested that, in theory, it would have been simple for a local garda to fire a shot, slip the spent cartridge from their weapon into their pocket and say nothing about it.

Top gardaí were utterly appalled at the suggestion. They pointed to the garda code, the binding oath taken at Templemore always to hand in a weapon that has been fired. Senior garda after senior garda took the stand and refuted the possibility of any officer doing such a thing. But such arguments carried little weight in a time when the gardaí were the subject of two Tribunals and 'Prime Time' specials were questioning the honesty of the force. There was no forensic proof to say the local gardaí were innocent of such a deed, and Barr was not going to be easily dissuaded from pursuing the possibility.

John Rogers repeatedly objected to the suggestion, and the matter of a possible undeclared fifth bullet became the overriding issue at the inquiry for weeks. After months of scant media coverage, the possibility that a local officer at Abbeylara had fired a fifth bullet at Carthy, but kept quiet about it, brought the tribunal back into the headlines. But more than the actual suggestion itself, it was the sparring between Barr and Rogers that was really grabbing the interest of journalists. The tension that had been building between the two men in the first months of the inquiry looked as though it were about to come to a head.

Rogers: 'I object to you putting this proposition. It is an outrageous comment and conjectural to suggest a fifth shot was fired.'

Barr: 'It could be that they [the local officers] were not necessarily telling the truth. It is up to me to find out. This is an investigation conducted by me, it is not a trial. It may be that someone fired another shot.'

Rogers told the chairman that he should leave the issue to the senior counsels, and allow them to deal with it. The advice was not appreciated.

Barr: 'I don't need you to give me advice. You are being positively insulting. Sit down, like a good chap.'

The tribunal was nearing the eve of its Christmas break in 2003 when the eruption finally came, and to the shock of all present, John Rogers made the decision to walk away. The exchanges between himself and the chairman had reached a new level of resentment and bitterness, and in those circumstances, the senior counsel walked out of the inquiry, throwing the entire tribunal into disarray and confusion.

Speculation was rife. Was he gone for good? How could the tribunal move forward if the gardaí were without their main legal contender? There was even talk of Rogers going to the High Court in an attempt to have the tribunal halted because of the apparent problems his clients had with Justice Barr.

The inquiry adjourned early for Christmas in the hope that when it returned, tensions between Rogers and Barr would have eased. In the event, the chairman did the necessary. He brought Harbison back after the Christmas break, and they explored other possible causes of the controversial wound. Harbison agreed that the wound on Carthy's calf could have been a ricochet wound or a re-entry scar from one of the other four bullets that grazed his calf after it emerged from his body.

Barr issued a ruling saying that he no longer suspected foul play on the part of the local gardaí. Rogers then returned to his corner of the chamber, and despite a few snipes here and there, the chairman and the senior counsel kept their thoughts and their disagreements to themselves.

21.

'I don't believe the operation struggled. I believe that overall the operation went quite well.'

(Superintendent Joe Shelly, scene commander at Abbeylara)

Several months of the inquiry were taken up with the experts' module, a process that saw police experts from around the world and psychiatric experts from around the country being brought to the Tribunal at great expense. They came from Britain, New Zealand and America, and the module took several weeks to complete. This was one of the more inefficient elements of the proceedings. One expert would disagree with what another had said; they all had their own views on John Carthy and the situation that had evolved at Abbeylara. Even the paper of record, the *Irish Times*, stopped covering the inquiry during those monotonous months.

There was one highlight of the experts' module, however, and that came in the form of former FBI negotiator, Frederick J Lanceley. Mr Lanceley is what many would describe as 'a character', and his appearance on the stand granted the tedium of those weeks some comic relief. Flamboyant and dramatic, he jetted in from the United States to give his opinion on the whole affair, and through a combination of huge gestures, graphs and heartfelt pleas he left an indelible impression.

His career with the FBI had been fraught with controversy and marked by some of the most controversial siege situations seen in the US over the past twenty years. In April 1993, Lanceley was the chief negotiator at the now notorious fifty-one day siege in Waco, Texas, involving David Koresh and the Branch Davidian cult. Less than eight months earlier, in August 1992, he was also the chief negotiator outside the house of Randy Weaver, a former Green Beret, at Ruby Ridge, Idaho, a siege that developed following Weaver's refusal to attend a court hearing on gun charges brought against him. Armed US marshals were sent to Weaver's house. The stand-off spiralled into chaos with the shooting dead of Weaver's wife, Vicki, who was holding their ten-month old daughter Elishiba in her arms at the time. The siege ended after ten days when Weaver gave himself up.

Lanceley had much experience in negotiating, had an immense knowledge of hostage and crisis situations, and was the author of a book entitled *On-Scene Guide for Crisis Negotiators*, but the fact that he was involved in both Waco and Ruby Ridge held his track record up to scrutiny. Newspapers that had little interest in the Barr Tribunal up to now suddenly ran articles on Lanceley's participation in the inquiry, asking why he had been chosen to give any opinion on the Abbeylara incident. But for the media at the inquiry every day, the baggage that came with Lanceley was soon largely overtaken by the soundbites he provided once he took the stand. Chief amongst them was the term 'Suicide by Cop'.

The 'Suicide by Cop' theory describes a phenomenon where a person has a death wish and wants to die at the hands of police officers. It refers to situations where a person purposely draws armed officers on themselves and provokes them until they open fire. It's a phenomenon that has been recognised in the States for a number of years, and police in the UK estimate that twelve police shootings there every year now have all the hallmarks of 'Suicide by Cop'.

Lanceley felt that John Carthy's death was a classic 'Suicide by Cop' case, and in his time at the tribunal he attempted to persuade Justice Barr that Carthy had been planning his death for a long time; that he had decided to die on the same day as his father and grandfather, but to go out with a bang, by getting the gardaí to shoot him, thus scarring the reputation of the force he so hated.

Lanceley pointed to indicators that suggested Carthy had been thinking out some plan for a few weeks. There was the alleged remark remembered by Mary Ireland: that Carthy had told a fellow labourer in Longford a few weeks beforehand that he was 'going to do something people would read about and hear about'. There was also the odd comment he made to Alice Farrell when she came to visit the Carthys the night before the incident began, when he said, 'The party is over. There'll be no more laughing. The guards won't be here again.' Lanceley interpreted these as symbolic of a plan, an intention on Carthy's part to end his life in a dramatic manner. It is reckoned that people who plan to commit suicide often talk about it beforehand, and in a similar way, Lanceley believed that such comments by Carthy were indicative of a forthcoming event.

Addressing Carthy's behaviour during the actual siege, Lanceley identified certain key elements in his gestures and speech to back up his elaborate theory. Specifically, he referred to the fact that towards the end of the incident, just before he emerged, Carthy began glancing at his watch in an obsessive manner. Gardaí on the front line described him as pacing impatiently in front of the kitchen window, looking at his watch every few steps. In Lanceley's mind, this was in keeping with one of the most common signs of a 'Suicide By Cop' intention – that the person will set a deadline for when they will launch the provocative behaviour that will lead to their death. Carthy's obsession with the time corresponded to such a theory.

Lanceley also cited some of the comments made by Carthy during the incident as other indicators of a 'Suicide by Cop' death wish, for instance, his frequent invitations to the gardaí to 'come in and get me', and his later taunts to 'shoot me, shoot me'. Some psychiatrists have associated such statements with the grandiose feelings of bravado that can occur in periods of mania, but Lanceley had different ideas. He said he felt certain that Carthy meant what he said, and when all his big talk didn't pay off, he eventually made the ultimate in provocative moves. He came out of the house with his loaded shotgun.

This was Carthy's big plan, in the FBI man's opinion. After months and months of dwelling on his wrongful arrest, after hearing the taunts and jeers of locals and having been spurred on by a worsening manic state, Carthy decided to get even with the gardaí in the best way possible – he would have them shoot him, and let them live to deal with the repercussions of having shot a mentally ill man. This was to be his revenge on the police force he hated, and perhaps even a type of revenge on those who had made a mockery of him. Were that his plan, Lanceley said, few could disagree that he pulled it off well.

'I think any of the gardaí at the back of the room today would agree that John Carthy got even with the gardaí in a very big way.'

Asked about the requests for cigarettes and a solicitor,

Lanceley was dismissive. Those were toe-in-the-water type chances, he said, an example of Carthy seeing to what extent he could control the gardaí. He wanted them to run errands for him, Lanceley said, because that was a smaller step towards revenge.

'The delivery of cigarettes and the solicitor were not what he wanted. Something else was going on. He did seem delighted that the gardaí were running errands for him.'

He made the point that if Carthy really did want a solicitor, he would have picked up the phone and got one himself. He wasn't without resources in his home, and getting legal advice would have been easily done, if he was so inclined.

'If I thought people outside were about to kill me, I'd be on the phone to a solicitor saying "get your ass down here". My question is why he didn't call one himself. If I want something badly, I don't rely on my enemies to do it.'

The 'Suicide by Cop' theory is dramatic and well known in the US but Justice Barr was unconvinced of its application in this case. It was considered unlikely that John Carthy had planned this and put it into action. There was little or no awareness of the 'Suicide by Cop' phenomenon in Ireland. In any event, Carthy would be well aware that the majority of the Garda Síochána is unarmed. Could he ever have expected that his actions would have drawn down the ERU?

Psychiatric experts also found it difficult to accept some of Lanceley's opinions, most pointing out that the FBI man had made no allowances for Carthy's mental state. They brought things back to the core point at the centre of this whole fiasco – that Carthy was very sick at the time of this incident. His illness had reached a state where little made sense to him. Thought processes that would logically occur to the normal person would probably not have entered his head. He may well have had moments of clarity, but for the most part, he was lost and powerless to the worst onslaught of his disease.

It was elements like the experts' module that made the inquiry seem inefficient at times. Asking police officers from around the world for their opinion on Abbeylara was a waste of time, given the differences in culture and policing between Ireland and other countries. Lanceley freely admitted that had the Abbeylara situation occurred in the US, Carthy would have been shot as soon as he walked out the door, and he would quite possibly have been shot hours before that, while he was still inside the house. Like all the other experts, Lanceley's opinions were based on his experience of policing in a totally different environment. His theories and suggestions were spawned from years of working in a force of officers who are trained to kill. They are not the product of the Templemore school of policing, and the two worlds are too far apart even to attempt to try and compare their approaches in dealing with incidents on every level.

At regular intervals during his time on the stand, Lanceley would make a big play of turning around in his seat to address the gardaí who were gathered at the back of the room. He would gesture towards them, signifying a unity with the work they do, a mutual respect and a shared knowledge of what they were going through. He said he was concerned at the lack of appreciation by the Irish people for the work the gardaí do, and he was worried for the safety of the force.

'I must say, throughout this case and others I'm aware of in Ireland, I find, and it greatly concerns me, a lack of appreciation for the level of danger these officers are in. There does not seem to be an appreciation of the danger they were in. I find it frightening on the part of the garda. I'm afraid that some of the gentlemen at the back of this room are going to die unless some changes are made. I find that frightening, absolutely frightening.'

Lanceley seemed to have much sympathy for Jackson in particular, and he commended the Abbeylara negotiator on the way he had handled Carthy. He took the view that rather than looking at the fact that the negotiator was eventually the officer who fired the first shot at Carthy, he would look at it from the more positive angle that rather than initiating Carthy's death in the twenty-fifth hour, he had managed to keep Carthy alive for twenty-four hours up to that. He said he felt Jackson had acted above and beyond the call of his duty.

'They didn't pay me enough to die on this job [as a negotiator], and I suspect they didn't pay Mr Jackson enough to die on the job either.'

♎   ♎   ♎

In the first weeks of the tribunal, Justice Barr announced his intention to include a media module in the inquiry. The issue of the garda dealings with the media as well as the conduct of journalists at the scene was arising in evidence, and the chairman decided it would be best if an entire segment of the tribunal was devoted to looking at the media handling of the incident.

When the module did come around, it quickly became clear that rather than being a media module, it was an RTÉ module, dealing solely with the national broadcaster's coverage of Abbeylara and the conduct of both Paul Reynolds and Niall O'Flynn.

Reynolds was an impressive witness, presenting himself as

a competent and careful journalist, who engaged only in the facts of a story rather than in the hype surrounding it. While he did not recall the details of all the conversations he had with Garda Press Officer John Farrelly and Niall O'Flynn, he impressed Justice Barr with his honesty.

The issue of the Five-Seven-Live broadcast was the only subject on which both the representatives of the gardaí and the family agreed for the entire duration of the inquiry. Both were damning in their summations of the lack of a unified policy across RTÉ that day to make it clear to all departments that John Carthy would not be named.

'It is submitted that there was no proper journalistic or public service justification for the broadcasting of John Carthy's name by RTÉ during the currency of the siege on the Five-Seven-Live programme. It is submitted that none of the content of the vox pops, and in particular the use of personal information in relation to the break-up with the girlfriend, the drinking and smoking and the appeal to John Carthy and the naming of him, was relevant to the alleged justification of RTÉ's responsibility to report and analyse matters of public importance and to inform the general public of such matters.' (Diarmuid McGuinness, Counsel for the Garda Commissioner)

When Niall O'Flynn took the stand he was confident in his delivery, convinced that he did the right thing and had no reason to feel guilty about his Five-Seven-Live report. He won himself few friends with his approach to his evidence, quickly creating a less than favourable impression in the eyes of the chairman with what appeared to be his utter lack of sensitivity when it came to John Carthy.

In cross-examination by Margaret Nerney, counsel for the

gardaí, O'Flynn revealed his true feelings on being brought in front of the tribunal, saying that he was being used as a distraction, to take the focus away from the gardaí.

'Ms Nerney, your clients knew John Carthy suffered from a mental illness, I did not. Your clients had critical information from the Carthy family. They chose to withhold that information not only from me, but from their own press officer. If the media had not been there, the full story might never have emerged. Now four years later on, what you want to do is shoot the messenger.'

The reporter was taken to task by Justice Barr on the content of the vox pops, asking him did he feel it was in any way right or proper for him to reveal such private details about anyone. Barr contended that John Carthy had a right to his privacy, regardless of what trouble he was in that day. O'Flynn dismissed the idea, saying his listeners were his top priority and Carthy had lost all rights to privacy when he fired the first shots at the garda car.

'John Carthy put himself at the centre of public events. In so doing, he lost his anonymity,' he said.

Ω   Ω   Ω

The Barr Tribunal finally wound to a close at the end of December 2004.

22.

The Closing Submissions

'It is submitted that it is equally clear that, even after all of the extensive written and oral evidence provided by a range of psychiatric and psychological experts, we are now no nearer to a firm or probable answer to the question: why did John Carthy behave as he did on the 19th and 20th April, other than the ultimately unsatisfactory answer: because he was mentally ill'.

(Diarmuid McGuinness, Counsel for the Garda Commissioner)

'There can be no doubt from the evidence that Mr Carthy harboured deep-seated animosity and resentment towards a number of local people who lived in and around the village of Abbeylara, and, in particular, Mr Willie Crawford, as a result of their cruel taunting and "slagging" of Mr Carthy in relation to the mascot incident and the fact that this was kept up for a very considerable period after Mr Carthy had been totally absolved of any suspicion in relation to the matter by the gardaí.'

(Margaret Nerney, Counsel for the Gardaí)

'If there is any question that has been completely unanswered touching on this siege, it is the peculiar and universal failure to address the issue of John Carthy's desire for a solicitor. The extent to which that desire was not met, investigated or even communicated to the Carthy family and friends is such as to give rise to a well founded inference that the gardaí were determined to call the shots and for reasons wholly unexplained were unwilling to have the advice of and presence of a legal professional at the scene.'

(Patrick Gageby, Counsel for the Carthy family)

'There has been a suggestion that there was some panic when Mr Carthy emerged from the house. It is submitted that the evidence of the armed personnel at the scene is abundantly clear and can only lead to the conclusion that there was no panic within that group. It is remarkable to note that even though the situation was extremely tense, only one person fired a weapon at any given time and Detective Sergeant Jackson ceased firing when he heard another weapon being discharged. There can be no clearer evidence that the armed personnel operated with great coolness, restraint and deliberation and were acutely aware of what was going on around them.'

(Margaret Nerney, Counsel for the Gardaí)

'In psychiatry, one of the best predictors of future behaviour is a person's past behaviour and the context in this case was that John Carthy had fired thirty shots.'

(Diarmuid McGuinness, Counsel for Garda Commissioner)

'We suggest that Sergeant Jackson was unfamiliar with his training, failed to apply the procedures and demonstrated the rigidity or inflexibility which is the very reverse of the true skill of a negotiator.'

(Patrick Gageby, Counsel for the Carthy family)

The closing summation from the Garda team came from Pat O'Connell, SC.

O'Connell: 'My clients perceive themselves as having been

cast in the role of the accused and they also feel that the manner of their questioning throughout has differed utterly from that of other witnesses.'

Barr: 'If the rest of this is that sort of abuse, I think you can take it as read and sit down.'

O'Connell: 'I intend to finish my submissions, sir.'

Barr: 'Well, I won't listen to it, if that is the sort of thing it is. Are you going to on in that vein?'

O'Connell: 'These are the submissions that are generally held by my clients and have had to suffer at the hands of yourself, sir, over the course of the Tribunal in many many ways. I think I should be allowed to finish my submission. It is very short.'

Barr: 'If it contains any more of that sort of abuse, the answer is no.'

O'Connell: 'Are you making a ruling, sir, I can't finish my submission?'

Barr: 'I will read it, you may now sit down.'

O'Connell: 'Sir, I wish to finish my submission.'

Barr: 'You may sit down. Does it contain – I haven't read it – does it contain more abuse of the sort that you have just embarked on?'

O'Connell: 'It contains my clients' submissions which I say I am entitled to put before the tribunal, as each and every other party have.'

Barr: 'You are not entitled to make the sort of abusive observations that you are doing, particularly where there isn't justification. I have explained and ruled in the clearest terms what I perceive my function is. This is not a court of law. This is an investigation and I have been participating and taking, I have no hesitation in saying, a hands-on part in that investigation. That, I am afraid, is something that your clients will have to live with. But I have not made up my mind on any issue, nor will I until I finally carry out a great deal of research that will now be necessary and consider the various submissions, including on behalf of your clients and then I will come to conclusions. I haven't reached them yet. So to talk to me, to refer to me as being an accuser of your clients is grossly offensive.'

O'Connell: 'Well, sir…'

Barr: 'Now if you are going on with that, sit down, because I won't listen to you.'

O'Connell: 'There are matters– '

Barr: 'Do you want to continue in that vein?'

O'Connell: 'I want to continue my submissions, sir.'

Barr: 'In that vein?'

O'Connell: 'I want to continue my submission.'

Barr: 'Are you going to go on in that vein or not?'

O'Connell: 'Well, I don't know what you mean by "that vein".'

Barr: 'Do you speak the King's English?'

O'Connell: 'I wish to complete my submissions, that is all I ask your indulgence on.'

Barr: 'Answer the question. Is it going to continue more abuse on the lines that you have already embarked upon?'

O'Connell: 'I don't consider it to be abuse. I consider it to be–'

Barr: 'I don't care whether you consider it abuse or not. Is it? If it is, I am not going to listen to it.'

O'Connell: 'It is a truthful account of how my clients feel they have suffered at your hands.'

Barr: 'Alright, I shall read it all in due course.'

O'Connell: 'So you are refusing to allow me to finish my submissions?'

Barr: 'Yes, sit down. I shall read it, it won't be wasted. But you won't get a platform for abuse, Mr O'Connell.'

Justice Barr did eventually allow Pat O'Connell to complete the final three lines of his submission on the following and final day at the inquiry.

23.

At the height of the silly season in the summer of 2006, it emerged that the Barr Report was finally ready for publication. It was a welcome turn of events, especially for the Carthy family, who had now been waiting more than six years for this special brand of closure. Initial expectations had predicted that the Report would be out by the time the family marked John's fifth anniversary, but the wait for answers dragged on for more than a year after the initial due date.

The mid-summer timing of the release of the Report, on 20 July 2006, meant it attracted far more media attention than might have been the case if it had been brought out during the autumn when the Dáil is in full session and stories are in plentiful supply. In July the TDs are on holidays and news is thin on the ground. About thirty press people jostled for room on the steps outside the Tribunal door, under pressure to get the Report, rapidly skim through it, and present the findings.

Finally, the doors were opened, and there was one for everyone in the audience. Tribunal staff handed out copies of the Report, and its sheer size and weight made many wish they had brought a wheelbarrow to transport the tome back to the office. Seven hundred and forty-four pages of analysis, criticisms, some praise and many recommendations. Enough reading to fill several weeks, but before the analysis commenced, people wanted to see the man himself.

Justice Barr agreed to see the journalists in groups of five or six in his comfortable chambers. He was in placid form; the eighteen months that had passed since the Tribunal hearings ended, and the extensive work he had done in the meantime, had not taken their toll on his appearance. He obeyed the photographers' orders to stand this way and that, holding the Report in one hand, then in the other, standing by the window, sitting at his desk. He joked with them that he had never been so popular.

Speaking with the reporters, Barr quickly got to the point. He wanted to explain the delay, why it had taken more than a year and a half to complete a task that he had initially thought would only take a few months. First of all, he asked for understanding and an acknowledgement that the workload had been immense. Twenty thousand pages of typed transcript were the tools he had to work with in compiling his Report, and that took an enormous amount of time in both reading and in consideration of the testimonies of every single witness.

The second reason for the delay was more personal. He revealed he had been hospitalised on two separate occasions in the past months. He did not go into the detail on the nature of his health problems, but admitted it had set him back in his work. As the journalists left his chamber, reports in hand, he jokingly asked them to go easy on him.

℧ ℧ ℧

Seven hundred and forty-four pages. Within the first ten, the Report marked itself out as a considered, detailed and insightful account of twenty-five hours in the life of one troubled young man, and the careers of several senior and junior gardaí. Barr had looked at everything, and the version of events that he set forth told the story in all its tragedy and confusion. He was realistic in his analysis, reminding the reader first off that 'the crisis presented by [Carthy] at his home in Abbeylara was unique in Irish police experience; was potentially extremely difficult to contend with and was a very far cry from the crisis situations for which the ERU and the Garda Síochána are trained to contend.'

But that did not excuse everything, and throughout the Report, the criticisms of An Garda Síochána were many. Barr condemned not only elements of the actual incident itself, but also expressed the view that previous garda dealings with John Carthy in relation to both the burning of the goat mascot and the confiscation of his shotgun were also inappropriate and unhelpful to the situation that arose at Abbeylara in the year 2000.

Justice Barr stated that the wrongful arrest and 'physical abuse' of Carthy when he was taken into custody following the arson attack on the goat, as well as the 'premature' and unjustified confiscation of his gun were both crucial factors in Carthy's response to Detective Sergeant Michael Jackson and other members of the gardaí during the stand-off. Both of these clashes with the local gardaí were the cause of 'Carthy's distrust of and antagonism towards the gardaí, which loomed large at Abbeylara.'

However, Barr accepted that there were certain factors both in Carthy's personality and in his life situation at the time of the incident that were beyond the control of the gardaí who responded to the incident. The break-up with Kathleen, the tenth anniversary of his father's death and the imminent demolition of the family home all contributed to a 'massive manifestation of his bipolar mental condition', which turned his usually placid manner into one of aggression and violence. This was something that the gardaí could not control. But it was something they should have been aware of and should have taken into consideration in their handling of the incident.

'The evidence indicates clearly that the combination of the foregoing tragedies carried John Carthy into a massive manifestation of his bipolar mental condition and, as already stated, introduced a protracted violent conduct which he had never engaged in before. Defence of the old home against all-comers appears to have become the vehement objective of his behaviour. The arrival of the police and commencement of the siege added another dimension of the distress and resurrected in John Carthy's mind his deep animosity towards the Garda Síochána arising out of the wrongful seizure of his gun and the goat mascot episode in 1998, including his allegation of physical assault by police interrogators at the time. The end result was readily apparent from his conduct in shooting frequently in the direction of garda officers and his negative response to the repeated efforts of Detective Sergeant Jackson, that John Carthy would not negotiate with the police and, in particular, that he would not surrender his gun to them or be seen to capitulate to the gardaí. Did the scene commanders, their superiors and the negotiator understand the realities of the situation as it emerged and how should they have responded?'

A lack of either training or experience on the part of almost every garda at the scene was singled out by Barr as being the foremost 'inhibiting' factor that handicapped the members who were on duty at Abbeylara. The negotiator, Detective Sergeant Michael Jackson had never negotiated at an incident before. A number of the local armed gardaí had never used a firearm while on duty before. The scene commanders had never policed an armed siege before. And apart from Detective Sergeant Russell, who had trained as a psychiatric nurse, none of the officers at the scene had any real knowledge of the intricacies of a mental illness.

'Neither of the scene commanders (Superintendents Shelly and Byrne) had any prior experience of dealing with an armed siege or of any event involving a dangerous armed person. Their training as scene commanders comprised one short course only at the time of promotion some years before the event. They had no training in or experience of dealing with violent conduct motivated by mental illness. The local armed officers at the scene were similarly inexperienced and none had had any prior occasion to use a firearm while on active duty.'

Contrary to what some may have been expecting from the report, Justice Barr placed very little blame on the frontline ERU men for the tragedy that unfolded at Abbeylara. With regard to the negotiator, Detective Sergeant Michael Jackson, Barr states that the ERU man made a great effort to help Carthy, and expresses praise for the novice negotiator, saying he made 'very real efforts to achieve a resolution of the impasse, but lack of resources and experience militated against his prospect of success.'

The one real area which drew criticism of Jackson was in relation to the cigarettes and the failure of gardaí to grant a packet of '20 Major', as was requested by Carthy. Barr states that Jackson was too rigid in his approach to this issue and that he was too determined not to make any concession to Carthy unless he gave something in return. He is also highly critical of the 'safe method of delivery', which Jackson claimed he tried to advance with Carthy.

'The negotiator ought to have realised the futility of alleging to John Carthy, that in the interest of the safety of the gardaí delivering cigarettes to the house, it would be necessary for the subject to put his gun down on the floor and display his hands at the kitchen window. He [Jackson] knew or ought to have realised at that stage that Mr Carthy was greatly antagonistic towards and distrustful of the police ...The strong probability is that the subject would be fearful that the true objective of that strategy may have been to create a situation which would enable a garda to jump through the kitchen window, or having gained entry to the house unknown to Mr Carthy, an attacker might burst into the kitchen while the gun was on the floor and in either event the subject would be overpowered before being able to retrieve his weapon.'

Considering the mental anxiety that was clearly dogging Carthy over the course of the event, and considering the negative impact which nicotine withdrawal would have had on such a heavy smoker as Carthy, Barr states clearly that cigarettes could and should have been delivered to the house. He states there is 'no doubt that cigarettes could have been delivered by leaving them at the hall door at any stage during the siege while John Carthy was under observation in the kitchen where in fact he spent nearly all of his time.'

But Jackson regained the respect of Barr when the Chairman turned his attention to the events that unfolded when Carthy emerged from his house, and the particular action of the negotiator in deciding against his training to shoot to injure rather than kill. Barr judged this to be an indication of the 'humanity' of the negotiator, and he commended him for it.

'He [Jackson] demonstrated a high degree of dedication, humanity and a real effort to resolve the impasse created by John Carthy, who was a sick man. I note in particular that when the deceased emerged onto the road from his house; removed one cartridge from his gun and then commenced walking towards Abbeylara with his weapon apparently at the ready, Sergeant Jackson observed that the deceased had not threatened any of the nearby ERU officers and he [Jackson], who was first to fire, elected to shoot at John Carthy's legs and he was struck twice in that area. Unfortunately, both bullets passed through soft tissue. If a bone had been struck it is probable that the subject would have fallen immediately thus removing any need for further shots. I commend Sergeant Jackson for his course of action in contending with the final difficult situation presented by John Carthy. I have no doubt that throughout the event, he did his best.'

Similarly, Barr does not criticise Detective Garda McCabe for firing the fatal bullet at Carthy after he emerged from his home. Barr said he accepted McCabe's testimony that he believed Carthy was still walking and was still posing a threat to the members of the force further up the Abbeylara Road. Taking into account the training armed officers receive, and the international best police practice which dictates that officers must fire at the central body mass of an armed subject, Barr judged that he could not in all honesty say that McCabe acted unlawfully in shooting and killing John Carthy.

Ω   Ω   Ω

According to Barr, the death of John Carthy was not the fault of those gardaí who actually fired shots that day. It was the fault of the scene commanders, Superintendents Joe Shelly and Michael Byrne, and to a lesser extent, the fault of the ERU

Tactical Commander, Detective Sergeant Gerry Russell. Because in Barr's opinion, the killing of Carthy did not just happen in the thirty seconds in which he emerged from his home on to the road. According to Justice Barr the writing was on the wall for Carthy long before that, due to a series of errors on the part of the senior officers who were in charge of the incident.

Barr particularly highlights the failure of Superintendent Shelly to uncover vital information on the circumstances of John Carthy. Shelly appointed himself intelligence officer at the scene, requiring him to do everything in his power to uncover as much vital information on Carthy as possible. The role of intelligence officer was very important at Abbeylara. It would usually have been entrusted to a senior officer at the scene, and their job would be to interview everyone in Carthy's circle, to compile a written log of all the information gathered, and to provide that information to the negotiator and the front line officers who were dealing with the incident. Shelly however, did not choose to appoint another intelligence officer.

Barr highlights several basic elements in John Carthy's situation that Shelly failed to uncover. The fact that Shelly never spoke to Dr Cullen himself at any point during the incident; the fact that it took so long to discover that Carthy had a treating psychiatrist; the fact that he never elected to personally contact Kevin Ireland for his direct account of what Carthy said to him in that phone call were all singled out by Barr to highlight the inadequacies of Shelly as an intelligence officer. In short, he states that 'Shelly appears to have done very little, if anything, in his adopted role of intelligence coordinator.'

Barr claims that Shelly's negligence in these key areas meant that Detective Sergeant Jackson, as negotiator, was deprived of vital information that would have greatly aided him in his attempts to win the trust of John Carthy. This was especially true in relation to the failure to debrief Kevin Ireland fully in relation to the phone call he had with Carthy just hours before his death. Barr states that this was a 'major mistake' on the part of the gardaí, and that it was obvious that the scene commander as well as the other senior officers at the scene all failed to recognise the importance of responding to Carthy's request for legal assistance. Had Mr Ireland been directly contacted, the gardaí would have discovered that Carthy had told him he would give himself up if he was provided with a solicitor.

'The backing and encouragement of a solicitor he trusted for ending the stand-off on the foregoing basis, without the humiliation of arrest at the scene, may have provided a catalyst for achieving success. It is surprising that so little was done to respond to John Carthy's apparently insistent request to provide him with a solicitor. It was patently negligent not to contact the subject's own local attorney or, failing that, the family solicitor, as a matter of urgency and to secure the assistance of that person at the scene.'

Barr suggests there was a possibility that the gardaí did not want to bring a solicitor to the scene for their own reasons – a suggestion which had been made on numerous occasions by the Carthy family and their legal representatives.

'One possible explanation for failure to respond to Mr Carthy's request for a solicitor is that such a person, unlike the other civilians, could not be orchestrated by the police regarding the line he should take with the subject and there was some risk that his participation could be discomforting for the gardaí.'

In questioning the failure of Shelly to interview Dr Cullen at any point throughout the incident, Barr identified this as one of the 'crucial command mistakes' at the scene. The chairman stated that Shelly's 'negligence' in not interviewing Dr Cullen was 'extraordinary'. It is in this regard that Justice Barr probes the reasons why Shelly chose to appoint himself as Intelligence Officer in the first place.

'Although Superintendent Shelly had the pivotal role of scene commander in a difficult situation of which he had no previous experience, he decided, contrary to his training, to take on personally the important function of intelligence coordinator rather than to appoint ... some other experienced officer ... to perform that task.'

Justice Barr put forward two possible explanations for Shelly's failure to interview Dr Cullen. The first was the possibility that this failure was simply a 'product of gross negligence' born out of the superintendent's lack of experience of dealing with such a situation. The second possible explanation is more damning and it draws in the controversial issue of the alleged assault on John Carthy after he was wrongfully arrested over the burning of the goat. While Shelly alleged he did not learn of this until late in the incident, Barr suggests that the scene commander was well aware of this from an early stage, writing:

'The unexplained and unnecessary decision to burden himself with a major additional chore which could have been performed by other competent officers, is credible if his motivation was to ensure as well as he could that embarrassing information was not obtained from Dr Cullen by another intelligence coordinator if one had been appointed.'

ᘯ   ᘯ   ᘯ

But it was the failure of the gardaí to plan adequately for the possibility that John Carthy might emerge from his house that drew the most criticism from Barr. This, he said, was the real reason that John Carthy was killed. Because the gardaí had failed to think through what might happen if Carthy came out, in a matter of seconds the decision had to be taken by both Detective Sergeant Jackson and Detective Garda McCabe to fire at the twenty-seven-year-old.

The scene on the Abbeylara road when John Carthy emerged was one of 'substantial confusion and some panic'. Armed and unarmed local officers had been allowed to congregate in the area just up the road from the Carthy driveway for the duration of the incident. Barr deems this to have been the most fatal error on the part of the garda management at the scene, and their failure to keep the road clear meant that there was no other choice left to the ERU officers other than to kill Carthy.

This was a fact borne out by the evidence of the two officers who fired at Carthy. Both Jackson and McCabe stated that it was because of the scene that lay before them further up the Abbeylara road that they took the decision to shoot Carthy so as to minimise the risk to the lives of those gardaí further up the road.

Barr contends that, first of all, once the ERU arrived there was very little need for so many local officers to have remained at the scene. At most 'three or four' local armed officers may have been required. The rest should have been moved away from the immediacy of the scene. The continued presence of so many officers on the road 'created a potential disaster situation, which ought to have been adverted to' by the senior officers at the scene. Barr states that the failure of the scene commanders and of the ERU tactical commander to foresee the potential difficulties of this indicated that they had not properly considered the possibilities for 'disaster'.

'There is no doubt that the scene commander, the tactical commander, the negotiator, the ERU officers and other local gardaí, armed and unarmed, at the scene were taken entirely by surprise when John Carthy suddenly emerged from his house without any prior warning. The consequent confusion and the negligence of those in command led to the tragedy of his death which would not have happened if the Abbeylara road had been kept clear of vehicles and all personnel, which ought to have been the case … The greatest Garda mistake at Abbeylara was not preparing for an uncontrolled exit by Mr Carthy from his house as actually happened; in not keeping the road clear of vehicles and all personnel and in not ensuring that all officers at the scene remained safely concealed and under cover at all times. It is evidence that the foregoing failures gave rise to the fatal shooting of Mr Carthy by presenting him with apparent targets which should not have been there, i.e., allowing a situation to exist whereby exposed officers appeared to be in danger of being killed or injured by the subject, thus causing Garda McCabe to shoot him with fatal consequences in order to remove that risk.'

Barr places the blame for this lack of planning squarely on the shoulders of the two men who were in charge of the operation, Superintendent Shelly as the main scene commander and Superintendent Michael Byrne as the night-time scene commander. Their failure to appreciate the danger that existed in allowing members to 'clutter the road' in the area outside the house 'amounted to a high degree of negligence'. In short, their inaction led to the death of John Carthy.

'Superintendent Shelly and Superintendent Byrne as scene commanders had primary responsibility for the circumstances which led to Mr Carthy's death ...'

' ... In the end John Carthy took matters into his own hands by leaving his house and walking towards Abbeylara with only one cartridge in his gun and having ignored the armed ERU men around him. Was his intention simply to buy cigarettes or perhaps to meet Dr Shanley and his sister who he knew were at the scene and surrender his gun to them or had he some other motive in leaving the house? We will never know the answer to those questions either. For reasons which I have already expressed, his death should not have happened.'

Ω   Ω   Ω

The media quickly devoured the main conclusions in the Report, but of even greater personal interest to many of them was that section of the Report that dealt with the media handling of the incident, and in particular the judgement Justice Barr had made on the Five-Seven-Live broadcast of Niall O'Flynn.

What they found in that section of the Report was an emphatic condemnation of the journalism of O'Flynn. Justice Barr stated the report was 'irresponsible', and he also questioned O'Flynn's claim that he had not heard anything of Carthy's mental illness or any suggestion that Carthy had a radio in his home that day.

'It is not credible that Mr O'Flynn, the series producer of Five-Seven-Live from June, 1999 and a long-time experienced news and current affairs reporter who had spent six hours at the scene investigating events at Abbeylara, did not learn from any of the large number of media personnel present or from locals who he interviewed in connection with his proposed programme, that John Carthy was suffering from depression.'

Justice Barr went on to say that while O'Flynn denied there was any ulterior motive in his broadcasting such personal details about Carthy or that his aim was to 'inject personal drama and interest' into the story, he believes that O'Flynn's objective was to upstage his journalistic rivals by airing a sensationalist report.

'Mr O'Flynn's conduct seems to indicate the likelihood of a desire on his part to steal a march on his news colleagues in RTÉ and the media generally by titillating his Five-Seven-Live audience with some details of John Carthy's recent, unhappy love life and to suggest that a lost intimate relationship might be revived ... The Five-Seven-Live Abbeylara broadcast as orchestrated by O'Flynn was irresponsible and should not have happened.'

♎   ♎   ♎

These were just some of the criticisms and conclusions reached by Barr in the course of his long Report. They made headline news, along with the revelation that the Minister for Finance on behalf of the taxpayer was to be hit with a bill of 18 million to cover the proceedings of the inquiry from its first day of hearings until the day the Report was finally released.

24.

The Barr Report brought to the public more than just a critique of the garda operation at Abbeylara. While the task handed down to Justice Barr centred on the death of John Carthy, the chairman also had the responsibility of making recommendations on the future direction of An Garda Síochána, and the changes that had to be made to ensure that such a tragedy would never happen again.

The most important element of this section of the Report centred on what are known as 'less than lethal' weapons, devices which can be used to disable rather than fatally wound a person. The range of 'less than lethal' weapons encompasses a wide assortment of devices, all of which are designed to stun, overpower or inflict mild injury. But the overarching requirement of such weapons is that they would successfully and peacefully defuse a situation such as the one that was created when John Carthy emerged from his home on to the Abbeylara road on the day he died.

When the officers from the Emergency Response Unit left their headquarters to respond to the incident at Abbeylara, they brought with them Sig Sauer pistols, Uzi sub-machine guns, a Heckler & Koch .33 rifle, and a Bennelli semi-automatic shotgun. At that time they did not have access to any 'less than lethal' devices. In the year 2000, no such weapons had been acquired by An Garda Síochána.

In the aftermath of the shooting, the Garda Commissioner

was ordered to establish a working group to consider the 'less than lethal' options that might be available to gardaí in the future and to make recommendations to the Minister for Justice regarding the purchase of such weapons. Eighteen months after John Carthy had been killed, a report was submitted to the Commissioner, recommending that the gardaí should be supplied with three different 'less than lethal' devices – a bean bag cartridge, an OC/CS shotgun cartridge, and pepper spray aerosol projectors.

Each of these devices has its own advantages when it comes to disabling rather than killing. The bean bag cartridge (a fabric pouch filled with either plastic or rubber pellets) is a device that, when ejected from a 12-gauge shotgun, will strike, but not penetrate, the body. The bag creates a severe blow of 120lb – about the same as a boxer's punch – winding its intended target and possibly causing mild injury. Ideally, the discharge of a bean bag round would give the officer enough time to approach and overcome the subject.

The OC/CS shotgun cartridge is essentially a projectile which, when discharged, will release an amount of either pepper spray (referred to technically as OC gas) or tear gas (known technically as CS) into the atmosphere around the target. Tear gas, as the name suggests, causes an irritation of the eyes, but depending on its strength, it can also cause immediate vomiting and collapse. Again, in a case such as Abbeylara, it would be hoped the discharge of tear gas would cause sufficient disorientation to the subject of an incident to allow officers time to disarm and carry out an arrest.

The pepper spray aerosol projector works on a similar basis to the OC shotgun cartridge. Pepper spray causes an irritation and pain in the eyes and is known to be very effective. The projector recommended by the Working Group would be capable of delivering a high volume discharge of the spray to a target up to thirty feet away.

In November 2002, the then newly appointed Minister for Justice, Michael McDowell, approved the introduction of the three recommended weapons. But that approval was not followed by any action towards actually acquiring the devices. By 2004, there was still no sign of the weapons. There was some concern amongst the garda authorities about the new proposed devices – a concern that has been mirrored in police forces across Europe. While the weapons are supposed to be 'less than lethal', they are dangerous nonetheless, and can be fatal if used incorrectly.

The gardaí have since been supplied with the bean bag cartridges.

In his Report, Justice Barr gave his approval to the purchase and use of such 'less than lethal' weapons by members of An Garda Síochána. He could not say for definite that had any of those devices been deployed at Abbeylara the outcome would have been different, but stated that in theory all could have been in some way 'advantageous' to the gardaí at the incident.

Ω   Ω   Ω

Justice Barr also outlined recommendations with regard to the potential use of garda dogs at the scene of an armed siege. Several expert police witnesses from around the world expressed the opinion in the course of the Tribunal that the use of what are known as 'non-compliant' police dogs at Abbeylara would have helped bring a peaceful ending to the incident. Non-compliant dogs, usually Alsatians or Dobermans, are trained to bite or attack people on command.

At the time of the incident at Abbeylara, the Garda Dog Unit was made up of compliant general purpose dogs only – animals that are used for drug sniffing, searching for missing persons and for pursuing fleeing criminals. This is still the case today. At present, the Garda Dog Unit has nineteen trained dogs, none of which are non-compliant.

It is common practice now in most parts of the UK and in countries such as New Zealand for these firearms support dogs and two handlers to be deployed to the scenes of armed incidents. This practice has been extremely successful, in spite of various incidents where the subjects of such sieges have shot and killed the animals before they had the chance to attack. In his Report, Justice Barr stated that he believed 'the use of firearms support dogs is a valuable less lethal option with a substantial incidence of success in an Abbeylara type situation'.

Justice Barr did not believe that the presence of the general compliant dog at Abbeylara would have been of any benefit to the operation. Compliant dogs will only pursue a target that appears to be fleeing from them. In the case of Abbeylara, where John Carthy emerged and walked at normal pace up the road, it is unlikely that the compliant dog would have been willing to overpower him.

By contrast, if two non-compliant dogs along with trained handlers had been at the scene, Justice Barr stated that the outcome could have been very different.

'If two such dogs were available at the scene, Mr Carthy, having a single cartridge in his gun after discarding the other one, could have shot only one dog if he had been attacked by two. It seems likely that in such circumstances, either the uninjured dog would have overpowered him or he would have

been overpowered by one or more of the nearby ERU officers as some of them were aware that he had only one
cartridge in his gun having discarded the other one on
reaching the road.'

Ω Ω Ω

Justice Barr also addressed the issue of gun licensing law in
Ireland, and suggested possible improvements in that law,
relating in particular to the handling of such weapons by
people suffering from a mental illness.

The Firearms Act, 1925 lays down the provisions of the main
gun licensing issues in this country. In relation to the issue of
licences to mentally ill persons, Section 4 of this Act states,
amongst other things, that before granting a firearm certificate
to any person, the Garda Superintendent must be satisfied
that the applicant 'can be permitted to have in his possession,
use and carry a firearm without danger to the public safety or
to the peace'. Section 8 of the Act provides a long list of persons who should not be allowed to possess a deadly weapon.
Included in this list is 'any person of intemperate habits, any
person of unsound mind and any person who is subject to the
supervision of the police.' The Act however does not define
what is meant by this reference to 'unsound mind'.

Analysing the current legislation on firearms, Justice Barr
made an interesting comparison with the law governing the
awarding of drivers' licences in this country. As it stands, any
application for a driving licence must be accompanied by a
health and fitness 'checklist', completed and signed by the applicant as a declaration of their being fully capable of holding
such a licence. There is no such provision in the firearm legislation. In fact, applicants for a gun licence in this country are

not required to provide any information regarding their mental or physical health.

Barr recommended a number of changes in this regard. Firstly, he advised that a revised detailed application form should be drafted, including a number of new questions to be asked of anyone seeking a gun licence. Under the new application system, the applicant would be required to provide a full medical history, including details of any mental health problems. Where there has been a history of depression or any such issue, the applicant would also be required to furnish the names and contact details of his or her GP and any specialists that they have attended.

Barr appreciated that there would technically be no onus on an applicant to provide this kind of information, and they could be particularly reluctant to do so if they felt it would work against their application. To this end, he recommended that all applicants for gun licences be accompanied by reports from two referees, one from an adult close relative and the other from a person over the age of thirty who has known the applicant for more than five years.

Up to this point, the decision on who is awarded a gun licence and who is rejected has been made by individual superintendents, acting on their own judgement of the applicant. Barr recommended that this practice be streamlined in some way, and that formal guidelines be set down to guide superintendents in their assessments of applications.

Justice Barr suggested a number of other recommendations in this area, chief amongst them a suggestion that there should be greater cooperation between the gardaí and the National Association of Regional Game Councils, which represent gun clubs nationwide. He also recommended that a provisional gun licence be introduced for novice applicants, who would be required to undergo a degree of training before being awarded a full licence.

To remedy the lack of police training evident at Abbeylara, Barr recommended several changes in the instruction of new garda recruits and refresher courses for existing members. In particular, he advised that members should be given some knowledge of mental health issues and how they should be handled. He also stressed the importance of establishing a formal working arrangement between the gardaí and state psychologists, so that negotiators at any future version of Abbeylara could have the benefit of a mental health expert at the scene.

♌ ♌ ♌

Within hours of its release, the Barr Report had been dissected by the broadcast media and a full-scale analysis for the following day's newspapers was underway. The story to be carried was obvious. Justice Robert Barr had declared that John Carthy's death should not have happened and had expressed the view that the 'disaster at Abbeylara' was the fault of the scene commanders, and in particular Superintendent Joe Shelly.

Journalists went in search of reaction. Reaction from the family. Reaction from the Minister for Justice, Michael McDowell, and reaction from the Garda Commissioner, Noel Conroy.

That evening, the media gathered in Buswell's Hotel to hear the verdict from the first most interested party, the Carthys. Marie entered the room to give a brief press conference, and those who had not seen her since she made her first ever public appearance just after the shooting had to look twice to make sure it was really her. On that day, in the Longford Arms Hotel, Marie had kept very much in the background, hugging herself inside a big jumper, her face partly hidden by a mane of untamed hair. Six years later, she strode into Buswell's a different, confident person.

Seeking justice for her brother had become her driving force, and the image she now presented was born out of frequent appearances on television and in the press over the years. She had become the public face of the Carthy family. The day of the release of the Report was the culmination of six years work, and she was ready for it. The press conference at Buswell's was handled by a PR company, hired by Marie to deal with press queries in the run-up to and the aftermath of the release of Report.

Marie took her place in front of the microphone, beside the family solicitor, Peter Mullan. She was now stylish and confident both in her manner and appearance, a sign that while life stood still in the moment her brother was shot dead, life had also moved on.

The statement she read out was brief. It centred on a feeling of lingering grief for her lost brother, and also a feeling of gratitude that closure had finally come. She did not revel in the findings of Justice Barr. His declaration that John should never have been killed may have been big news and a revelation for the Irish public, but that was a fact of which she and her family had been sure for years. She reminded the gathered journalists that John was a 'beloved son, brother, nephew, cousin, neighbour and friend', and said that they would always remember him as a 'great character'.

There was nothing bitter in her voice. She said she understood that the garda who had fired the fatal shot, Detective Garda Aidan McCabe, was a family man, who on that day in Abbeylara thought he was doing his job, and she knew he would have to live with that action for the rest of his life. For her family, this was a welcome conclusion to the tragedy, the long road had now been travelled, and the answers had finally been provided.

The Report however had also brought personal vindication for Marie. In dealing with the media coverage of both the event and its aftermath, Justice Barr stated he believed that certain negative articles that had appeared in the press had been orchestrated by members of the gardaí in an effort to create in the public consciousness a suggestion that Marie Carthy was not on good terms with her brother. This referred specifically to a front page *Sunday Independent* article which ran at Hallowe'en 2004. The article, by journalist Maeve Sheehan, declared that the newspaper had found 'Dramatic New Evidence in Abbeylara Case', and carried a subheading 'Abbeylara family row over land may have affected siege victim Carthy's state of mind prior to his death'. The article suggested there was a possibility of 'family friction' within the Carthys over land, a claim that was based on inaccurate information supplied to the journalist.

Justice Barr pointed out that the article was 'heavily slanted' towards the arguments of the legal representatives of the gardaí, and in particular the arguments of John Rogers, SC. Because of this, he formed the view that the likely source for Sheehan's article was a member of An Garda Síochána, who purposely leaked the information to the journalist in the hope that it would discredit the relationship between the Carthy siblings.

'It is probable that the person or persons directly or indirectly responsible for orchestrating the story and for putting in train a scheme whereby Ms Sheehan was informed of information helpful to the garda case providing titillating "new" evidence likely to be of particular interest to her as a *Sunday Independent* journalist, was a member of the Garda Síochána or someone associated with the police.'

This, Justice Barr stated, was an attempt by the gardaí to counteract Marie's grievance that she was never allowed to speak with her brother during the siege.

'I note that strenuous efforts have been made in the interest of the gardaí to downgrade Ms Carthy's potential importance as an intermediary with her brother. This has extended to dishonestly obtaining erroneous press coverage suggesting that she did not have a good relationship with him.'

Such statements by Justice Barr came as a bonus for Marie and Rose Carthy. Following publication of the *Sunday Independent* article, they initiated libel proceedings against Independent Newspapers, and just weeks before the release of the Report, they received compensation from the news group, as well as a front-page apology.

Ω   Ω   Ω

On the day the Barr Report was released, Minister Michael McDowell and Garda Commissioner Noel Conroy sat side-by-side surveying the new troops. They were guests of honour at a passing out ceremony at Templemore Garda College, and once the formalities were done, both waited for the questions on what they made of this latest independent examination of the conduct of the gardaí. Their reactions were very different.

Minister McDowell selected a tone that was measured, sympathetic, yet protective of the gardaí. He said the State owed 'an expression of profound regret' to the family of John Carthy, but also pointed out that the gardaí at the scene in Abbeylara were faced with a very dangerous and threatening situation. He said that nobody, not even Justice Robert Barr, could be sure that things would have ended differently no matter how the gardaí had dealt with it, and criticising the management at the scene was only a matter of subjection.

'I do agree with Mr Justice Barr that a more professional approach to the management of the scene could have avoided the particular outcome as a matter of probability, but not with certainty. You just don't know,' he said.

The Minister said that he found Justice Barr's findings in relation to the assault on John Carthy while he was in garda custody over the burning of the goat to be 'a very serious matter', and also said he intended to take on board many of the recommendations that had been made by the chairman in relation to the gun licensing issue and the training of the ERU in relation to less than lethal weapons.

The tone set by McDowell was not shared by Garda Commissioner Noel Conroy. His remarks mirrored the general reaction of the garda authorities to the Report, reminding the public of the pressure that was put upon the gardaí at Abbeylara. Commissioner Conroy said the ERU was a force of well-trained, committed officers who frequently put their lives on the line. While Justice Barr had years to consider how the situation should have been dealt with, the ERU men who shot John Carthy only had seconds to make their difficult choice of whether to kill or not to kill.

'If you go back and look at what the ERU have been doing on

behalf of the Irish people and the force generally during the terrorist campaign in this country, I can assure you all those people put their lives on the line time and time again,' he said.

The Commissioner did not offer anything in the way of an apology to the Carthy family, a fact for which he would be criticised in the days and weeks to come. He did, however, assure the Irish public that he would ensure that the recommendations made by Justice Barr would receive careful consideration.

⚖ ⚖ ⚖

The day of reckoning was over. Now aged seventy-six, Justice Barr officially began his retirement, and at the Harcourt Square headquarters of An Garda Síochána, work began on sifting through the Barr Report and figuring out how the gardaí could best implement his recommendations. This was the new direction for their policing: less than lethal weapons; extra training; sensitivity to mental illness. All that was very good on paper. Implementation would be another thing altogether.

For the Carthy family, tough decisions lay ahead. Now that it had been confirmed that John's death should not have happened, the option of legal action was open to them if they so wished. Where one drama ended, another version of the same story was about to unfold.

Epilogue

Almost three weeks after the release of the Barr Report, Rose Carthy was alone in the house in Toneymore when a letter was hand delivered to her door. It was the long-awaited letter of apology from the Garda Commissioner, Noel Conroy. The Commissioner had been slow to offer an apology on behalf of his force, but under growing pressure from the Minister for Justice, he finally put pen to paper. The letter was short and simple. In it Commissioner Conroy said An Garda Síochána was 'truly apologetic' for the death of John Carthy at Abbeylara.

Responsibility had now been accepted. From the top down – from Taoiseach, to Minister for Justice to Garda Commissioner – all had apologised for what had happened. What remained to be seen was how the Carthy family would respond.

On 9 October 2006 the Carthys should have been celebrating with John. Had he lived, this would have been his thirty-third birthday. Instead, the day brought a different sort of milestone to Marie and Rose: another step in their fight for justice. They chose this day to issue their claim in the High Court, initiating proceedings for damages against the Garda Commissioner, the Minister for Justice and the Attorney General.

The date was also marked by a strange coincidence. Hours after the Carthy family had initiated their proceedings against the pillars of justice in the capital, an armed forty-year-old man barricaded himself into his home on Crowe Street in Gort, County Galway, having evicted his family, and began firing shots out of the windows and doors.

Within hours of the first shots being fired, around fifty gardaí had responded to the incident, evacuating the residents and cordoning off the area. The Emergency Response Unit was called in, and an operation similar to that at Abbeylara was put in full swing. But what followed differed greatly to the incident that had unfolded in response to the actions of John Carthy six years previously.

The negotiator at the incident attempted to make contact over the phone. He did not approach the immediacy of the area, and while it took several hours, he did eventually succeed in cajoling the man inside the house into talking to him on the phone. Garda dogs were deployed. And when the man came out, after a twenty-one-hour standoff, he was fired at with the 'less than lethal' bean bag round. Unfortunately, the bean bag round did not deter the armed man from continuing to fire his gun, and gardaí were forced to discharge their lethal weapons. A bullet to the chest injured him, but he was rushed to hospital and survived.

The siege in Gort was reminiscent of the events that had unfolded at Abbeylara, except for some key factors that were in no small way encouraged by the questions and recommendations that were made in the years after the shooting of John Carthy. The presence of garda dogs and the fact that the ERU had bean bag rounds in their possession are both highly significant.

The short letter that Rose Carthy received from the Garda Commissioner that day did more than apologise to the family. It also offered them the full commitment of the gardaí towards implementing all of the recommendations that had been made by Justice Robert Barr. That assurance was important, and if and when all of those recommendations are indeed put in place, the force as a whole will be all the better for it.

Perhaps this will be the legacy of John Carthy.